CCSP®
Certified Cloud
Security Professional
Practice Exams

ABOUT THE AUTHOR

Daniel Carter, CCSP, CISSP, CISM, CISA, is currently working as a senior systems engineer at Johns Hopkins University & Medicine. An IT security and systems professional for almost 20 years, Daniel has worked extensively with web-based applications and infrastructure, as well as LDAP and federated identity systems, PKI, SIEM, and Linux/Unix systems. He is currently working with enterprise authentication and single sign-on systems, including cloud-base deployments. Daniel holds a degree in criminology and criminal justice from the University of Maryland, and a master's degree in technology management, with a focus on homeland security management, from the University of Maryland, University College.

About the Technical Editor

Gerry Sneeringer, CISSP, has been an IT professional with the University of Maryland for the past 30 years. He has been involved in customer support, systems programming, system administration (including the operation of one of the Internet's root domain name servers), and network engineering. For the past 16 years, Gerry has been the head of security in the university's central IT office. He currently serves as the university's chief information security officer, overseeing the protection of university computing services hosted locally and in the cloud. Gerry holds a bachelor's degree in computer science from the University of Maryland.

CCSP®

Certified Cloud
Security Professional
Practice Exams

Daniel Carter

New York   Chicago   San Francisco
Athens   London   Madrid   Mexico City
Milan   New Delhi   Singapore   Sydney   Toronto

Cataloging-in-Publication Data is on file with the Library of Congress

McGraw-Hill Education books are available at special quantity discounts to use as premiums and sales promotions, or for use in corporate training programs. To contact a representative, please visit the Contact Us pages at www.mhprofessional.com.

CCSP® Certified Cloud Security Professional Practice Exams

1 2 3 4 5 6 7 8 9   QFR   21 20 19 18

ISBN: Book p/n 978-1-260-03133-1 and CD p/n 978-1-260-03134-8
of set 978-1-260-03135-5

MHID: Book p/n 1-260-03133-0 and CD p/n 1-260-03134-9
of set 1-260-03135-7

Sponsoring Editor	**Technical Editor**	**Composition**
Wendy Rinaldi	Gerry Sneeringer	Cenveo Publisher Services
Editorial Supervisor	**Copy Editor**	**Art Director, Cover**
Janet Walden	Bart Reed	Jeff Weeks
Project Manager	**Proofreader**	
Surbhi Mittal,	Rick Camp	
Cenveo® Publisher Services	**Production Supervisor**	
Acquisitions Coordinator	Lynn M. Messina	
Claire Yee		

This book is dedicated to my children—Zachariah, Malachi, Alannah, and Ezra. I love you all so much, and look forward to seeing how each of you four very unique souls will change the world for the better!

CONTENTS

ACKNOWLEDGMENTS

The *CCSP Certified Cloud Security Professional All-in-One Exam Guide* was my first entry into the community of authors, and I first want to thank Matt Walker for connecting me with this opportunity and encouraging me to take it on.

I want to thank Gerry Sneeringer for his efforts as technical editor on this project first and foremost, but also for all the knowledge and experience he has bestowed on me for the almost 20 years I have known him. My background and expertise have never been in networking, and the knowledge in that area I do have I owe almost exclusively to Gerry. I also owe him enormous thanks for getting me into IT security from my original job as a systems administrator working on middleware systems.

I worked with David Henry for many years at the University of Maryland, and learned much about middleware and systems architecture from him. Much of my philosophy and approach to IT challenges today I owe to things I learned working for and with him. There are so many others from my days at the University of Maryland from whom I learned so much (so don't be mad if I leave anyone out), but I specifically want to call out John Pfeifer, David Arnold, Spence Spencer, Kevin Hildebrand, Fran LoPresti, Eric Sturdivant, Willie Brown, and Brian Swartzfager.

From my time at the Centers for Medicare & Medicaid Services, I want to thank Jon Booth and Ketan Patel for giving me the opportunity to move into a formal security position for the first time, and for trusting me to oversee incredibly public and visible systems. I also want to thank Zabeen Chong for giving me the opportunity to join CMS and expand beyond my roots in the academic world. Also, I could never leave out Andy Trusz, who from my first day at CMS showed me the ropes of the workplace and became a very close personal friend. Sadly, he lost his battle with cancer the very day I left CMS for HPE. I will never forget his friendship and all he showed me!

Thank you to everyone I worked closely with at HPE/DXC, including Joe Fuhrman, Steve Larson, BJ Kerlavage, David Kohlway, Seref Konur, Ruth Pine, Brian Moore, and the aforementioned Matt Walker, for always being an amazing team and showing me so many different perspectives and new approaches to challenges! I also have to thank some colleagues from other companies I have worked closely with on projects over the years for all their support and encouragement—specifically, Anna Tant, Jason Ashbaugh, and Richie Frieman.

Thank you to Andy Baldwin, my new director at Johns Hopkins, for giving me an opportunity to return to the academic community. A special thanks to my new team and colleagues at Johns Hopkins University, from whom I have already learned so much: Patrick Le, Etan Weintraub, Kevin Buckley, Robert Kuryk, Stephen Molczyk, Anthony Reid, Michael Goldberg, Phil Bearman, and Phil Gianuzzi.

Last and most certainly not least, I want to thank my amazing wife, Robyn, for always being supportive with everything I have done professionally and personally. With four young kids at home, I would have never been able to even consider this project without all her help, assistance, and understanding—and for running interference with all our kids and pets!

INTRODUCTION

Starting a few years ago, the term *cloud* took its place within the modern lexicon and became commonly used in everyday dialogue, even by lay persons with no connection to, training for, or expertise in the IT industry. It has become common in commercials targeting the public at large, and is often used as a main selling point for services and offerings. Even those who do not understand what cloud computing is, let alone how it works, have largely come to understand it as a positive feature, feeling that it means higher reliability, faster speed, and overall a more beneficial consumer experience. Also, many companies are flocking to the benefits and features of cloud computing at a rapid pace.

With this enormous paradigm shift in the industry, the need for skilled professionals who understand cloud computing has grown at a similarly rapid pace. This demand applies to professionals in all facets of computing, but the unique aspects and features of cloud computing make the need for skilled security personnel paramount to any organization in order to properly safeguard and protect their systems, applications, and data.

Cloud computing represents a new dynamic in how IT experts—and certainly IT security experts—look at protecting data and the various techniques and methodologies available to them. Some of you approaching this certification will be experienced security professionals and already hold other certifications such as the CISSP. For others, this certification may be your first as a security professional. Some of you have been working with cloud computing from its onset, while others will be learning the cloud basics for the first time. This volume of practice exams is designed to complement the *CCSP Certified Cloud Security Professional All-in-One Exam Guide* and aims to aid anyone approaching this challenging exam, regardless of background or specific experience in security or general computing.

These practice exams, along with the *CCSP Certified Cloud Security Professional All-in-One Exam Guide,* will give you the information you need to pass the CCSP exam, as well as hopefully expand your understanding and knowledge beyond just being able to answer specific exam questions. My hope is that you find both serve you long past the exam as comprehensive desktop references for the core concepts and approaches to cloud computing and cloud security.

The structure of the *All-in-One Exam Guide* is closely aligned with the subjects of the official exam guide from (ISC)², and the practice exams are designed in the same manner.

Regardless of your background, experience, and other certifications, I hope you find the world of cloud computing and its unique security demands to be enlightening, challenging, and intellectually stimulating. Cloud represents a very dynamic and exciting new direction in computing, and one that seems likely to be a major paradigm for the foreseeable future.

Why Get Certified?

Obtaining an industry standard certification that is widely respected and recognized will serve the career of any IT professional. With cloud computing growing rapidly and more organizations clamoring to leverage its potential, the CCSP will serve as an independent verification of your skills and understanding of these concepts to any employer or regulatory agency. The CCSP can benefit anyone working in IT security at any level, from starting security analysts up to an organization's chief information security officer (CISO). Although the CCSP will in many cases complement other security certifications, such as the CISSP, it can also serve as a first or stand-alone certification as well.

How to Get Certified

The following steps and requirements for the CCSP were valid at the time of writing, but as with anything in the IT industry and its rapidly changing landscape, you should always verify directly with (ISC)² as to the most current requirements. The website for the CCSP can be found at https://www.isc2.org/ccsp.

The following are the requirements to obtain the CCSP certification:

- **Experience** A candidate must have five years of fulltime IT work experience. Within this five years, they must have three years minimum experience in IT security, and at least one year minimum in at least one of the CCSP domains. If a candidate has the CCSK certificate from the CSA, it can be substituted for the CCSP domain experience requirement, and the CISSP from (ISC)² can be used solely to fulfill the entire experience requirement for the CCSP.

- **Exam** The candidate must register for and pass the CCSP certification exam. Information about registration and the fees required can be found on the CCSP website listed earlier. The exam is four hours in duration, with 125 questions. A candidate must successfully pass the exam with a scaled score of 700 out of 1000 points.

- **Endorsement** Upon meeting the experience requirements and successfully passing the exam, a candidate must have their application endorsed by a current (ISC)² certification holder. This endorsement must be done by someone who knows the candidate and can attest to the validity of their experience and professional credentials.

- **Maintenance** After being awarded the CCSP, a certification holder must complete specific continuing professional education (CPE) requirements and pay annual maintenance fees (AMFs). Refer to the official (ISC)² site for current information about both requirements.

CCSP Domains

While it is assumed that you have studied and prepared for this exam using a resource such as the *CCSP Certified Cloud Security Professional All-in-One Guide*, the following is a brief introduction to each domain covered by the CCSP exam (it can also serve as a brief refresher).

Domain 1: Architectural Concepts and Design Requirements

The Architectural Concepts and Design Requirements domain lays the foundation for a strong understanding of the basics of cloud computing. These building blocks and foundations are based on the ISO/IEC 17788 standard. The domain defines the different and crucial roles that individuals and other entities will play within a cloud implementation, from the perspective of both the cloud service provider and the cloud service customer. It outlines the key characteristics of cloud computing, including on-demand self-service, broad network access, multitenancy, rapid elasticity and scalability, resource pooling, and measured service. It also introduces the key building blocks for a cloud environment, such as virtualization, storage, networks, and the underlying infrastructures that host and control them.

Domain 2: Cloud Data Security

The Cloud Data Security domain delves into the design, principles, and best practices for systems and applications to protect data, taking into account all types of systems, services, virtual machines, networks, and storage technologies within the hosting environment. Domain 2 outlines the cloud data lifecycle, which shows how data flows from its creation through its disposal, and how it is handled through various uses and activities while it remains within a system or application.

Domain 3: Cloud Platform and Infrastructure Security

A cloud environment consists of both a physical and virtual infrastructure, and both carry with them unique security concerns and requirements. Whereas cloud systems are built on virtualization and virtual components, underneath those virtualization layers are physical hardware and security requirements, the same as with a traditional data center. This includes access to physical systems, such as the BIOS and hardware layers, as well as the software that hosts and maintains the virtualized environments on top of them. Any breach of security or controls on the physical layer could put all virtual hosts managed within it at risk as well. Security controls within a cloud environment apply to the standard set of resources: network and communications, storage, and computing. However, the use of virtualization also requires the consideration of security in regard to the management plane that is used to control and manage the virtual machines. Domain 3 delves into the cloud-specific risks, the risks associated with virtualization, and the specific countermeasure strategies that can be employed to offset them.

Domain 4: Cloud Application Security

Using cloud environments and cloud technologies is quickly gaining in popularity for both their cost and flexibility. Cloud environments offer incredible efficiencies and ease with quickly bringing environments and virtual machines online for developers, and costs are incurred only while they are live and operating; the lead time and costs associated with procuring environments or test servers in a traditional data center are largely mitigated in a cloud environment. In order for optimal cloud development to be leveraged, especially with security in mind, the Cloud Security Professional and the developers will need a solid understanding of the realities of cloud environments, what is required to secure them, as well as the common threats and vulnerabilities facing the cloud.

Domain 5: Operations

The Operations domain outlines the planning for data centers, including both the physical and logical layers and technologies employed. This also incorporates how environmental concerns and needs are addressed along with physical requirements, including reliable and redundant access to cooling and electrical resources, as well as adequate protection from natural disasters and environmental issues.

Domain 6: Legal and Compliance

Domain 6 is focused on the legal and regulatory compliance requirements for IT systems, including how they are specifically related to cloud computing and its many unique facets. Cloud computing presents many distinct risks and challenges because it often spans different regulatory or national borders, and as such is subjected to many different requirements, which sometimes are in conflict with each other. The domain covers legally mandated controls from the perspective of multiple jurisdictions, as well as legal risks specific to cloud computing. The particular definitions and legal requirements for personal information and privacy as they relate to jurisdictional controls are included, as well as the differences between contractual and regulated personal data protections.

Architectural Concepts and Design Requirements Domain

Domain 1 is focused on the following topics:

- Cloud computing players and terms
- Cloud computing essential characteristics
- Cloud service categories
- Cloud deployment models
- Security concepts relevant to cloud computing
- Certifications
- Cloud cost–benefit analysis
- Cloud architecture models

Domain 1, which covers architectural concepts and design requirements, forms the basis for cloud computing technologies and defines their key components and characteristics. Cloud computing is a model for enabling ubiquitous, convenient, on-demand network access to a shared pool of configurable computer resources (e.g., networks, servers, storage, applications, and services) that can be rapidly provisioned and released with minimal management effort or service provider interaction. This cloud model is composed of five essential characteristics, three service models, and four deployment models.

Differing from the classic data center model of server hardware, network appliances, cabling, power units and environmental controls, cloud computing is predicated on the concept of purchasing "services" to comprise various levels of automation and support based on the needs of the customer at any various point in time. Compare that to the classical data center model, which requires a customer to have purchased and configured systems to their maximum capacity at all times, regardless of the need due to business cycles and changing demands.

1. Which concept of cloud computing pertains to the ability for a cloud customer and users to access their services through a variety of different devices and locations?

   A. Interoperability

   B. Open source

   C. Broad network access

   D. Single sign-on

2. Your new contract with a customer requires the certification of cryptographic modules used within your systems and applications. Which certification framework would be the *MOST* appropriate to utilize to comply with the contractual requirements?

   A. FIPS 140-2

   B. NIST SP 800-53

   C. SOC 2

   D. ISO/IEC 27001

3. Which of the following aspects of an application is *MOST* likely to be a component of measured service with all SaaS implementations?

   A. CPU

   B. Storage

   C. Number of users

   D. Memory

4. In a traditional data center, resources are owned, controlled, and maintained by a single entity for their exclusive use for services and systems. Within a cloud environment, this infrastructure is shared among many different customers. What is this concept called?

   A. Co-location

   B. Elasticity

   C. System sharing

   D. Resource pooling

5. Which of the following concepts, pertaining to cloud computing, allows the cloud customer to provision services with minimal assistance or involvement from the cloud provider?

   A. On-demand self-service

   B. Auto-scaling

   C. Elasticity

   D. Customer self-provisioning

6. Which concept of cloud computing pertains to the ability to reuse components and services of an application for other purposes?

   A. Portability

   B. Interoperability

   C. Resource pooling

   D. Elasticity

7. Which of the following threat types is mostly likely to occur as a result of an organization moving from a traditional data center to a cloud environment?

   A. Insufficient due diligence

   B. Data breach

   C. Insecure APIs

   D. System vulnerabilities

8. Which of the following types of software is a Type 2 hypervisor dependent on that a Type 1 hypervisor isn't?

   A. VPN

   B. Firewall

   C. Operating system

   D. IDS

9. Which cloud service category brings with it the most expensive startup costs, but also the lowest costs for ongoing support and maintenance staff?

   A. IaaS

   B. SaaS

   C. PaaS

   D. DaaS

10. Which type of cloud service category would having a vendor-neutral encryption scheme for data at rest (DAR) be the *MOST* important?

   A. Public

   B. Hybrid

   C. Private

   D. Community

11. Although encryption can help an organization to effectively decrease the possibility of data breaches, which other type of threat can it increase the chances of?

   A. Insecure interfaces

   B. Data loss

   C. System vulnerabilities

   D. Account hijacking

12. Which of the following auditing or reporting types pertains *ONLY* to financial statements and reporting?

   A. SOC 1

   B. NIST SP 800-53

   C. SOC 2

   D. FIPS 140-2

13. Which of the following roles works to obtain new customers and secure contracts?

   A. Cloud service manager

   B. Cloud service broker

   C. Cloud service deployment manager

   D. Cloud service business manager

14. Which of the following is a security consideration of a Type 2 hypervisor that is *NOT* a security concern of a Type 1 hypervisor?

   A. Operating system

   B. Firewall

   C. VLAN

   D. Access controls

15. Which of the following is *NOT* considered an effective method of mitigation for the systems vulnerability threat?

   A. Patching

   B. Monitoring

   C. Scanning

   D. Virtualization

16. Most modern web-based applications, especially those hosted within a cloud environment, rely heavily on web services and consumable resources. Which of the following is the most widely used security protocol to protect these types of technologies?

   A. IPSec

   B. VPN

C. HTTPS

D. SSH

17. Your company is focused on software development, and your main focus is keeping the costs of development as low as possible to maximize profit. Which cloud service category would be the most appropriate to use for this goal?

   A. Infrastructure

   B. Software

   C. Platform

   D. Desktop

18. Which of the following aspects of cloud computing makes data in transit (DIT) between internal servers more of a risk than in a traditional data center?

   A. Multitenancy

   B. Portability

   C. Interoperability

   D. Broad network access

19. Data is modified from its original form by an application or user. Which phase of the cloud secure data lifecycle would this action be classified under?

   A. Use

   B. Share

   C. Archive

   D. Modify

20. In a cloud environment, many different users and organizations have access to the same resources, and the cloud provider has systems staff who have access to storage systems where virtual machine images are housed. Which of the following, based on that information, is necessary to protect and isolate data to only those authorized?

   A. Encryption

   B. Sandboxing

   C. VLANs

   D. Reversibility

21. Which of the following data sanitation methods would be the *MOST* effective if you needed to securely remove data as quickly as possible in a cloud environment?

   A. Zeroing

   B. Cryptographic erasure

   C. Overwriting

   D. Degaussing

22. Which of the following descriptions of a Type 1 Hypervisor is *MOST* correct?

   A. It runs on as an application on top of an operating system to host virtual machines.

   B. It runs on a separate management server and interacts with a virtualization appliance.

   C. It runs directly on top of the hardware and serves as the sole layer between the hardware and virtual machines.

   D. It runs directly on top of the hardware and runs an additional software layer to host virtual machines.

23. When a user accesses a system, what process determines the roles and privileges that user is granted within the application?

   A. Authorization

   B. Authentication

   C. Provisioning

   D. Privilege

24. Which of the following technologies has been deprecated and deemed unsafe to use for secure communications and data?

   A. TLS

   B. AES

   C. DNS

   D. SSL

25. Which concept pertains to cloud customers paying only for the resources they use and consume, and only for the duration they are using them?

   A. Measured service

   B. Auto-scaling

   C. Portability

   D. Elasticity

26. Which of the following aspects of cloud computing is a more prominent feature of PaaS versus IaaS?

   A. Availability

   B. Auto-scaling

   C. Portability

   D. Broad network access

27. Which role, on behalf of the cloud customer, is responsible for the testing of cloud services?

   A. Cloud service user

   B. Cloud service administrator

C. Cloud service business manager

D. Cloud service integrator

28. Your company has undertaken a full study of moving services to a cloud environment, but due to budget constraints, the project has been delayed. You now have received budget money and a demand that the cloud services be set up as soon as possible. Which cloud service category would be your best option under the circumstances?

    A. Private

    B. Community

    C. Hybrid

    D. Public

29. What is the main drawback to having a remote key management service in production use, versus a local one?

    A. The cloud provider will have full control over the keys.

    B. The software may be insecure.

    C. Availability is crucial.

    D. Incompatibility issues.

30. Which cloud service category is *MOST* likely to use a client-side key management system?

    A. IaaS

    B. SaaS

    C. PaaS

    D. DaaS

31. Which of the following is *NOT* part of the determination of the account provisioning process?

    A. Regulations

    B. Contracts

    C. Organizational policies

    D. Privacy notices

32. Which of the following threats against a system is the *MOST* difficult to mitigate when the cloud service category is removed as part of the consideration?

    A. Insufficient due diligence

    B. Malicious insiders

    C. Account hijacking

    D. Data loss

33. Which of the following methods of attack, used in a SaaS environment, poses the biggest threat to the exposure of data across different customers?

   A. DDoS

   B. XSS

   C. JSON

   D. XSLT

34. Which concept is focused on ensuring that users are given the appropriate rights to data and functions within an application?

   A. Authentication

   B. Authorization

   C. Privilege

   D. Provisioning

35. Which of the following concepts would *MOST* likely apply specifically to a private cloud deployment model?

   A. Portability

   B. Reversibility

   C. Ownership

   D. Resource pooling

36. Which of the following concepts pertains to the ability to verify that proper controls and policies are in place on a system or application?

   A. Auditability

   B. Governance

   C. Regulation

   D. Elasticity

37. Which security certification serves as a general framework that can be applied to any type of system or application?

   A. ISO/IEC 27001

   B. PCI DSS

   C. FIPS 140-2

   D. NIST SP 800-53

38. Which group developed, maintains, and controls the PCI DSS standards and controls?

   A. NIST

   B. ISO/IEC

C. EU

D. Credit card companies

39. Which cloud service category offers the most customization options and control to the cloud customer?

    A. PaaS

    B. IaaS

    C. SaaS

    D. DaaS

40. The NIST Cloud Technology Roadmap contains a component focused on the minimum requirements to meet satisfactory contractual obligations between the cloud provider and cloud customer. Which of the following encapsulates this concept?

    A. Accountability

    B. Governance

    C. SLA

    D. Auditing

41. For optimal security, where should the authorization process of user access and permissions be performed?

    A. Account provisioning

    B. Throughout use of the application

    C. Immediately after authentication

    D. As part of the change management process

42. Which of the following would *NOT* be a reason a customer could be "locked in" to a particular cloud provider?

    A. Software versions

    B. Developers

    C. Application environments

    D. Regulations

43. Within a cloud environment, which network location would be the *LEAST* effective for a cloud customer to expect the implementation of security controls?

    A. Border perimeter

    B. DMZ

    C. Between VLANs

    D. Between the data and application zones

44. Your IT security director has asked you to evaluate a cloud provider to determine whether its security practices match with current organizational policy in regard to data sanitation processes. Compared to your traditional data center, which of the following options is unlikely to be available with a cloud provider?

   A. Degaussing

   B. Cryptographic erasure

   C. Overwriting

   D. Zeroing

45. Which of the following types of threats is often made possible via social engineering tactics?

   A. Data loss

   B. System vulnerabilities

   C. Advanced persistent threats

   D. Insufficient due diligence

46. If you are bidding on contracts with the US federal government, which security framework will you need to be knowledgeable of or familiar with?

   A. PCI DSS

   B. NIST SP 800-53

   C. SOC 2

   D. ISO/IEC 27001

47. Which of the following cloud concepts encapsulates the security concerns related to bring your own device (BYOD) that a cloud security professional must always be cognizant of?

   A. Portability

   B. Broad network access

   C. On-demand self-service

   D. Interoperability

48. Which of the following is *NOT* considered a building block technology for cloud computing?

   A. CPU

   B. Memory

   C. Storage

   D. Servers

1. C	**17.** C	**33.** B
2. A	**18.** A	**34.** B
3. C	**19.** A	**35.** C
4. D	**20.** A	**36.** A
5. A	**21.** B	**37.** A
6. B	**22.** C	**38.** D
7. A	**23.** A	**39.** B
8. C	**24.** D	**40.** C
9. B	**25.** A	**41.** B
10. B	**26.** B	**42.** B
11. B	**27.** B	**43.** A
12. A	**28.** D	**44.** A
13. B	**29.** C	**45.** C
14. A	**30.** B	**46.** B
15. D	**31.** D	**47.** B
16. C	**32.** B	**48.** D

Comprehensive Answers and Explanations

1. Which concept of cloud computing pertains to the ability for a cloud customer and users to access their services through a variety of different devices and locations?

   A. Interoperability

   B. Open source

   C. Broad network access

   D. Single sign-on

   ☑ **C.** Broad network access pertains to the availability of cloud resources from virtually any network location, and through any type of device. This can be from corporate networks or from the public Internet on virtually any type of connection. In regard to devices, while many cloud services are accessed via web browsers and mobile applications, it is possible to use any type of thick or thin desktop client that is appropriate as well.

   ☒ **A** is incorrect because interoperability refers to the ease with which one can move or reuse components of an application or service. For systems and applications with a high level of interoperability, the customer is not bound or locked in to a particular cloud provider, and has the option to move between them. This allows far great flexibility for a cloud customer, and the ability to continually shop for the best financial and feature options from different cloud providers.

   ☒ **B** is incorrect because "open source" refers to a style and methodology of software development and distribution, not the manner in which the applications themselves are accessed once deployed. With open source software, the full source code is available for distribution to anyone who wants it, even if binary distributions are offered as well. This allows for understanding or auditing of the source code, as well as for those interested to contribute to the software development. It also offers the opportunity for someone to modify the source code for their particular needs. Many commonly used applications are open source, such as Apache, Perl, PHP, MySQL, and even the Linux operating system.

   ☒ **D** is incorrect because, although single sign-on is very often a component of cloud-based applications, it is not a requirement, nor does it refer specifically to the manner in which applications or services are accessed. Single sign-on systems offer the ability for users to sign into one source and then, through cookies, tokens, or some other method of maintaining state, pass from one application to another without having to authenticate again for each one.

2. Your new contract with a customer requires the certification of cryptographic modules used within your systems and applications. Which certification framework would be the *MOST* appropriate to utilize to comply with the contractual requirements?

   A. FIPS 140-2

   B. NIST SP 800-53

C. SOC 2

D. ISO/IEC 27001

☑ **A.** The Federal Information Processing Standard (FIPS) 140-2 publication, authored by the National Institutes of Standards and Technology (NIST) of the United States, is a process by which cryptographic modules are evaluated and certified. It applies to both the hardware and software components used during cryptographic processes, and it's based on the particular needs for confidentiality and integrity of the data being protected. It is composed of four levels, with increasing intensities of security controls and implementations of them.

☒ **B** is incorrect because the NIST SP 800-53 is a publication and set of guidelines that governs security controls for all IT systems of the US federal government, except those pertaining to national security systems. It is designed and intended to serve as an aid for federal agencies in the governance of the IT systems and data, specifically in regard to the implementation of federal laws and policies related to them.

☒ **C** is incorrect because Service Organization Controls (SOC) Type 2 reports serve as more general framework evaluations of the security controls and postures of an organization, and not specifically focused on the evaluation or certification of cryptographic modules. SOC 2 reports focus on a core collection of trust principles, including security, processing integrity, availability, privacy, and confidentiality.

☒ **D** is incorrect because the ISO/IEC 27001 is considered a broad and general "gold standard" for security certification and guidance. It comprehensively covers all areas of security controls and policies, and is not specifically focused on cryptographic modules or their certification.

3. Which of the following aspects of an application is *MOST* likely to be a component of measured service with all SaaS implementations?

A. CPU

B. Storage

C. Number of users

D. Memory

☑ **C.** Within a Software as a Service (SaaS) implementation, cloud customers are acquiring and paying for services that are explicitly tied to the use of a fully operational application package that is completely designed, maintained, and implemented by the cloud provider. Billing is often measured based on the number of users or the number of transactions the organization does with the application, rather than traditional computing resources associated with other service categories.

☒ **A** is incorrect because CPU resources are the responsibility of the cloud provider within a SaaS implementation, to ensure they are sufficiently allocated to support and meet the requirements of the customers.

☒ **B** is incorrect for the same reasons as CPU. However, in some circumstances, depending on the actual software application and the needs of the customer, there could be incremental storage costs, but these are handled on a case-by-case basis and are not necessarily something that is universal across SaaS implementations. The main exception to this would be for public SaaS implementations such as iCloud, Dropbox, and OneDrive, where the services at a base level are free, with incremental charges for additional storage capacity.

☒ **D** is incorrect because memory and CPU, in this sense, would be similar in that it is incumbent on the cloud provider to ensure appropriate computing resources are allocated and available to the applications and users.

4. In a traditional data center, resources are owned, controlled, and maintained by a single entity for their exclusive use for services and systems. Within a cloud environment, this infrastructure is shared among many different customers. What is this concept called?

   A. Co-location

   B. Elasticity

   C. System sharing

   D. Resource pooling

   ☑ **D.** Resource pooling is largely what separates a traditional data center from a cloud in regard to computing resources. In a traditional data center, resources are allocated to specific systems or applications, and for the most part are not shared. Within a cloud, the entire hardware infrastructure is viewed as an aggregate and then allocated accordingly to the various cloud customers and applications hosted within it. This is typically a massive pool of resources that not only can handle the typical operational load of the hosted applications, but also allow for expansion through auto-elasticity or cyclical loads of some applications.

   ☒ **A** is incorrect because co-location refers to the hosting of multiple applications or systems within the same physical hardware, but not necessarily through the use of pooled and allocated resources. This can also be done within a traditional data center, where any level of hardware can be shared, including networking, physical floor space, cooling, and power. The typically dedicated nature of resources within a co-location setup is what differentiates it from resource pooling within a cloud environment.

   ☒ **B** is incorrect because elasticity refers to the ability for systems, services, and applications to automatically expand or shrink to meet actual needs at the time. If the applications are written to support elasticity, then as load changes are detected in the environment and meet predefined thresholds, the cloud environment can dynamically and rapidly resize the resources allocated to meet exactly what is needed, rather than having enormous resources on standby to handle any sudden increase in demand.

   ☒ **C** is incorrect because system sharing is provided as an erroneous answer. Although it is a similar type of answer to resource pooling, it is not a typically used or official term for anything related to cloud computing, or this specific question.

5. Which of the following concepts, pertaining to cloud computing, allows the cloud customer to provision services with minimal assistance or involvement from the cloud provider?

A. On-demand self-service

B. Auto-scaling

C. Elasticity

D. Customer self-provisioning

☑ **A.** Cloud services can be requested, provisioned, and put into use by the customer through automated means, without the need to interact with support personnel of the cloud provider. This is typically offered to the cloud customer through a web portal, but can also be exposed through API calls or other programmatic means. As services are changed, billing is adjusted based on the changing nature of the currently allocated resources.

☒ **B** is incorrect because auto-scaling refers to the automatic and programmatic ability for a cloud environment to dynamically adjust to current demands. Although this is similar in some ways to on-demand self-service, the difference is with the automatic nature of the processes. On-demand self-service is something originated and requested by the cloud customer at the time, rather than something that is programmed with thresholds and rulesets to execute automatically.

☒ **C** is incorrect because elasticity refers to the ability of a cloud or application environment to change resources as demand changes. An application or service must be designed in such a way to allow for easy expansion of resources, and implemented in such a way that programmatic means can be used to do so.

☒ **D** is incorrect because customer self-provisioning is an erroneous answer that is similar to the actual answer of on-demand self-service. Although the terms sound very similar, it is not the official or commonly used term for such capabilities.

6. Which concept of cloud computing pertains to the ability to reuse components and services of an application for other purposes?

A. Portability

B. Interoperability

C. Resource pooling

D. Elasticity

☑ **B.** Interoperability is the ease with which one can move or reuse components of an application or service. The main concept is to not have such dependencies on the underlying operating system, hosting environment, libraries, or APIs that lock in a service to one particular set of hosts or solutions. Services with a high degree of interoperability can easily move between cloud providers, hosting configurations, and cloud service categories, and give enormous flexibility to an organization. This allows different services to leverage applications and APIs for different purposes, along with the modularization of components for reuse.

☒ **A** is incorrect because portability, while similar to interoperability, focuses solely on the ability to move between cloud providers, and not on the ability to use components or modules from a particular service for other or extended purposes. For portability, the main focus is not on reuse or repurposing, but rather solely on the ability to freely and easily move.

☒ **C** is incorrect because resource pooling refers to the sharing of resources within the cloud environment, where the entire hardware infrastructure is viewed as an aggregate and then allocated accordingly to the various cloud customers and applications hosted within it. This is typically a massive pool of resources that not only can handle the typical operational load of the hosted applications, but also allow for expansion through auto-elasticity or cyclical loads of some applications.

☒ **D** is incorrect because elasticity refers to the ability of a cloud or application environment to change resources as demand changes. An application or service must be designed in such a way to allow for easy expansion of resources, and implemented in such a way that programmatic means can be used to do so.

7. Which of the following threat types is mostly likely to occur as a result of an organization moving from a traditional data center to a cloud environment?

   A. Insufficient due diligence

   B. Data breach

   C. Insecure APIs

   D. System vulnerabilities

   ☑ **A.** When an organization is considering moving its systems and applications from a traditional data center model to a cloud environment, it must evaluate a lot of variables and factors to determine if the move to a cloud system is appropriate or feasible. Without proper and thorough evaluation of its systems, designs, and controls, an organization may unintentionally expose itself to more security risk and vulnerabilities by moving to a cloud environment.

   ☒ **B** is incorrect because a data breach occurs when there is an unauthorized exposure of sensitive or private data to a party that is not entitled to have it. This can occur either from accidental exposure or from hacking or other malicious activity. Within a cloud environment, because of multitenancy, there is a higher exposure and risk than in a traditional data center with isolated systems.

   ☒ **C** is incorrect because insecure APIs occur when there are not proper controls or validation of services utilizing and accessing them. Cloud environments make heavy use of APIs for everything from consumer cloud services to the backbone management, automation, and orchestration of the cloud, and their security is of the utmost importance.

   ☒ **D** is incorrect because system vulnerabilities are related to the patching, configuration, and monitoring of all IT systems, whether in a cloud environment or not. With any system vulnerabilities, threats can be expanded to other services by gaining unauthorized exposure to resources, and strong policies and practices are needed to ensure compliance with configuration and patching of systems, and monitoring for noncompliance is always extremely important.

8. Which of the following types of software is a Type 2 hypervisor dependent on that a Type 1 hypervisor isn't?

   A. VPN

   B. Firewall

   C. Operating system

   D. IDS

   ☑ **C.** A Type 2 hypervisor runs on top of a host operating system as a software application, and then the virtual machines are deployed within it. With a Type 1 hypervisor, the software is tied directly to the underlying hardware and does not rely on a host operating system to function.

   ☒ **A** is incorrect because a virtual private network (VPN) is a method for securing network traffic and communications, and does not have any impact on hypervisors or the type that is used.

   ☒ **B** is incorrect because a firewall is used for network security and the limiting of traffic across a network, but is not specifically related to a hypervisor or the type of hypervisor used.

   ☒ **D** is incorrect because an intrusion detection system (IDS) is a network security device to monitor for specific types of traffic or patterns against a set of signatures for known attacks and vulnerabilities. It is not related to, or dependent on, a hypervisor or the specific type of hypervisor used.

9. Which cloud service category brings with it the most expensive startup costs, but also the lowest costs for ongoing support and maintenance staff?

   A. IaaS

   B. SaaS

   C. PaaS

   D. DaaS

   ☑ **B.** A Software as a Service (SaaS) solution will typically have the highest startup and licensing costs, as the customer is buying a fully developed, integrated, secured, and production-ready software application. This means that the upfront costs are directly financial (and not as staff intensive as the others), but over its lifetime an SaaS solution will have the lowest costs in support staff and maintenance because the cloud provider will be responsible for those activities.

   ☒ **A** is incorrect because Infrastructure as a Service (IaaS) will have the lowest financial costs upfront, as most of the activities related to getting a system up and running involve staff. It is the responsibility of the cloud customer to configure and deploy the virtual machines and all components, but also the application and its security. Over the lifetime of the hosting arrangement, the staff costs will be the highest with IaaS implementations, while the actual licensing and hosting costs from a purely financial standpoint will be the lowest.

⊠ **C** is incorrect because Platform as a Service (PaaS) represents a balance between upfront financial costs and licensing, as well as the staff costs on behalf of the cloud customer. With PaaS, the cloud provider delivers the virtual machine, with the application framework and dependencies ready to use, but it is up to the cloud customer to deploy, secure, and test its software applications and services.

⊠ **D** is incorrect because Desktop as a Service (DaaS) is very similar to PaaS, in that the cloud provider delivers the framework and platform, but it is up to the cloud customer to deploy and configure its specific applications and services that will run within the framework.

10. Which type of cloud service category would having a vendor-neutral encryption scheme for data at rest (DAR) be the *MOST* important?

A. Public

B. Hybrid

C. Private

D. Community

☑ **B.** With the hybrid cloud category, a vendor-neutral solution for encryption would be the most important because the application and data would span more than one cloud provider. There is little chance of success or scalability with the utilization of an encryption scheme from one cloud provider, and it wouldn't likely port or work well with another. By using a vendor-neutral solution, a cloud customer can maintain maximum flexibility going forward with a hybrid cloud solution.

⊠ **A** is incorrect because a public cloud solution is with a single cloud provider, which might provide built-in or proprietary encryption schemes that work optimally in its environment. Care needs to be taken to ensure the application and systems do not get effectively locked into that provider because a loss of portability and interoperability can occur.

⊠ **C** is incorrect because many private cloud solutions offer their own encryption schemes that are designed to work within their environment. Care needs to be taken to ensure the application and systems do not get effectively locked into one provider because a loss of portability and interoperability can occur.

⊠ **D** is incorrect because a community cloud may be constructed with toolsets that work optimally within it and are likely geared toward similar organizations and needs. Care needs to be taken to ensure the application and systems do not get effectively locked into one provider because a loss of portability and interoperability can occur.

11. Although encryption can help an organization to effectively decrease the possibility of data breaches, which other type of threat can it increase the chances of?

    A. Insecure interfaces

    B. Data loss

    C. System vulnerabilities

    D. Account hijacking

    ☑ **B.** Data loss occurs when an organization either loses data or loses access to it. This is different from a data breach, where it is exposed to unauthorized parties. Although the use of encryption will serve as a strong mitigation against data breaches, the reliance on keys, and access to them, increases the possibility of data loss. If the keys were to be lost or destroyed, the organization would lose access to the data.

    ☒ **A** is incorrect because "insecure interfaces" refers to having APIs or other services improperly secured, and thus subject to being compromised or abused. Insecure interfaces would render any application and its data less secure and more vulnerable, and as such, would not fit what this question is looking for.

    ☒ **C** is incorrect because system vulnerabilities would always lead to less secure applications and data, and they would not under any circumstances decrease the possibility of data breaches.

    ☒ **D** is incorrect because account hijacking refers to situations where an attacker is able to access a system or cloud environment through a valid account, perhaps not even on the same application, and then use that access to eavesdrop or to access other data. This is not unique to a cloud environment, but due to multitenancy, the risk level is higher and not under control of an individual cloud customer.

12. Which of the following auditing or reporting types pertains *ONLY* to financial statements and reporting?

    A. SOC 1

    B. NIST SP 800-53

    C. SOC 2

    D. FIPS 140-2

    ☑ **A.** The Service Organization Control (SOC) Type 1 reports focus on the controls in place at an organization and pertain to financial reporting and the types of information useful with a financial audit. SOC 1 focuses on the management structure of the organization, the target customer base, and the regulations that an audit would be guided by and subjected to.

☒ **B** is incorrect because NIST SP 800-53 is on security controls for US federal government IT systems, with the exception of national security systems, and serves as a guide for federal agencies and contractors to conform to pertinent law and regulations. It is focused exclusively on government systems, and although it forms a comprehensive framework for security, some elements would likely be difficult for nongovernmental systems to comply with.

☒ **C** is incorrect because SOC Type 2 reports are structured by the same organization as SOC Type 1 reports. They go beyond just a review of controls and information pertinent to financial reports and statements, and include five additional areas: security, availability, processing integrity, confidentiality, and privacy.

☒ **D** is incorrect because FIPS 140-2 is a United States federal government publication that is focused on the certification and validation of cryptographic modules, and does not pertain to financial statements or reports in any way.

13. Which of the following roles works to obtain new customers and secure contracts?

   A. Cloud service manager

   B. Cloud service broker

   C. Cloud service deployment manager

   D. Cloud service business manager

   ☑ **B.** The cloud service broker obtains new customers, analyzes the marketplace, and secures contracts and agreements for cloud services.

   ☒ **A** is incorrect because the cloud service manager delivers, provisions, and manages cloud services.

   ☒ **C** is incorrect because the cloud service deployment manager gathers metrics on cloud services, manages deployment steps and processes, and defines the environment and processes.

   ☒ **D** is incorrect because the cloud service business manager oversees business plans and customer relationships, as well as processes financial transactions.

14. Which of the following is a security consideration of a Type 2 hypervisor that is *NOT* a security concern of a Type 1 hypervisor?

   A. Operating system

   B. Firewall

   C. VLAN

   D. Access controls

   ☑ **A.** Rather than interacting directly with the underlying hardware as a Type 1 hypervisor does, a Type 2 hypervisor runs on top of an operating system. This creates an additional layer of security considerations because the security of the host operating system will also impact the hypervisor software, and the hypervisor is susceptible to any security vulnerabilities or threats to the operating system. With a Type 1 hypervisor, there is no additional layer, and security can be tightly controlled by the vendor.

☒ **B** is incorrect because firewalls, and their impact and importance on network security, would not be affected by the type of hypervisor employed to host virtual machines.

☒ **C** is incorrect because VLANs are logical network segments for organizing, segregating, and assisting with network security, and would not be impacted by the type of hypervisor being used.

☒ **D** is incorrect because access controls are a concern of all hypervisors and the hosts that run within them, and would not be impacted by the use of either type of hypervisor.

15. Which of the following is *NOT* considered an effective method of mitigation for the systems vulnerability threat?

A. Patching

B. Monitoring

C. Scanning

D. Virtualization

☑ **D.** Virtualization would not be a method or effective tool for the mitigation of system vulnerabilities. When running, a virtual machine is subjected to the same security concerns and vulnerabilities as a physical server and operating system would be. Additionally, because the virtual machine is merely an image residing in storage, there are extra vulnerabilities in regard to securing the image, and the reality is that an image can be attacked or compromised even when not running.

☒ **A** is incorrect because patching is one of the key components and most effective ways for mitigating system vulnerabilities. As security vulnerabilities are discovered, vendors publish and distribute patches to fix or mitigate the vulnerabilities within their software. By installing these patches as soon as possible, administrators can decrease the likeliness of their systems being compromised.

☒ **B** is incorrect because the monitoring of systems is an effective method for mitigating and limiting system vulnerabilities and threats. Monitoring will give insight into the types of threats and attacks being employed against your systems, and you can discover when a potential exploit may have been successful and what steps can be taken to contain or limit any damage.

☒ **C** is incorrect because scanning is a very common tool used to discover any vulnerabilities on systems in need of mitigation. Scanning is commonly used to verify that patches have been applied, as well as to verify what settings and configurations have been properly implemented to limit threats and to disable unnecessary services and access.

16. Most modern web-based applications, especially those hosted within a cloud environment, rely heavily on web services and consumable resources. Which of the following is the most widely used security protocol to protect these types of technologies?

    A. IPSec

    B. VPN

    C. HTTPS

    D. SSH

    ☑ **C.** The Hypertext Transfer Protocol Secure (HTTPS) is the most commonly used protocol for securing communications and applications within a cloud environment, especially as most are web-based systems. HTTPS extends the traditional HTTP protocol used for web communications by adding security protocols and encryption.

    ☒ **A** is incorrect because although IPSec is a commonly used method for securing communications, it is not used nearly on the same scale as HTTPS. It is also used for server-to-server communications, adds substantial load to systems, and is not a method used for customer communications at all.

    ☒ **B** is incorrect because VPNs are often used for administrative and support communications; they are not commonly used for security web services. In situations where a VPN is used to protect communications, HTTPS is still almost always used in conjunction with it.

    ☒ **D** is incorrect because SSH is used for obtaining secure shell access to servers for administration and application support. In PaaS and SaaS service categories, the cloud customer will typically not have server access either. SSH is not commonly used to secure web services.

17. Your company is focused on software development, and your main focus is keeping the costs of development as low as possible to maximize profit. Which cloud service category would be the most appropriate to use for this goal?

    A. Infrastructure

    B. Software

    C. Platform

    D. Desktop

    ☑ **C.** With the Platform as a Service (PaaS) service category, a development company can focus exclusively on software development and deployment, rather than having to maintain, install, or configure hosting systems. It also would enable a development team to quickly try out different hosting platforms or cloud providers to find what works best for their applications.

    ☒ **A** is incorrect because although the startup costs with the cloud provider will be lower for Infrastructure as a Service (IaaS) than with PaaS, the costs with staff and time to build, install, configure, and secure virtual machines will be enormous. Having to build out and maintain infrastructure would take the developers away from their core focus.

☒ **B** is incorrect because Software as a Service (SaaS) offers a full application for a cloud customer, not something where development would be done (or even could be done).

☒ **D** is incorrect because Desktop as a Service (DaaS) would not be appropriate for development and deployment, as it is intended to host desktop applications in a cloud environment.

18. Which of the following aspects of cloud computing makes data in transit (DIT) between internal servers more of a risk than in a traditional data center?

   A. Multitenancy

   B. Portability

   C. Interoperability

   D. Broad network access

   ☑ **A.** Multitenancy, within a cloud environment, means having different customers, systems, and applications, all within the same physical systems and networks. Even with the use of secure communications and encryption, this poses an additional risk above a traditional data center because any compromise or malicious intent from one system could impact the other systems. Threats such as eavesdropping and internal attacks are a major concern with cloud computing and multitenancy.

   ☒ **B** is incorrect because portability refers to the capability to easily move between different cloud providers and hosting arrangements. It does not pose any security concerns in relation to data in transit, no with any production runtime systems.

   ☒ **C** is incorrect because interoperability refers to the capability of reusing and repurposing components and services. It gives an organization the ability to quickly deploy different applications and make modular components to assist with rapid development. As a capability, it does not pose any security concerns with data in transit or runtime environments.

   ☒ **D** is incorrect because broad network access refers to the capability of accessing cloud services from any location and from a variety of devices. This would be similar to accessing of services within a traditional data center, but does not necessarily pose additional security concerns by itself in the way that multitenancy can expose potential internal attacks from other compromised systems.

19. Data is modified from its original form by an application or user. Which phase of the cloud secure data lifecycle would this action be classified under?

   A. Use

   B. Share

   C. Archive

   D. Modify

   ☑ **A.** During the "use" phase of the cloud secure data lifecycle, the data is consumed and possibly modified from its original form by an application, either via programmatic means or by the direct actions of a user of the application.

☒ **B** is incorrect because the "share" phase of the cloud secure data lifecycle entails the data being available to view by users, customers, administrators, or other services.

☒ **C** is incorrect because the "archive" phase of the cloud secure data lifecycle pertains to the data being removed from active access and availability and then placed into a static state where it is preserved for a predefined period of time.

☒ **D** is incorrect because "modify" is not a phase of the cloud secure data lifecycle. The concepts that would most likely be placed under such a heading are already found in the "use" phase.

20. In a cloud environment, many different users and organizations have access to the same resources, and the cloud provider has systems staff who have access to storage systems where virtual machine images are housed. Which of the following, based on that information, is necessary to protect and isolate data to only those authorized?

    A. Encryption

    B. Sandboxing

    C. VLANs

    D. Reversibility

    ☑ **A.** With resource pooling and multitenancy, as well as the support staff of the cloud provider having privileged access throughout the entire environment, encryption is of particular importance to protect data. With the keys under the control of the cloud customer, even if a system is compromised, the data will be protected, which would also apply to virtual images that could be accessed via storage systems.

    ☒ **B** is incorrect because sandboxing is a way of segregating systems or applications for testing or security reasons, but would not provide additional protection for data on systems. It is mostly used to keep web services from interacting and to keep production and non-production systems from mixing together.

    ☒ **C** is incorrect because VLANs are used for logical network segregations, and although they can be used to provide additional security at the network level, they would not provide any additional security to data and storage methods.

    ☒ **D** is incorrect because reversibility refers to the ability of a cloud customer to remove all applications and data from a cloud environment, along with assurances from the cloud provider that everything was securely removed from its systems. This does not pertain to the security of data during a hosting arrangement.

21. Which of the following data sanitation methods would be the *MOST* effective if you needed to securely remove data as quickly as possible in a cloud environment?

    A. Zeroing

    B. Cryptographic erasure

    C. Overwriting

    D. Degaussing

☑ **B.** Cryptographic erasure works by destroying the keys that were used to encrypt the data. Although it does not delete the data in a traditional sense, with the keys destroyed, the data is unreadable and unrecoverable, thus giving the same effect. Because the focus is on the destruction of keys, it is also something that can be done very quickly and with minimal effort, whereas deleting large volumes of data and then verifying it has been deleted can be a very time-consuming process.

☒ **A** is incorrect because zeroing data refers to overwriting all data sectors with null values. Within a traditional data center with physical hardware, this is typically possible, but within a cloud environment and the way data is very dispersed, or in the case of object storage housed externally, zeroing data may not be possible. Even if it is possible, the process is very long, time consuming, and resource intensive.

☒ **C** is incorrect because overwriting refers to the replacement of valid data with garbage or random values, in order to verify that the data has been completely destroyed. Depending on the access and cloud configuration, overwriting may not even be possible in a cloud environment—and even if it is available, the process would be extremely resource intensive and time consuming.

☒ **D** is incorrect because degaussing refers to the demagnetizing of physical storage media. Although this is possible in a traditional data center, where an organization owns the media and can do so, degaussing would not be possible in a cloud environment at all.

22. Which of the following descriptions of a Type 1 Hypervisor is *MOST* correct?

   A. It runs on as an application on top of an operating system to host virtual machines.

   B. It runs on a separate management server and interacts with a virtualization appliance.

   C. It runs directly on top of the hardware and serves as the sole layer between the hardware and virtual machines.

   D. It runs directly on top of the hardware and runs an additional software layer to host virtual machines.

☑ **C.** A Type 1 hypervisor runs directly on top of the underlying hardware and is tightly tied to it, with both hardware and software from the same vendor.

☒ **A** is incorrect because the answer is describing a Type 2 hypervisor that runs on top of an operating system, not one tied directly to the underlying hardware.

☒ **B** is incorrect because it does not describe a Type 1 or Type 2 hypervisor.

☒ **D** is incorrect because although a Type 1 hypervisor does run directly on top of the hardware, it does not need an additional software layer to host virtual machines.

23. When a user accesses a system, what process determines the roles and privileges that user is granted within the application?

   A. Authorization

   B. Authentication

   C. Provisioning

   D. Privilege

☑ **A.** Authorization is the process by which a user is granted roles and access to an application, after successfully completing the authentication process. It is typically based on group and role memberships.

☒ **B** is incorrect because authentication is the process where a user proves and validates his identity, but it does not confer access or roles.

☒ **C** is incorrect because provisioning is the process where a user is identified and proven to a system in order to acquire authentication credentials and access.

☒ **D** is incorrect because privilege refers to a level of access a user has within a system, but it's a result of the authorization process.

24. Which of the following technologies has been deprecated and deemed unsafe to use for secure communications and data?

    A. TLS

    B. AES

    C. DNS

    D. SSL

    ☑ **D.** Secure sockets layer (SSL) version 3.0 was deprecated in June 2015 by RFC 7568 because it was considered insecure, and admins were instructed to move systems to TLS.

    ☒ **A** is incorrect because Transport Socket Layer (TLS) has replaced SSL and is now the standard security for network and web communications.

    ☒ **B** is incorrect because the Advanced Encryption Standard (AES) is a type of modern encryption, and many ciphers are used with TLS for securing communications.

    ☒ **C** is incorrect because Domain Name Service (DNS) is a protocol for mapping common names to IP addresses for network communications; it is not a security protocol or used to protect actual communications.

25. Which concept pertains to cloud customers paying only for the resources they use and consume, and only for the duration they are using them?

    A. Measured service

    B. Auto-scaling

    C. Portability

    D. Elasticity

    ☑ **A.** Measured service refers to cloud customers paying only for the resources they consume, and only for the time they are consuming them. This would typically refer to the building blocks of cloud computing: CPU, memory, storage, and possibly network. This differs from a traditional data center, where an organization would need to have all resources available at all times.

☒ **B** is incorrect because auto-scaling refers to the ability of a cloud provider to automatically and programmatically alter the resources allocated to a particular application, based on its current demands and load. Although it certainly plays a crucial role with measured service, it is a distinctly different process and one that is not required, or enabled, with all cloud applications.

☒ **C** is incorrect because portability refers to the capability of a cloud-based system or application to easily move between cloud providers, and does not play a direct role in anything regarding billing or payments for services.

☒ **D** is incorrect because elasticity is the capability of a cloud-based application to grow to meet current demands in an easy, and typically in a programmatic manner. It does not relate to billing for services, though the invocation of elasticity based on load would lead to a change in billing and charges for services.

26. Which of the following aspects of cloud computing is a more prominent feature of PaaS versus IaaS?

   A. Availability

   B. Auto-scaling

   C. Portability

   D. Broad network access

   ☑ **B.** With PaaS offering a full platform and framework, and just needing application code and data to function, auto-scaling is a prominent feature of the service category, and it's typically the service category being discussed with the topic.

   ☒ **A** is incorrect because availability pertains to all cloud service categories and would not be a prominent feature of one over the other.

   ☒ **C** is incorrect because portability refers to being able to easily move from one cloud environment to another, and it applies to all cloud service categories.

   ☒ **D** is incorrect because broad network access is one of the core concepts of cloud computing and applies to all cloud service categories equally.

27. Which role, on behalf of the cloud customer, is responsible for the testing of cloud services?

   A. Cloud service user

   B. Cloud service administrator

   C. Cloud service business manager

   D. Cloud service integrator

   ☑ **B.** One of the key tasks of the cloud service administrator is to test cloud services, but also to monitor services, administer security of services, provide usage reports, and address problem reports.

   ☒ **A** is incorrect because the cloud service user is the consumer of cloud services that are offered by the cloud customer or provider.

☒ **C** is incorrect because the cloud service business manager oversees business and billing administration, as well as purchases cloud services and requests audit reports, as necessary.

☒ **D** is incorrect because the cloud service integrator is responsible for connecting and integrating existing systems and services within a cloud environment.

28. Your company has undertaken a full study of moving services to a cloud environment, but due to budget constraints, the project has been delayed. You now have received budget money and a demand that the cloud services be set up as soon as possible. Which cloud service category would be your best option under the circumstances?

   A. Private

   B. Community

   C. Hybrid

   D. Public

   ☑ **D.** Public cloud services are the quickest and easiest to set up and begin using. Most public cloud systems will be totally automated from a self-service portal, with only the need for a credit card to establish an account and begin allocating resources.

   ☒ **A** is incorrect because a private cloud would be offered by an organization for its own internal services, or it would something that's procured via contract with a provider. It is not something that could be established as quickly and easily as a public cloud would.

   ☒ **B** is incorrect because a community cloud is established by similar organization to meet their common goals. It would not be something that an organization could easily or quickly join like it could with a public cloud.

   ☒ **C** is incorrect because a hybrid cloud spans multiple hosting providers and adds additional complexity, and would not be something an organization could quickly establish and begin using.

29. What is the main drawback to having a remote key management service in production use, versus a local one?

   A. The cloud provider will have full control over the keys.

   B. The software may be insecure.

   C. Availability is crucial.

   D. Incompatibility issues.

   ☑ **C.** A remote key service is one that is hosted apart and away from the applications and systems. This gives an organization much greater control over its keys and key practices, and also allows a great degree of portability. However, having the keys kept apart from the hosting provider and applications also means that availability is crucial. If the key system were to become unavailable or unreachable, the systems and applications that rely on these keys would effectively be down as far as the users are concerned because they would be unable to function.

☒ **A** is incorrect because the entire premise of having a remote key management system is for the cloud customer to maintain control over the keys, usage, and signing practices.

☒ **B** is incorrect because regardless of whether the key management system is local or remote, the same security considerations would apply.

☒ **D** is incorrect because compatibility concerns are an issue for any service, whether it is hosted locally or remotely, and neither solution would give an inherent benefit over the other concerning compatibility.

30. Which cloud service category is *MOST* likely to use a client-side key management system?

    A. IaaS

    B. SaaS

    C. PaaS

    D. DaaS

☑ **B.** A client-side key management system is one where the software for the key management system is supplied by the cloud provider but hosted and run from a location chosen by the cloud customer. This is most common with SaaS implementations, as the cloud provider would need to supply the software to ensure compatibility with the application.

☒ **A** is incorrect because a client-side key management system would be least likely with an IaaS implementation, as it would be incumbent on the cloud customer to pick and implement its own toolsets and practices.

☒ **C** is incorrect because a client-side key management system is one typically tied closely to an application, and with a PaaS implementation, although the cloud provider is supplying the framework and hosting environment, the actual application and code are provided by the cloud customer and are its responsibility.

☒ **D** is incorrect because DaaS would typically look and perform similar to a PaaS implementation, where the cloud provider is responsible for supplying the platform and framework, but not the actual application or toolset.

31. Which of the following is *NOT* part of the determination of the account provisioning process?

    A. Regulations

    B. Contracts

    C. Organizational policies

    D. Privacy notices

☑ **D.** Privacy notices are publicly posted, on a website typically, and disclose to the users of the site how their information is collected and used. They are not part of the account provisioning process at all and would have no bearing on it.

☒ **A** is incorrect because regulations can play a central role in account provisioning. Many regulatory frameworks have specific requirements for how users must be validated prior to having credentials provisioned, including the information they must present or what kind of background check must be completed.

☒ **B** is incorrect because contracts will typically play a key role in account provisioning. Going beyond regulatory requirements, contracts often articulate and document who is to be granted access, how they will be verified, and what level and type of access they are provisioned.

☒ **C** is incorrect because organizational policies also play a key role in account provisioning. Policies may dictate to whom credentials are provisioned, as well was what the process is, what must be verified, and how long credentials are valid for.

32. Which of the following threats against a system is the *MOST* difficult to mitigate when the cloud service category is removed as part of the consideration?

   A. Insufficient due diligence

   B. Malicious insiders

   C. Account hijacking

   D. Data loss

   ☑ **B.** Malicious insiders are typically individuals who have valid access and authorization to a system, application, or data, and then use that valid access for reasons outside the intended purpose. It is especially difficult to mitigate against malicious insiders because they have valid credentials and authorization for what they are accessing, and are using it for inappropriate purposes.

   ☒ **A** is incorrect because insufficient due diligence occurs when an organization does not properly plan or evaluate IT systems for configurations, vulnerabilities, security, monitoring, and so on. This can lead to insufficient controls or misconfigurations, resulting in vulnerabilities or performance problems.

   ☒ **C** is incorrect because account hijacking refers to an attacker gaining access to a system through valid credentials and then using those credentials to launch attacks or attempt to compromise other systems within the same infrastructure as the launching pad. Other countermeasures, such as multifactor authentication, can be employed to largely mitigate the chances of account hijacking from occurring.

   ☒ **D** is incorrect because data loss refers to a situation where an organization loses actual data or loses access to it. This most commonly occurs when data is deleted or hardware fails and backups have not been performed, but it can also occur with encrypted data should the keys become lost or corrupted without backup.

33. Which of the following methods of attack, used in a SaaS environment, poses the biggest threat to the exposure of data across different customers?

   A. DDoS

   B. XSS

   C. JSON

   D. XSLT

☑ **B.** Cross-site scripting (XSS) poses a big risk with any environment, but especially within a SaaS implementation, where it is very likely that data from multiple customers is housed and accessible within the same software application.

☒ **A** is incorrect because a distributed denial of service (DDoS) attack is against the availability of a system or application, not against the confidentiality of its data.

☒ **C** is incorrect because JavaScript Object Notation (JSON) is a data-interchange format that is often used with web services. It is not a security measure, nor is it focused on data confidentiality.

☒ **D** is incorrect because Extensible Stylesheet Language Transformations (XSLT) is used for transforming documents in XML format to other formats, and is not used for security or data confidentiality processes.

34. Which concept is focused on ensuring that users are given the appropriate rights to data and functions within an application?

A. Authentication

B. Authorization

C. Privilege

D. Provisioning

☑ **B.** Authorization, performed after successful authentication, is the process by which appropriate roles and permissions are granted to the user or service account. This is based on the attributes of the account holders, such as group membership, employment status, location, or any other type of variable, and then is matched against roles for access.

☒ **A** is incorrect because authentication is the process by which a user or service proves its identity to a system or application based on its specific requirements.

☒ **C** is incorrect because privilege refers to elevated (typically administrative) access within a system or application.

☒ **D** is incorrect because provisioning is the process by which credentials are verified and proven, and then an authentication object or token is granted for access.

35. Which of the following concepts would *MOST* likely apply specifically to a private cloud deployment model?

A. Portability

B. Reversibility

C. Ownership

D. Resource pooling

☑ **C.** Within the private cloud service category, in many circumstance the cloud will be owned by the organization, or done via a contract, where a level of ownership is maintained over hardware, systems, or processes that would not be available with other cloud service categories.

☒ **A** is incorrect because portability is a key cloud concept that pertains to the ability to move services and applications between different cloud providers, and it applies to any service category or hosting model and is not different with a private cloud versus other models.

☒ **B** is incorrect because reversibility is a key cloud concept that pertains to the ability to easily and comprehensively remove applications and data from a cloud environment, and it applies to any cloud deployment model.

☒ **D** is incorrect because resource pooling is one of the key characteristics of cloud computing that relates to the aggregate system sources and their allocation among different customers and services; it does not pertain to a specific cloud deployment model.

36. Which of the following concepts pertains to the ability to verify that proper controls and policies are in place on a system or application?

    A. Auditability

    B. Governance

    C. Regulation

    D. Elasticity

    ☑ **A.** Auditing is a process of testing and verifying the security controls and configurations in place on a system or application and then comparing them to the requirements from regulations or configuration baselines that define what they should be. How easy or difficult this type of testing and verification on a system is to complete is the auditability of that system.

    ☒ **B** is incorrect because governance refers to the connection between IT management and the business focus of a company and ensuring that resources and configurations are allocated with an eye toward business needs. The distinction between governance and auditability is that the latter is focused on security controls and configurations based on regulations or baselines, not on the specific business needs used to define them.

    ☒ **C** is incorrect because regulation pertains to requirements that an organization must follow based on the type and usage of its particular data, and it is governed by the pertinent jurisdiction where the organization is located. Regulations will typically be used to form the basis of audits and guidelines for the implementation of security controls and system configurations.

    ☒ **D** is incorrect because elasticity refers to the ability of a cloud system to dynamically change the resources available to a system or application based on its current needs; it does not pertain to the auditing or evaluation of controls in any way.

37. Which security certification serves as a general framework that can be applied to any type of system or application?

    A. ISO/IEC 27001

    B. PCI DSS

C. FIPS 140-2

D. NIST SP 800-53

☑ **A.** The ISO/IEC 27001 standard, and its most current iteration ISO/IEC 27001:2013, serves as a general security framework for any type of system or application, regardless of its purpose and specific type of data. It is widely considered the "gold standard" for international security certification, even if it is does not specifically pertain to cloud computing.

☒ **B** is incorrect because the Payment Card Industry Data Security Standard (PCI DSS) is a standard developed and enforced by the major credit card companies for systems that interact with their networks and process transitions under their auspices. It is specific to these types of systems and data and is not a general framework for IT security.

☒ **C** is incorrect because FIPS 140-2 is a US federal government certification standard for cryptographic modules. It is focused specifically on that use and purpose and is not a general framework for systems.

☒ **D** is incorrect because NIST SP 800-53 is a publication for US government security requirements for all government IT systems, with the exception of national security systems. It is not intended for a general framework for security and only pertains to government systems within the United States.

38. Which group developed, maintains, and controls the PCI DSS standards and controls?

A. NIST

B. ISO/IEC

C. EU

D. Credit card companies

☑ **D.** The PCI DSS standards were developed and are enforced by the major credit card companies and pertain to the systems that interact with their networks and process transactions on their behalf.

☒ **A** is incorrect because although the NIST, part of the US federal government, does publish many pertinent security standards and regulations, it does not publish the PCI DSS standards, or any other standard pertaining to proprietary financial transactions.

☒ **B** is incorrect because although the joint commission between the International Organization for Standardization (ISO) and the International Electrotechnical Commission (IEC) does publish many pertinent security standards and regulations, it does not publish the PCI DSS standards or any other standard pertaining to proprietary financial transactions.

☒ **C** is incorrect because although the European Union (EU) does publish many pertinent security standards and regulations, it does not publish the PCI DSS standards or any other standard pertaining to proprietary financial transactions.

39. Which cloud service category offers the most customization options and control to the cloud customer?

   A. PaaS

   B. IaaS

   C. SaaS

   D. DaaS

    ☑ **B.** The Infrastructure as a Service (IaaS) category allows for the most customization and control by the cloud customer; the cloud provider merely provides the virtualized environment to deploy virtual machines and virtual network devices within, but then leaves it to the cloud customer to deploy and configure those specific items.

    ☒ **A** is incorrect because the Platform as a Service (PaaS) category provides the operating system and application framework to the cloud customer, who then only deploys and configures the applications within it. PaaS does not have the same level of customization available as IaaS.

    ☒ **C** is incorrect because the Software as a Service (SaaS) category provides a full application to the cloud customer, where the only level of customization available is typically some branding or default settings for users.

    ☒ **D** is incorrect because Desktop as a Service (DaaS) is very similar to the PaaS service category, where the framework is provided within which to deploy applications. DaaS does not have the same level of customization available as IaaS.

40. The NIST Cloud Technology Roadmap contains a component focused on the minimum requirements to meet satisfactory contractual obligations between the cloud provider and cloud customer. Which of the following encapsulates this concept?

   A. Accountability

   B. Governance

   C. SLA

   D. Auditing

    ☑ **C.** The service level agreement (SLA) forms the basis for evaluating control compliance between the cloud customer and cloud provider. It documents and articulates specific requirements for availability, processes, customer service, support, security controls, auditing, reporting, and any other area deemed important by company policy or regulation from the cloud customer.

    ☒ **A** is incorrect because although accountability refers to circumstances similar to the ones the SLA covers (specifically meeting obligations and response times), it is not a facet of the NIST Cloud Technology Roadmap.

    ☒ **B** is incorrect because governance refers to the connection between IT management and the business focus of a company, and ensuring that resources and configurations are done with an eye toward business needs. The distinction between it and auditability is that the latter is focused on security controls and configurations based on regulations or baselines, not on the specific business needs that were used to define them.

☒ **D** is incorrect because auditing refers to the process of testing and evaluating system controls and configurations against regulatory requirements or policy, but not the performance metrics or response times that would be included with an SLA.

41. For optimal security, where should the authorization process of user access and permissions be performed?

   A. Account provisioning

   B. Throughout use of the application

   C. Immediately after authentication

   D. As part of the change management process

   ☑ **B.** Although initial authorization decisions are made when a user authenticates to an application, optimally they should be reevaluated as the user accesses different functions or data within the application. This will prevent attacks where users may find ways to elevate privileges after authentication, and it also catches cases where a user's access may have changed since he initially authenticated.

   ☒ **A** is incorrect because the account provisioning process is where the user's identity is provided and verified to get authentication credentials issued. It does not play a role in the authorization of a user as he accesses an application or data.

   ☒ **C** is incorrect because authorization will typically be performed upon successful authentication, but doing so only at that point leaves data susceptible to elevation-of-privilege attacks, and therefore it is not an optimal solution.

   ☒ **D** is incorrect because the change management process may be used to grant roles and access initially, especially in the case of privileged or administrative users, but it would not play any role in system operations as that access is being used.

42. Which of the following would *NOT* be a reason a customer could be "locked in" to a particular cloud provider?

   A. Software versions

   B. Developers

   C. Application environments

   D. Regulations

   ☑ **B.** A customer can become "locked in" to a particular cloud provider for a variety of reasons, but the developers who are responsible for their code and applications would not be such a reason. Applications are designed to work within specific frameworks or technologies, not with specific hosting providers.

☒ **A** is incorrect because if a specific software version is required, this would limit the customer to only cloud service providers that offer that specific software and version. Depending on how specific or rare the required software version is, a cloud customer could be limited to a small number of cloud providers, or even to a single cloud provider.

☒ **C** is incorrect because application environments are required to run code and runtimes, and being dependent on a specific one can lock an organization into specific cloud providers. Depending on how specific or rare the required application environment is, a cloud customer could be limited to a small number of cloud providers, or even to a single cloud provider.

☒ **D** is incorrect because regulations, especially ones specific to certain data, may dictate that specific cloud providers, or even a single cloud provider, must be used in order to maintain compliance.

43. Within a cloud environment, which network location would be the *LEAST* effective for a cloud customer to expect the implementation of security controls?

   A. Border perimeter

   B. DMZ

   C. Between VLANs

   D. Between the data and application zones

   ☑ **A.** In a traditional data center, the border perimeter of the network is a common place for security devices and controls to be implemented, to stop traffic of certain types or from certain origins from even getting to the IT systems hosted within it. However, in a cloud environment, especially with multitenancy, the ability to place anything at a network perimeter will likely be completely impossible, and even if it is possible, it will be extremely limited.

   ☒ **B** is incorrect because a DMZ can still be implemented within logical network segmentations and virtual network devices in a cloud environment.

   ☒ **C** is incorrect because VLAN segmentation is available and heavily used to logically separate network within a cloud environment. Between VLANs would be an effective location for security controls or devices.

   ☒ **D** is incorrect because logical network zones can be created within a cloud environment and would be a very common and strategic place for security controls or devices to be implemented.

44. Your IT security director has asked you to evaluate a cloud provider to determine whether its security practices match with current organizational policy in regard to data sanitation processes. Compared to your traditional data center, which of the following options is unlikely to be available with a cloud provider?

   A. Degaussing

   B. Cryptographic erasure

C. Overwriting

D. Zeroing

☑ **A.** Degaussing is the process of physically altering or removing the magnetic nature of storage hardware, and as such would not be available within a cloud environment. This is due to resource pooling and multitenancy, as well as the dynamic nature of a cloud, where data can be moved and stored in different places constantly.

☒ **B** is incorrect because cryptographic erasure involves the destruction of the keys used to encrypt the data, and it's available on any type of system. It is a very commonly used method within cloud environments for secure deletion of data.

☒ **C** is incorrect because overwriting involves writing over the sectors where the data was written and stored. Although this is trickier in a cloud environment based on the dynamic nature of data, overwriting may be available in situations where physical destruction of media would not be.

☒ **D** is incorrect for the same reasons as overwriting, as zeroing is the same process but involves writing null values to data sectors.

45. Which of the following types of threats is often made possible via social engineering tactics?

A. Data loss

B. System vulnerabilities

C. Advanced persistent threats

D. Insufficient due diligence

☑ **C.** Advanced persistent threats occur when an attacker is able to gain access to a system and reside there for a long period of time without being detected. This is usually done to snoop on traffic or collect information over time. Often it is accomplished through social engineering tactics to gain access to valid and real accounts so that access can be performed without detection.

☒ **A** is incorrect because data loss refers to an organization losing access to data or the data becoming corrupted, without appropriate backups or means of access. This typically occurs due to hardware or system failure or due to the destruction or corruption of encryption keys.

☒ **B** is incorrect because system vulnerabilities can occur based on misconfigurations or poor patching practices; they do not involve the actions of a malicious actor.

☒ **D** is incorrect because insufficient due diligence occurs when an organization has not properly planned a system deployment or migration, and therefore has left itself vulnerable to security threats.

46. If you are bidding on contracts with the US federal government, which security framework will you need to be knowledgeable of or familiar with?

    A. PCI DSS

    B. NIST SP 800-53

    C. SOC 2

    D. ISO/IEC 27001

    ☑ **B.** The NIST SP 800-53 publication governs the requirements for the security of US government systems, with the exception of national security systems. Anyone bidding on such contracts will need to be very familiar with its requirements because they are very specific in how hardware configurations must be done and will be crucial for any contract proposal.

    ☒ **A** is incorrect because PCI DSS applies only to credit card payment systems and interactions across the networks and systems of the major credit card companies. It does not apply to government systems.

    ☒ **C** is incorrect because SOC Type 2 reports pertain to financial reporting and the security controls used within them. They do not apply to US government systems.

    ☒ **D** is incorrect because the ISO/IEC 27001 security certification and framework is a general security program and does not apply to US government systems.

47. Which of the following cloud concepts encapsulates the security concerns related to bring your own device (BYOD) that a cloud security professional must always be cognizant of?

    A. Portability

    B. Broad network access

    C. On-demand self-service

    D. Interoperability

    ☑ **B.** Broad network access is a key concept of cloud computing, where services and applications are accessible across the public Internet and through a variety of clients and devices. This particularly applies to BYOD situations and the large number of clients and configurations that may interact with cloud services and data.

    ☒ **A** is incorrect because portability refers being able to easily move services or applications between different cloud providers and does not relate to issues involving BYOD.

    ☒ **C** is incorrect because on-demand self-service pertains to a cloud customer being able to provision and allocate resources from a portal, without needing to interact with cloud provider staff. It does not pertain to BYOD.

    ☒ **D** is incorrect because interoperability refers to being able to reuse components or services for other purposes and does not pertain to BYOD.

48. Which of the following is *NOT* considered a building block technology for cloud computing?

 A. CPU

 B. Memory

 C. Storage

 D. Servers

☑ **D.** Servers are not a key building block technology of a cloud environment, because the focus is on computing resources, not the number of actual servers being used.

☒ **A** is incorrect because CPU is a major building block technology of cloud computing and is one of the major billable items.

☒ **B** is incorrect because memory is a major building block technology of cloud computing and is one of the major billable items.

☒ **C** is incorrect because storage is a major building block technology of cloud computing and is one of the major billable items.

CHAPTER 2

Cloud Data Security Domain

Domain 2 is focused on the following topics:

- The cloud data lifecycle
- How storage systems differ between cloud hosting models
- How to design security strategies for data protection within a cloud environment
- The process of data discovery and how it relates to data classification
- Privacy acts and how they relate to cloud environments
- Data rights management and information rights management concepts
- The identification and collection of even data within a cloud environment, and how to leverage and analyze it for business value and regulatory compliance

As with any application or system, the data contained within is the most important and valuable aspect to a company or organization. Although many of the principles of data security and protection will be the same within a cloud environment as a traditional data center, a cloud environment presents some unique differences and challenges.

1. Which of the following pieces of data about an individual would be considered a direct identifier?

   A. Job title

   B. Educational history

   C. Income

   D. Phone number

2. When DLP is used to protect data in use, where would the DLP solution and software be deployed?

   A. On the client

   B. On the application server

   C. Network perimeter

   D. Data layer

3. Which cloud storage type uses an opaque value or descriptor to categorize and organize data?

   A. Volume

   B. Object

   C. Structured

   D. Unstructured

4. Although content analysis is the least efficient and slowest of the available data discovery methods, which of the following aspects of the data make discovery the most challenging?

   A. Size

   B. Throughput

   C. Quality

   D. Source

5. Which of the following actions do *NOT* fall under the "create" phase of the cloud data lifecycle?

   A. Newly created data

   B. Data that is imported

   C. Data that is archived

   D. Data that is modified

6. You are working as a forensic investigator and collecting information on a potential system breach by a malicious insider. Which of the following is essential for you in order to ensure evidence is preserved and admissible?

   A. Confidentiality

   B. Privacy

   C. Chain of custody

   D. Aggregation

7. Which storage type is typically used by the cloud provider to house virtual machine images?

   A. Volume

   B. Structured

   C. Unstructured

   D. Object

8. When a DLP solution is used to protect data in transit, where is the optimal place to deploy the DLP components?

   A. On the server originating the traffic

   B. At the network perimeter

   C. Between VLANs

   D. On the server receiving the data

9. Which of the following types of solutions is often used for regulatory compliance reporting?

   A. SIEM

   B. DLP

   C. IRM

   D. IDS

10. Encryption solutions can be embedded within database operations that will serve to protect data in a manner that is not noticeable to the user. What kind of encryption strategy is this?

    A. Transparent

    B. Passive

    C. RSA

    D. Homomorphic

11. Which phase of the cloud data lifecycle also typically entails the process of data classification?

   A. Use

   B. Store

   C. Create

   D. Archive

12. Your application generates large volumes of data based on customer input. With the large volume of incoming data, you need to be able to determine data discovery and classification as quickly and efficiently as possible. Which of the following methods for data discovery would be your best choice?

   A. Content analysis

   B. Labels

   C. Metadata

   D. Authorization

13. When using an e-commerce site, you see your credit card information with all but the last four digits replaced with asterisks. What kind of data masking is being employed by the application?

   A. Dynamic

   B. Homomorphic

   C. Static

   D. Replication

14. During which phase of the cloud data lifecycle would technologies such as DRM and DLP be most appropriately utilized?

   A. Use

   B. Share

   C. Store

   D. Archive

15. In order to move quickly from your traditional data center to a cloud environment, you want your storage to resemble the same directory structure you currently have. Which cloud storage type will be your best option?

   A. Object

   B. Structured

   C. Volume

   D. Unstructured

16. Which of the following concepts refers to having logs available from throughout a system or application within a single source?

    A. Consolidation

    B. Correlation

    C. Aggregation

    D. Archiving

17. Which key storage solution would be the *BEST* choice in a situation where availability might be of a particular concern?

    A. Internal

    B. External

    C. Hosted

    D. Embedded

18. Digital right management is an extension of information rights management, but is focused on which particular type of data?

    A. Health records

    B. Academic records

    C. Consumer media

    D. Financial data

19. Which of the following is a law in the United States that protects healthcare information and privacy?

    A. HIPAA

    B. PII

    C. PHI

    D. ACA

20. Which of the following technologies or concepts could be used for the preservation of integrity?

    A. DNSSEC

    B. Encryption

    C. Tokenization

    D. Anonymization

21. Although indirect identifiers cannot alone point to an individual, the more of them known can lead to a specific identity. Which strategy can be used to avoid such a connection being made?

   A. Masking

   B. Anonymization

   C. Obfuscation

   D. Encryption

22. Which type of cloud-based storage is IRM typically associated with?

   A. Volume

   B. Unstructured

   C. Structured

   D. Object

23. Which of the following is the sole responsibility of the cloud customer within an IaaS service category?

   A. Physical security

   B. Network security

   C. Hypervisor security

   D. Data security

24. Your new project and its data have regulations that dictate what type of records must be maintained and for how long. Which term refers to this concept?

   A. Data retention

   B. Data archiving

   C. Data preservation

   D. Data warehousing

25. Which type of new and emerging encryption allows for the manipulation and accessing of data without having to unencrypt it first?

   A. Dynamic

   B. Homomorphic

   C. Parallel

   D. Heterogeneous

26. Which concept refers to the ability to confirm and validate the original source of data or an operation to sufficiently meet the required level of assurance?

   A. Nonrepudiation

   B. Integrity

C. Authentication

D. Availability

27. Within a PaaS implementation, which of the following is *NOT* the responsibility of the cloud provider?

   A. Physical environment

   B. Infrastructure

   C. Application framework

   D. Data

28. Which of the following is a functionality and tool offered by IRM solutions, but not available with traditional permissions and security settings?

   A. Confidentiality

   B. Expiration

   C. Integrity

   D. Copying

29. When an organization implements an SIEM solution and begins aggregating event data, the configured event sources are only valid at the time it was configured. Application modifications, patching, and other upgrades will change the events generated and how they are represented over time. What process is necessary to ensure events are collected and processed with this in mind?

   A. Continual review

   B. Continuous optimization

   C. Aggregation updates

   D. Event elasticity

30. Applying restrictions on certain activities requires the use of information rights management (IRM). Which of the following would *NOT* require an IRM solution?

   A. Copy

   B. Rename

   C. Read

   D. Print

31. Which cloud service category is object storage associated with?

   A. Software

   B. Infrastructure

   C. Desktop

   D. Platform

32. Which of the following is *NOT* a common component of a DLP implementation process?

   A. Discovery

   B. Monitoring

   C. Revision

   D. Enforcement

33. Which of the following operations can be controlled and prevented with an IRM solution but would not be possible with traditional authorization mechanisms?

   A. Read

   B. Delete

   C. Modify

   D. Distribution

34. Which of the following concepts is *NOT* one of the key components of a data-archiving program?

   A. Format

   B. Size

   C. Regulations

   D. Testing

35. Which of the following activities is *NOT* something typically performed by an SIEM solution?

   A. Deletion

   B. Alerting

   C. Correlation

   D. Aggregation

36. Which of the following would be considered an indirect identifier?

   A. Name

   B. ZIP Code

   C. Educational history

   D. Address

37. Which of the following is *NOT* a method for protecting data in transit?

   A. HTTPS

   B. IPSec

   C. DRM

   D. TLS

38. You are reviewing literature from a cloud service provider and its main pitch to you involves its offerings for a "fully installed and implemented application hosting and deployment framework." Based on your understanding of cloud features, which storage types are you expecting to see offered with this solution?

A. Volume and object

B. Structured and unstructured

C. Container and object

D. Volume and structured

39. Which of the following methods or strategies is *NOT* a method for protecting sensitive data from data sets?

A. Zeroing

B. Anonymization

C. Tokenization

D. Obfuscation

40. Which of the following areas is *NOT* part of the CCM framework and represented as a domain?

A. Mobile security

B. Human resources

C. Governance

D. Financial audit

41. The final phase of the cloud data lifecycle is the destroy phase, where data is ultimately deleted and done so in a secure manner to ensure it cannot be recovered or reconstructed. Which cloud service category poses the most challenges to data destruction or the cloud customer?

A. Platform

B. Software

C. Infrastructure

D. Desktop

42. During data discovery and classification, the use of metadata is a primary means for analysis. Which of the following would *NOT* be considered metadata?

A. Column names

B. Content

C. Filenames

D. Headers

43. Different types of cloud deployment models use different types of storage from traditional data centers, along with many new types of software platforms for deploying applications and configurations. Which of the following is *NOT* a storage type used within a cloud environment?

   A. Docker

   B. Object

   C. Structured

   D. Volume

44. When data is required to be archived and retained for extended lengths of time, which of the following becomes the most pressing concern over time?

   A. Encryption

   B. Size

   C. Restoration

   D. Availability

45. Which of the following data protection methodologies maintains the ability to connect back values to the original values?

   A. Tokenization

   B. Anonymization

   C. Obfuscation

   D. Dynamic mapping

46. Which of the following is not a commonly accepted strategy for data discovery?

   A. Labels

   B. Metadata

   C. Signature hashing

   D. Content analysis

47. Although the preservation and retention of data are the most important concepts that usually come to mind when you're considering archiving, what process is equally important to test regularly for the duration of the required retention period?

   A. Recoverability

   B. Portability

   C. Encryption

   D. Availability

48. You are reviewing the standard offerings from a prospective cloud provider, and one area of log collection promises full and complete access to operating system logs for all provisioned systems. Which cloud service category is this *MOST* likely referring to?

A. Platform

B. Desktop

C. Software

D. Infrastructure

49. Which of the following will always serve as the starting point for the minimum period of data retention?

 A. Contract

 B. Regulation

 C. System resources

 D. Company policy

50. Which type of masking would be appropriate for the creation of data sets for testing purposes, where the same structure and size are of importance?

 A. Dynamic

 B. Structured

 C. Tokenized

 D. Static

1. D	18. C	35. A
2. A	19. A	36. C
3. B	20. A	37. C
4. C	21. B	38. B
5. C	22. D	39. A
6. C	23. D	40. D
7. D	24. A	41. B
8. B	25. B	42. B
9. A	26. A	43. A
10. A	27. D	44. C
11. C	28. B	45. A
12. C	29. B	46. C
13. A	30. C	47. A
14. B	31. B	48. D
15. C	32. C	49. B
16. C	33. D	50. D
17. A	34. B	

Comprehensive Answers and Explanations

1. Which of the following pieces of data about an individual would be considered a direct identifier?

   A. Job title

   B. Educational history

   C. Income

   D. Phone number

   ☑ **D.** A phone number is considered a direct identifier because it is unique to a residence or individual. With a phone number as a sole piece of information, a specific individual can be readily and quickly identified, meeting the precise definition of a direct identifier.

   ☒ **A** is incorrect because a job title is not specific enough to identify an individual in almost all circumstances. With most job titles, unless attached to a specific organization, the description could easily apply to a large number of individuals and therefore cannot be tied directly to a specific person.

   ☒ **B** is incorrect because educational history, including schools attended and degrees conferred, would not be specific enough to tie to an individual and would apply to a large number of possible people. Therefore, it would not be considered a direct identifier.

   ☒ **C** is incorrect because income would be a seemingly arbitrary number that could apply to a very large number of jobs and individuals and therefore, by itself, would not be a direct identifier to a specific individual.

2. When DLP is used to protect data in use, where would the DLP solution and software be deployed?

   A. On the client

   B. On the application server

   C. Network perimeter

   D. Data layer

   ☑ **A.** For a DLP solution to work for data in use, it would need to be installed on the actual client where the processing was taking place. This could be anything from a mobile device to a desktop computer, laptop, or software client. By being installed at the client level, the DLP solution would be able to closely watch how the data was being used and processed and to apply policies appropriately.

   ☒ **B** is incorrect because the application server is under control of the organization and the data owner, so how it is used can be tightly controlled. When on a client, a user has a broad range of things he can do with the data, but an application server will be limited to what it is programmed to do and is controlled by the application owner.

☒ **C** is incorrect because installing DLP at the network perimeter would be appropriate for controlling and monitoring data in transit, not data in use, as there is no processing or use of the data at the network perimeter level.

☒ **D** is incorrect because the data layer is where data at rest would be applicable, not where the data is being actually used or consumed as it would be on a client.

3. Which cloud storage type uses an opaque value or descriptor to categorize and organize data?

   A. Volume

   B. Object

   C. Structured

   D. Unstructured

   ☑ **B.** Object storage works by utilizing a flat file system, where each item is housed with an opaque handler or descriptor. When files are accessed, the object storage is called with the descriptor or opaque value and then presented to the application or client.

   ☒ **A** is incorrect because volume storage provisions a logical storage container to the virtual machine, where it is then utilized much as a traditional file system, with directory structures and file-naming conventions chosen by the application developers or administrators, rather than through the use of an opaque value.

   ☒ **C** is incorrect because structured storage, used with PaaS, resembles database storage, where items are categorized in a logical and consistent manner.

   ☒ **D** is incorrect because unstructured storage is used with PaaS and is employed to store files and objects that do not fit within the structured storage type—typically, support files or web files such as images, style sheets, and so on.

4. Although content analysis is the least efficient and slowest of the available data discovery methods, which of the following aspects of the data make discovery the most challenging?

   A. Size

   B. Throughput

   C. Quality

   D. Source

   ☑ **C.** With any content analysis, the quality of the data poses the biggest challenge to data discovery. Content can be freeform and may come in a variety of formats, with little to no consistency. Variations in spelling and word use can also make content analysis very challenging because there is no standardization to build concrete discovery rules against.

   ☒ **A** is incorrect because the size of the data by itself does not pose any direct challenges to data discovery. Although large data sets will require more time or processing to evaluate, the size does not correlate necessarily to the quality problems that do pose a significant challenge.

☒ **B** is incorrect because throughput may impact performance and processing time but does not pose the type of challenge in the evaluation of content that quality does.

☒ **D** is incorrect because the source of the data has no direct bearing on the quality of data or the ability to evaluate it.

5. Which of the following actions do *NOT* fall under the "create" phase of the cloud data lifecycle?

    A. Newly created data

    B. Data that is imported

    C. Data that is archived

    D. Data that is modified

    ☑ **C.** Data that is archived involves taking already existing data and capturing a read-only static copy of it for long-term preservation. Although the data may be new to a particular storage medium, especially if it's archived on a system external from its original location, the format or content of the data is not changed during the process, and as such it's not newly created or modified data.

    ☒ **A** is incorrect because newly created data is the main and simplest focus of the create phase of the cloud data lifecycle.

    ☒ **B** is incorrect because data that is imported is new to the system accepting the import. Because it is new to the system importing it, the data is effectively being created on that system and entered into its storage and classifications. This differs from archiving because importing implies future use and processing of the data, rather than capturing a static copy.

    ☒ **D** is incorrect because data that is modified is considered new data due to its new form or format, so it has been created as part of the initial phase within the system.

6. You are working as a forensic investigator and collecting information on a potential system breach by a malicious insider. Which of the following is essential for you in order to ensure evidence is preserved and admissible?

    A. Confidentiality

    B. Privacy

    C. Chain of custody

    D. Aggregation

    ☑ **C.** In order for evidence to be considered properly preserved and admissible for legal proceedings, the chain of custody is essential. The chain of custody catalogs the life of the data, including its capture, being passed through various parties, any modifications or tests run against it, and any other information pertinent to everything and everyone who has touched it or accessed it. The chain of custody serves to preserve confidence in the data, as well as giving the ability to question or challenge it based on its handling and preservation.

☒ **A** is incorrect because confidentiality is not important for all data as part of its preservation. Obviously, some data that is sensitive has confidentiality requirements, but those are separate from the requirements of chain of custody to catalog the handling of data since its collection.

☒ **B** is incorrect for the same reason as confidentiality, in that privacy does not apply to all data and does not preserve its handling processes or procedures.

☒ **D** is incorrect because aggregation refers to collecting data, typically event data, into a single index and storage system. Aggregation does not apply directly to data preservation at all.

7. Which storage type is typically used by the cloud provider to house virtual machine images?

   A. Volume

   B. Structured

   C. Unstructured

   D. Object

   ☑ **D.** Object storage utilizes a flat hierarchy and catalogs data with an opaque file handler or descriptor. When storing virtual machine images, cloud providers typically use object storage because there is no reason to maintain an organized file structure, and an opaque descriptor works perfectly for virtual machine images and provides easy access to call them.

   ☒ **A** is incorrect because volume storage resembles a traditional file system structure, with organization and filenames, and would not serve an appropriate or necessary purpose for the storage of virtual machine imagines. Volume storage also is logically attached to a specific instance and would not be broadly accessible throughout and environment like object storage is.

   ☒ **B** is incorrect because structured storage resembles a database-type organization and is used specifically with PaaS implementations; it would not be used for virtual image storage throughout a cloud infrastructure.

   ☒ **C** is incorrect because unstructured storage is used within a PaaS implementation for support objects such as images and web files; it would not be used for the storage of virtual machines for use throughout a cloud infrastructure.

8. When a DLP solution is used to protect data in transit, where is the optimal place to deploy the DLP components?

   A. On the server originating the traffic

   B. At the network perimeter

   C. Between VLANs

   D. On the server receiving the data

   ☑ **B.** When protecting data in transit, a DLP solution would optimally be deployed at the network perimeter. Within a network, extensive monitoring can be used in conjunction with other security controls on the data, but the network perimeter represents the last hop before leaving the application for external use, and would be the appropriate place to have a DLP implementation.

☒ **A** is incorrect because the server originating the traffic represents a first hop of network transmission, and the data may pass through other systems and network devices before leaving for external use. It would not be the optimal place for a DLP implementation.

☒ **C** is incorrect because firewalls and other network-monitoring solutions are used between VLANs, which by nature are internal to a network and do not represent when data leaves for external use.

☒ **D** is incorrect because the server receiving the data would be a client where data in use becomes the appropriate stage; it is no longer data in transit once it reaches its destination.

9. Which of the following types of solutions is often used for regulatory compliance reporting?

   A. SIEM

   B. DLP

   C. IRM

   D. IDS

☑ **A.** A security information and event management (SIEM) solution is used to collect, aggregate, and process event data throughout an application or even an entire infrastructure. It is often used to produce auditing and compliance reports based on the data that is collected and aggregated, and most SIEM solutions have very robust reporting, alerting, and dashboard capabilities.

☒ **B** is incorrect because a data loss prevention (DLP) solution is used to protect sensitive information and how it is processed, handled, and disseminated. It is not used for reporting.

☒ **C** is incorrect because information rights management (IRM) solutions are used to control how information is accessed and used, and is not a reporting tool or solution.

☒ **D** is incorrect because an intrusion detection system (IDS) is used to monitor data transmissions against known signatures and patterns, and to alert application owners or developers to anomalies or suspicious circumstances. It is not used for regulatory or compliance reporting.

10. Encryption solutions can be embedded within database operations that will serve to protect data in a manner that is not noticeable to the user. What kind of encryption strategy is this?

   A. Transparent

   B. Passive

   C. RSA

   D. Homomorphic

☑ **A.** Transparent encryption is used within a database to protect data as it is being stored and processed, but it's done as an integrated database function and is not something that needs input from the application. The application doesn't even need to be aware it is being done. Transparent encryption is an effective tool because applications do not need to be rewritten or modified to handle encryption activities.

☒ **B** is incorrect because passive encryption is not a method of embedding encryption within a database system and its operations.

☒ **C** is incorrect because RSA refers to a specific type of encryption algorithm, not to a specific implementation of encryption. A transparent encryption system may use RSA as its cryptographic algorithm, but RSA itself is not applicable to the question.

☒ **D** is incorrect because homomorphic encryption is a cutting-edge technique that allows for accessing and processing encrypted data without the traditional step of having to unencrypt it first. It is a type of encryption rather than a specific implementation, which is what the question is asking.

11. Which phase of the cloud data lifecycle also typically entails the process of data classification?

   A. Use

   B. Store

   C. Create

   D. Archive

   ☑ **C.** Data classification should optimally be done immediately as part of the "create" phase. As soon as data is created, it is subjected to regulatory and other protection requirements, so classification must be applied immediately.

   ☒ **A** is incorrect because the "use" phase is where data is first consumed and processed; however, because the data has already been stored, classification needs to have already been applied. In some instances, the "store" phase may be momentary, and in others the data may reside in storage for a while before entering the "use" phase, so classification is needed earlier.

   ☒ **B** is incorrect because data needs to have a classification attached before it enters the "store" phase, as many security controls are implemented based on the way data is stored and protected. The manner in which the data is stored may also be highly dependent on its classification.

   ☒ **D** is incorrect because the "archive" phase is a much later part of the overall process, and data will have gone through storage, usage, and sharing long before it reaches archiving, so classification would need to take place much earlier.

12. Your application generates large volumes of data based on customer input. With the large volume of incoming data, you need to be able to determine data discovery and classification as quickly and efficiently as possible. Which of the following methods for data discovery would be your best choice?

A. Content analysis

B. Labels

C. Metadata

D. Authorization

☑ **C.** Metadata uses attributes about the data itself, such as creator, application, type, data, or any other type of information to determine classification. Metadata is typically known as "data about data." By using metadata, where possible, you can make very quick and efficient determinations on classification.

☒ **A** is incorrect because content analysis is a very intensive and slow process for analyzing data to determine classification. It is also highly subjective because the data may not be normalized and consistent enough to accurately determine classification with any type of efficiency.

☒ **B** is incorrect because applying labels, although much quicker than content analysis, is highly subjective and is often done inconsistently. Labels rely on a process or require users to correctly apply them in a consistent manner, whereas metadata uses attributes about the data itself.

☒ **D** is incorrect because authorization is the process of granting privileges and access to data or functions within an application; it is not related to the classification process at all.

13. When using an e-commerce site, you see your credit card information with all but the last four digits replaced with asterisks. What kind of data masking is being employed by the application?

A. Dynamic

B. Homomorphic

C. Static

D. Replication

☑ **A.** Dynamic masking is implemented between the data and application layers, and is applied in real time as data is requested and processed. This allows for showing only portions of a credit card number, for example, rather than the entire number that is contained in storage.

☒ **B** is incorrect because homomorphic refers to a type of cutting-edge encryption where data can be accessed and utilized without the traditional need to unencrypt the data set first. Although systems may use homomorphic encryption throughout any type of process, it does not specifically relate to masking.

☒ **C** is incorrect because static masking creates a set of data, typically used for testing in non-production environments. It is done as a separate process and outputs a distinct set of new data with masked values, and it's not done on a live system such as the one presented in the question.

☒ **D** is incorrect because replication refers to making multiple copies of data for either redundancy, high availability, or any use where a secondary copy is needed. It is not related specifically to masking, as replication involves making identical copies of data and not outputting one with masking in place.

14. During which phase of the cloud data lifecycle would technologies such as DRM and DLP be most appropriately utilized?

   A. Use

   B. Share

   C. Store

   D. Archive

   ☑ **B.** During the "share" phase, data is allowed outside of the original system and consumed by external users or services. This point, where data is leaving systems and consumed by others, is ideal for the inclusion of DRM and DLP technologies to control how data is disseminated and ultimately used, as well as to control how far and wide it can be distributed.

   ☒ **A** is incorrect because the "use" phase is still within a controlled application and environment, where more stringent controls can be applied without relying on services and technologies such as DRM and DLP.

   ☒ **C** is incorrect because the "store" phase relies on different technologies for security, such as server controls, network controls, and encryption. DRM and DLP are focused on where data is transmitted or consumed and would be more appropriate during the "share" phase.

   ☒ **D** is incorrect because archiving involves static copies of data for preservation, where technologies such as encryption would be appropriate. The use of DRM or DLP would not be necessary or appropriate because the data is not being transmitted, shared, or consumed in this phase.

15. In order to move quickly from your traditional data center to a cloud environment, you want your storage to resemble the same directory structure you currently have. Which cloud storage type will be your best option?

   A. Object

   B. Structured

   C. Volume

   D. Unstructured

☑ **C.** Volume storage, used with Infrastructure as a Service (IaaS), is a logical storage volume that is mounted and used much like a traditional file system on a virtual machine. It allows for directory structures and naming conventions, the same as a legacy system, along with the same kind of file permissions and controls. It would make for the easiest and quickest transition for a system or application to a cloud environment.

☒ **A** is incorrect because object storage is an external storage system that uses an opaque file handler or descriptor to catalog and access items. It does not resemble a traditional directory structure and would not be applicable to this type of situation.

☒ **B** is incorrect because structured storage, used with Platform as a Service (PaaS), typically is a database-type system, which does not use file system organization or structure in a traditional server sense.

☒ **D** is incorrect because unstructured is a data storage type with PaaS that is used for objects that do not fit within a structured storage system (typically, support files, images, web objects, and so on). It is not used in the sense of a traditional file system's structure and configuration for this example.

16. Which of the following concepts refers to having logs available from throughout a system or application within a single source?

    A. Consolidation

    B. Correlation

    C. Aggregation

    D. Archiving

    ☑ **C.** Aggregation refers to the collection of event data and logs from throughout an environment and indexing them into a single source. It allows for quick and easy searching of events for trends of specific incidents across all systems, rather than having to go onto each individual system.

    ☒ **A** is incorrect because although consolidation is essentially the same concept as aggregation, the official term is aggregation.

    ☒ **B** is incorrect because correlation is the function of taking different data sources and finding commonalities or trends among them. Although this is typically done after aggregation, these are two separate and distinct concepts.

    ☒ **D** is incorrect because archiving is the long-term preservation of event data. This is often done on systems that do aggregation for simplicity; these concepts are not necessarily related or dependent upon each other.

17. Which key storage solution would be the *BEST* choice in a situation where availability might be of a particular concern?

    A. Internal

    B. External

    C. Hosted

    D. Embedded

☑ **A.** Internal key storage keeps the keys on the actual server or system where they are to be used. Although this will prevent the availability problems that an external key store may experience, it also makes security more challenging. If the server or system itself is compromised in a way where a malicious actor gains system access, he can also access the keys used to encrypt and protect the data on the system.

☒ **B** is incorrect because an external key system, although more secure in the case of a system breach, also carries with it the potential problems of availability. If network access to the external key store becomes unavailable, or if the external system experiences an outage, then the data will become inaccessible until access and availability are restored.

☒ **C** is incorrect because "hosted" is not a term typically applied to a key storage solution. In essence, all key systems are hosted; it is the delineation between internal and external that is important.

☒ **D** is incorrect because the term "embedded" refers to a type of encryption, not to a type of key storage system. The term is typically applied to encryption that is built into a system and is an integral part of it, rather than an external service or operation.

18. Digital right management is an extension of information rights management, but is focused on which particular type of data?

    A. Health records

    B. Academic records

    C. Consumer media

    D. Financial data

    ☑ **C.** Digital rights management (DRM) systems are similar to IRM solutions, with the main distinction being their focus on consumer media. They are intended to protect copyrights and the use of digital media after it is distributed. DRM systems can be used to prevent copying, enforce expirations of subscriptions, control what devices may be used to access the media, and many other types of operations.

    ☒ **A** is incorrect because health records are not a focus of DRM, although IRM solutions may be used to protect the data according to its specific regulations or requirements.

    ☒ **B** is incorrect because academic records are not a focus of DRM solutions, although IRM solutions may be used to protect the data as necessary.

    ☒ **D** is incorrect because DRM is focused on consumer media and not financial records, although IRM solutions may be used to protect financial records, as applicable.

19. Which of the following is a law in the United States that protects healthcare information and privacy?

    A. HIPAA

    B. PII

C. PHI

D. ACA

☑ **A.** The Health Insurance Portability and Accountability Act (HIPAA) is a United States law that is focused on health records, their protection, disclosure requirements, and how health records may be used or shared.

☒ **B** is incorrect because PII refers to personally identifiable information as a broad concept, rather than a specific law or regulation. The concepts of PII do certainly pertain to health records and their protection, though.

☒ **C** is incorrect because PHI refers to protected health information. It is a subset and section of the HIPAA law and defines what types of information must be protected. In other words, it's only a portion of the applicable law and now the law itself.

☒ **D** is incorrect because the Affordable Care Act (ACA) is a United States law pertaining to health insurance coverage and access, but it does not pertain to specific regulations for the handling and protection of heathcare data.

20. Which of the following technologies or concepts could be used for the preservation of integrity?

A. DNSSEC

B. Encryption

C. Tokenization

D. Anonymization

☑ **A.** DNSSEC is an extension on the traditional DNS protocol and allows for the signing and verification of DNS results. When a query is issued to the DNS servers, they sign the results using keys that can authenticate that they did come from an authoritative source. This strategy prevents DNS spoofing and redirecting attacks, and is implemented in a way that does not require additional lookups or calls.

☒ **B** is incorrect because encryption is used for preserving and protecting the confidentiality of data, but not for the integrity of it. There is nothing about encryption that would prevent the data from being altered against the encrypted blocks, even if it renders the data unreadable or unable to be unencrypted.

☒ **C** is incorrect because tokenization is the process of replacing sensitive data with key or opaque values that ultimately can be mapped back to the original values. It is used for protecting the confidentiality of data, not the integrity of it.

☒ **D** is incorrect because anonymization is the process of removing identifiers from a data set that would allow an individual identity to be determined from the various data. It is a method and strategy for protecting the privacy and confidentiality of data, not the integrity of it.

21. Although indirect identifiers cannot alone point to an individual, the more of them known can lead to a specific identity. Which strategy can be used to avoid such a connection being made?

   A. Masking

   B. Anonymization

   C. Obfuscation

   D. Encryption

   ☑ **B.** Anonymization is the process of removing identifiers that could ultimately be used to identity a specific individual. This process can include removing direct identifiers or a sufficient quantity of indirect identifiers in order to ensure a specific identification cannot be made.

   ☒ **A** is incorrect because masking is the process of replacing values in a data field, or additional characters can be added to alter the original values. This process can also be done by shifting values through predefined algorithms or deleting specific data fields or data sets altogether.

   ☒ **C** is incorrect because obfuscation is the process of replacing values in a data set, typically for producing sets to test applications in non-production and development environments. This is often done to meet regulatory compliance for test data.

   ☒ **D** is incorrect because encryption is used for protecting the confidentiality of data, not for altering values or ensuring the data cannot be tied through indirect identifiers to a specific individual.

22. Which type of cloud-based storage is IRM typically associated with?

   A. Volume

   B. Unstructured

   C. Structured

   D. Object

   ☑ **D.** Object storage is typical by used for data objects and downloads, to which IRM technologies and strategies are often applied. Other types of data are usually either too scattered and distributed across many files or used too internally to an application to really apply IRM to them. Object storage is ideal for IRM implementations because each object represents a single data package.

   ☒ **A** is incorrect because volume storage appears as a traditional file system and would not typically represent the kind of data that is extracted or downloaded, although it could be. Most cloud applications that implement IRM and offer that type of service defer to object storage, which is the more appropriate and correct answer here.

☒ **B** is incorrect because unstructured data is used within PaaS implementations, typically for support files or media needed by an application. It is not typically used for the type of data that would be extracted and consumed by an entity where the application of IRM would be useful or warranted.

☒ **C** is incorrect because structured data, used within PaaS, represents the type of data that is typically housed with a database system. It is used for the processing and support of the application, rather than the type of data that would be extracted or saved by a user or other entity. Therefore, the application of IRM would not be applicable or useful.

23. Which of the following is the sole responsibility of the cloud customer within an IaaS service category?

    A. Physical security

    B. Network security

    C. Hypervisor security

    D. Data security

    ☑ **D.** Within an IaaS implementation—and, in fact, with virtually all cloud hosting—data security is always the responsibility of the cloud customer. Cloud customers are responsible for ensuring that adequate controls and oversight are in place, either by implementing them themselves or through the use of contracts and SLAs to meet any policy or regulatory requirements.

    ☒ **A** is incorrect because physical security in all cloud service categories is always the responsibility of the cloud provider. The cloud provider is the only entity that has physical access to facilities—there is no reason for a cloud customer or user to even know or care where the provider is located. Although the cloud provider may make available to current and potential customers certain reports, specifications, or audits of physical security for regulatory compliance or to instill trust, it is extremely unlikely that much insight would ever be gained by cloud customers or that they would be allowed much input.

    ☒ **B** is incorrect because network security at the IaaS level is shared between the cloud customer and the cloud provider. With IaaS, the cloud customer handles much of network security through the deployment and configuration of virtualized network devices and the design of strategies such as VLAN implementation. The responsibility is ultimately shared with the cloud provider for border security and physical network security.

    ☒ **C** is incorrect because with all cloud service categories, hypervisor security is solely the responsibility of the cloud provider. At the hypervisor level, the cloud customer would never be allowed access or given insight beyond limited API and service calls made to the hypervisors via automated and secured tools authorized by the cloud provider.

24. Your new project and its data have regulations that dictate what type of records must be maintained and for how long. Which term refers to this concept?

 A. Data retention

 B. Data archiving

 C. Data preservation

 D. Data warehousing

☑ **A.** Data retention is the process of collecting, protecting, and storing records for a defined period of time. The exact duration of time will be established by either regulation or organizational policy, but the requirements from regulation will always form the basis for the minimum duration.

☒ **B** is incorrect because although the term "data archiving" is very similar to "data retention," it's not the official term. Archiving is a process that is part of data retention, but it's focused on the technical aspects, as opposed to the entire approach with management, policy, and regulation attached.

☒ **C** is incorrect because data preservation is only a part of an overall data retention program. Preservation includes the identification and collection of events and data. It culminates in the actual preservation of the data, but does not include the regulatory and policy considerations that data retention encompasses.

☒ **D** is incorrect because data warehousing refers to the process of consolidating and storing data in a centralized system, which can then be leveraged for business intelligence and other analysis. It does not refer to the long-term retention of data, nor the policies and regulations involved in it.

25. Which type of new and emerging encryption allows for the manipulation and accessing of data without having to unencrypt it first?

 A. Dynamic

 B. Homomorphic

 C. Parallel

 D. Heterogeneous

☑ **B.** Homomorphic encryption is a new, cutting-edge method that allows data to be accessed and processed without being unencrypted first. It allows operations to be performed against encrypted text, with the results directly generated in encrypted form. Unencrypting the resulting output will show the same results as if the data had been unencrypted when processed.

☒ **A** is incorrect because dynamic encryption involves the use of a cryptographic proxy. This is done because many systems where encryption is done, such as on personal computers, are not considered trusted environments where the encryption modules and processes are guaranteed to be safe, so the use of an external encryption proxy is intended to alleviate this problem.

☒ **C** is incorrect because parallel refers to multiple processes taking place simultaneously. This can involve encryption and decryption, or operations such as uploading and encrypting can be paired to occur at the same time. It does not refer to accessing or manipulating data without the need to decrypt it first.

☒ **D** is incorrect because heterogeneous encryption is not a real technology or concept. This option was merely provided as a choice similar to homomorphic encryption.

26. Which concept refers to the ability to confirm and validate the original source of data or an operation to sufficiently meet the required level of assurance?

  A. Nonrepudiation

  B. Integrity

  C. Authentication

  D. Availability

  ☑ **A.** Nonrepudiation is essentially the assurance and guarantee that something cannot be denied. This concept is applied to security and data in that the originating system or user cannot deny the validity or authenticity of data or transactions, thus guaranteeing a high level of assurance. This is of particular interest in digital forensics and the preservation of evidence.

  ☒ **B** is incorrect because integrity refers to ensuring that data has not been modified in an authorized manner or corrupted throughout its lifecycle. This is of particular importance with many types of transactions, especially financial, where correct data and processing are essential.

  ☒ **C** is incorrect because authentication refers to the process of establishing the identity of a user or service that is requesting access or performing operations to the satisfaction of a regulation or policy. Based on the type of data and its classification, the level of scrutiny and proof for authentication can vary greatly.

  ☒ **D** is incorrect because availability refers to data, systems, or services being accessible and functioning when needed, and in a secure manner. It does not address the confidentiality or integrity of the data or systems themselves, nor does it prove origination or identity.

27. Within a PaaS implementation, which of the following is *NOT* the responsibility of the cloud provider?

  A. Physical environment

  B. Infrastructure

  C. Application framework

  D. Data

☑ **D.** Under all cloud service categories, the security and protection of data is the sole responsibility of the cloud customer. Although the cloud provider will play a complimentary role with data security through the controls it implements and tools it provides throughout its entire cloud infrastructure, the ultimate responsibility for compliance and verification lies with the cloud customer as the owner or steward of the data.

☒ **A** is incorrect because the physical environment is always the responsibility of the cloud provider. This applies to all cloud service categories, and in almost all instances, the cloud customer will not have any insight into, or really any need to know, the physical security measures or even the locations of assets.

☒ **B** is incorrect because infrastructure within the PaaS service category is the responsibility of the cloud provider. With PaaS, the cloud provider offers a fully functional application framework and environment into which to deploy application code and data, and the cloud customer is not responsible for any operating system or infrastructure design, configuration, or maintenance.

☒ **C** is incorrect because the main focus of the PaaS service category is on providing an application framework for the cloud customer to deploy code and data into. The cloud customer will have considerable input into and contractual requirements for the application framework, but it is the responsibility of the cloud provider to meet and address those needs to meet SLA requirements.

28. Which of the following is a functionality and tool offered by IRM solutions, but not available with traditional permissions and security settings?

   A. Confidentiality

   B. Expiration

   C. Integrity

   D. Copying

☑ **B.** IRM allows for many extended security operations and functions that are not available with traditional permissions and settings. With traditional permissions, it is possible to limit who can read or modify a file, but with read permissions, a file can be copied very easily with no limitations, and once this is done, it can be used forever. Even if the permissions of the user are revoked at some point, if the user has copied or downloaded the data, he can still access it. With IRM layered on top, a file can be copied or downloaded but with expiration restrictions on it. After the expiration time has passed, the file will no longer be accessible.

☒ **A** is incorrect because confidentiality can be provided through traditional permissions and settings by limiting who can access or read data, as well as through mechanisms such as encryption. However, once the ability to access the data is allowed, there is nothing to prevent future use or copying of data.

☒ **C** is incorrect because integrity can be assured through traditional permissions by denying the ability to write or delete data. If permissions are granted to modify or delete data, through traditional permissions there is not any mechanism to limit how much of the data or what portions of it can be modified or for how long, as IRM could provide.

☒ **D** is incorrect because the ability to copy is inherent with the ability to read data. If a user can access a file to read it, he can also copy it, either directly copying the file as a whole unit or copying the data out of it and into another source. IRM is capable of preventing data from being copied even if the user can read it.

29. When an organization implements an SIEM solution and begins aggregating event data, the configured event sources are only valid at the time it was configured. Application modifications, patching, and other upgrades will change the events generated and how they are represented over time. What process is necessary to ensure events are collected and processed with this in mind?

   A. Continual review

   B. Continuous optimization

   C. Aggregation updates

   D. Event elasticity

   ☑ **B.** Continuous optimization is the process where event data is evaluated on an ongoing basis to catch any changes in formats or additional data sources to correct collection methods. Applications are always changing, and without continuous optimization, event data would likely become stale or incomplete before long.

   ☒ **A** is incorrect because the term "continual review," although it sounds similar to continuous optimization, is not the term used for what the question is asking.

   ☒ **C** is incorrect because while the term "aggregation updates" does sound similar and captures the essence of what continuous optimization does, it is not a real term or commonly used.

   ☒ **D** is incorrect because "event elasticity" is a made-up term for the purposes of the question, though it does capture the concept of event data and pairing with the elastic nature of cloud environments. However, it is not pertinent to the question.

30. Applying restrictions on certain activities requires the use of information rights management (IRM). Which of the following would *NOT* require an IRM solution?

   A. Copy

   B. Rename

   C. Read

   D. Print

☑ **C.** The ability to restrict who can read data or files does not require the use of an IRM solution and can be accomplished with traditional security controls or permissions settings. This can be done either through direct file permissions or the use of ACLs, or even by preventing a user or process from getting to the file at all.

☒ **A** is incorrect because a file that can be read can also be copied. Even if file permissions restrict the ability to insert files onto the file system, the contents of the file can be copied through a variety of methods.

☒ **B** is incorrect because files can typically be renamed if they can be read on a system. Though some file systems can prevent new files from being inserted, which will also prevent them from being renamed in most instances, it is not a universal capability and will typically require the use of an IRM solution.

☒ **D** is incorrect because printing is possible if a file can be read. Once the data is accessible, even if printing is not possible directly from the host system, there are a variety of ways to copy or move data that could expose it to being printed. IRM technologies can be used in a variety of ways to prevent printing.

31. Which cloud service category is object storage associated with?

    A. Software

    B. Infrastructure

    C. Desktop

    D. Platform

    ☑ **B.** Infrastructure as a Service (IaaS) uses object and volume storage. Object storage is where data is stored on a system through the use of an opaque descriptor or handler and then accessed with it, rather than through a traditional file system with naming conventions, folders, and so on.

    ☒ **A** is incorrect because Software as a Service (SaaS) uses its own storage mechanisms that are specific to its applications and not typically accessible by a cloud customer through any other means than the application interfaces. Even for instances where file objects are allowed to be stored, they are done so through application interfaces and are only accessible through those means.

    ☒ **C** is incorrect because Desktop as a Service (DaaS) uses storage in a similar way as SaaS. Storage is done by the cloud provider and is specific to the way its systems are implemented. DaaS typically functions as a SaaS implementation, where applications hosted on a cloud platform are accessed and used through a client.

    ☒ **D** is incorrect because Platform as a Service (PaaS) uses structured and unstructured storage types. Structured storage typically resembles a database-type system, where the organization and labels are well defined and used by the application, whereas unstructured storage serves to host support files such as images, web objects, configuration files, and so on.

32. Which of the following is *NOT* a common component of a DLP implementation process?

   A. Discovery

   B. Monitoring

   C. Revision

   D. Enforcement

   ☑ **C.** Revision is not a core component of a data loss prevention (DLP) process, though it would likely be part of an organization's larger change management or technical advisory processes. For any DLP strategy to be successful, an organization must include other processes in the workflow for revision over time as systems change and data evolves, but revision is not a core component of the actual DLP processes.

   ☒ **A** is incorrect because data discovery is a key component of a DLP implementation. DLP systems first need to discover the data they are intended to protect and monitor, either through specific configurations of data sources and storage systems or via predefined signatures and other discovery method to find new data as it comes into the system or is accessed.

   ☒ **B** is incorrect because monitoring is done constantly by DLP systems as data is access or moved. DLP systems, before enforcing polices and controls, need to constantly monitor data and network operations to match against rulesets or signatures.

   ☒ **D** is incorrect because the ultimate goal of DLP solutions is to enforce policies and controls on data as it is being used or moved.

33. Which of the following operations can be controlled and prevented with an IRM solution but would not be possible with traditional authorization mechanisms?

   A. Read

   B. Delete

   C. Modify

   D. Distribution

   ☑ **D.** An IRM solution can control what can be done with data beyond the capabilities of restricting its access. With traditional authorization systems, once someone can read and access data, there is little that can be done to prevent them from copying, printing, sharing, or otherwise distributing it. With an IRM solution, these other operations can be largely avoided or eliminated.

   ☒ **A** is incorrect because read operations can be controlled by traditional authorization and security controls and do not need an IRM solution. However, an IRM solution can extend those controls and augment how the data can be used or processed, even if read permissions are granted.

   ☒ **B** is incorrect because deletion can be prevented through modify or specific delete rights with traditional permission schemes and controls.

☒ **C** is incorrect because modify is a core capability of all file systems and authorization schemes, and IRM is not needed to control it, though IRM can certainly give far greater and more granular control over it.

34. Which of the following concepts is *NOT* one of the key components of a data-archiving program?

    A. Format

    B. Size

    C. Regulations

    D. Testing

    ☑ **B.** Many considerations are needed to develop a data-archiving program and establish the policies that govern it, but the size of archives is a technical consideration concerning implementation, not one to drive policy. Regulations especially focus on what needs to be preserved and for how long, but the size of the archives is never a consideration under regulatory frameworks.

    ☒ **A** is incorrect because the format of archives is a prime consideration. It ties directly to regulatory requirements for what must be preserved, as well as to considerations for ensuring it can later be restored and accessed for the duration of the required retention period.

    ☒ **C** is incorrect because regulations are the most central and important component of a data-archiving program. They define what needs to be preserved and what the retention period is. Company policies or other considerations may expand on the regulatory requirements, but the regulatory requirements will always form the minimum basis for retention.

    ☒ **D** is incorrect because testing is vital to ensure the success and compliance of an archiving program. Although identifying data that must be preserved and establishing processes to do so are vital, the testing of the restoration capabilities is equally as vital. Collecting data and archiving it will not fulfill regulatory requirements if the organization is later unable to restore or access it, should the need arise.

35. Which of the following activities is *NOT* something typically performed by an SIEM solution?

    A. Deletion

    B. Alerting

    C. Correlation

    D. Aggregation

    ☑ **A.** An SIEM solution will aggregate event data and allow for analysis and reporting on it. However, it functions as only a consumer of event data; it does not maintain the data from the source. Data is copied into an SIEM solution from agents running on devices or servers, or it is sent via syslog technologies, typically, and then is indexed for use. An SIEM solution does not maintain or prune the data that is being sent in at all; that is left to processes external to the solution. Because of this, the SIEM solution does not delete data.

☒ **B** is incorrect because alerting is a core function of an SIEM solution. Once data has been consumed and indexed by the SIEM solution, alerting can be performed based on any correlations or values found within it.

☒ **C** is incorrect because correlation of data from across an enterprise is a core function, and one of the main benefits, of an SIEM solution. With data from across the enterprise, it is easy to search across different devices or systems for common patterns and the flow of processes and data, which would not be possible on isolated servers.

☒ **D** is incorrect because aggregation is perhaps the most well known function of an SIEM solution, which collects data from many different devices, servers, and sources and then indexes it for use in a single repository and searching mechanism.

36. Which of the following would be considered an indirect identifier?

    A. Name

    B. ZIP Code

    C. Educational history

    D. Address

☑ **C.** Educational history is not considered a direct identifier. It is not specific enough to attach to an individual, as many others will have attended both the same institutions and obtained the same degrees or studied the same subjects.

☒ **A** is incorrect because a person's name is one of the most direct identifiers available. Although some common names are shared by many, this identifier makes for very quick identification of an individual, especially within a small population.

☒ **B** is incorrect because a ZIP Code is typically considered specific enough to be a direct identifier, especially with the ZIP+4 Code that is commonly used because it denotes an even more specific location. Although broader geographic terms (such as city) are not considered to be direct identifiers, a ZIP Code is, because it can be used to quickly narrow down and point to specific individuals.

☒ **D** is incorrect because an address is very specific to an individual or a residence. With the address alone, it is possible to very quickly focus on an individual directly.

37. Which of the following is *NOT* a method for protecting data in transit?

    A. HTTPS

    B. IPSec

    C. DRM

    D. TLS

☑ **C.** Data rights management (DRM) works by protecting how data is accessed and used, specifically relating to the use of digital and consumer media, such as movies, audio files, and images. It is not focused on data in transit, only on the actual use and access.

☒ **A** is incorrect because HTTPS is the main method for secure web and web service communications. It is widely used by both individuals and systems for communicating over networks, especially the public Internet, in a secure manner.

☒ **B** is incorrect because IPSec is used for securing communications directly between two servers via encrypted channels. It is solely focused on data in transit and its security.

☒ **D** is incorrect because TLS is now the default standard encryption and secure model for most network communications, but especially for web and web services. It has several methods for both securing and ensuring the authentication of data-in-transit communications.

38. You are reviewing literature from a cloud service provider and its main pitch to you involves its offerings for a "fully installed and implemented application hosting and deployment framework." Based on your understanding of cloud features, which storage types are you expecting to see offered with this solution?

    A. Volume and object

    B. Structured and unstructured

    C. Container and object

    D. Volume and structured

    ☑ **B.** The phrase "fully installed and implemented application hosting and deployment framework" describes the Platform as a Service (PaaS) cloud service category. With that in mind, the applicable storage types are structured and unstructured.

    ☒ **A** is incorrect because volume and object are applicable to Infrastructure as a Service (IaaS). They are not storage types used with PaaS, which is what the question asks for.

    ☒ **C** is incorrect because container and object are not recognized storage types associated with cloud services. Although object is applicable to IaaS implementations, container is typically used along with deployment technologies such as Docker rather in a specific storage context.

    ☒ **D** is incorrect because although both volume and structured are storage types used within cloud environments, they span two different cloud service categories. Volume storage is associated with IaaS, whereas structured storage is associated with PaaS; both are not applicable to the PaaS example represented in the question.

39. Which of the following methods or strategies is *NOT* a method for protecting sensitive data from data sets?

A. Zeroing

B. Anonymization

C. Tokenization

D. Obfuscation

☑ **A.** Zeroing involves replacing and overwriting data with zeros or null values. Although it is a successful strategy for guaranteeing the secure deletion of data, it would not be considered a method for protecting sensitive data, because it would actually destroy the data.

☒ **B** is incorrect because anonymization involves removing or masking indirect identifiers in data sets to prevent the identification of specific individuals. It is used to protect sensitive data from individual identification, and is often used in conjunction with other strategies.

☒ **C** is incorrect because tokenization involves replacing sensitive data with opaque or key values so that the original sensitive data is not presented. Although tokenization can allow linking back to the original values, it definitely is a method for protecting sensitive information.

☒ **D** is incorrect because obfuscation is typically used as a method for making data sets available for testing of development or non-production systems by removing sensitive data or replacing it with other values.

40. Which of the following areas is *NOT* part of the CCM framework and represented as a domain?

A. Mobile security

B. Human resources

C. Governance

D. Financial audit

☑ **D.** The Cloud Control Matrix (CCM) serves as a framework for cloud security and covers the areas that are pertinent to it. Although the matrix contains main domains and areas that are directly applicable to data security and cloud data systems, financial audit is not included as one of them.

☒ **A** is incorrect because mobile security is one of the domains listed as part of the CCM.

☒ **B** is incorrect because human resources is listed as one of the domains of the CCM, as it pertains directly to personnel security and the prevention of malicious insiders.

☒ **C** is incorrect because governance of IT data and resources is a core domain of the CCM.

41. The final phase of the cloud data lifecycle is the destroy phase, where data is ultimately deleted and done so in a secure manner to ensure it cannot be recovered or reconstructed. Which cloud service category poses the most challenges to data destruction or the cloud customer?

   A. Platform

   B. Software

   C. Infrastructure

   D. Desktop

   ☑ **B.** With Software as a Service (SaaS), data destruction often poses the most challenges because it is solely the responsibility of the cloud provider, but also because most platforms tend to be large implementations with many customers or tenants using them. This makes assurances of data destruction more challenging because the methods and resources available can be limited.

   ☒ **A** is incorrect because Platform as a Service (PaaS) is isolated to a specific cloud customer, and data destruction techniques can be used without interfering with others or causing possible conflicts. The destruction of the virtual machine wholesale also allows for options that are not available with SaaS.

   ☒ **C** is incorrect because Infrastructure as a Service (IaaS) is also focused on a specific customer, and the destroy phase can be done via the destruction of the virtual machine or the zeroing of data, which would not be possible with SaaS.

   ☒ **D** is incorrect because Desktop as a Service (DaaS) operates much as SaaS and carries with it the same concerns, but is more segregated by individual cloud customers.

42. During data discovery and classification, the use of metadata is a primary means for analysis. Which of the following would *NOT* be considered metadata?

   A. Column names

   B. Content

   C. Filenames

   D. Headers

   ☑ **B.** Metadata by definition is data about data, so the actual content of the data would not fit within this definition. Content analysis goes against the actual data and sources rather than against metadata.

   ☒ **A** is incorrect because column names are descriptive and structural information about the data, so they meet the definition of metadata. They do not contain actual data or information, only information about the data and how it is organized.

   ☒ **C** is incorrect because filenames are information about data, regardless of the naming convention, and as such are considered metadata.

☒ **D** is incorrect because headers are very similar column names and represent information about the data and how it is organized or categorized. They are also considered metadata and descriptive in nature.

43. Different types of cloud deployment models use different types of storage from traditional data centers, along with many new types of software platforms for deploying applications and configurations. Which of the following is *NOT* a storage type used within a cloud environment?

    A. Docker

    B. Object

    C. Structured

    D. Volume

    ☑ **A.** Docker is a container method for building, shipping, and running applications across different platforms and clients. It runs within its own agents and containers, is not a storage type under a cloud deployment model, and can be used with virtually any type of platform.

    ☒ **B** is incorrect because object storage, where data is stored as an opaque file handler or descriptor in a flat file system, is an official cloud storage type used with Infrastructure as a Service (IaaS).

    ☒ **C** is incorrect because structured storage, where data is stored in a database-type application, is an official cloud storage type used with Platform as a Service (PaaS).

    ☒ **D** is incorrect because volume storage, where data is stored on a logical partition resembling a traditional file system hierarchy, is an official cloud storage type used with Infrastructure as a Service (IaaS).

44. When data is required to be archived and retained for extended lengths of time, which of the following becomes the most pressing concern over time?

    A. Encryption

    B. Size

    C. Restoration

    D. Availability

    ☑ **C.** As time passes and organizations change out software and other technologies, it is imperative that the ability to restore archives is maintained. Given that some regulatory requirements are several years or longer, and with the rapid development of technology and upgrades, it is very possible without proper planning for an organization to end up deprecating the capability to restore archives before they have reached their minimum retention time. When this happens, an organization would likely have to contract with a third party, likely at a very high cost, for restoration services should the need arise.

☒ **A** is incorrect because the concern with encryption is the protection of keys over time, but the underlying technology and capabilities will still exist down the road. This is different than with software and other technologies used to create and store archives, where the prospects of being deprecated are much higher.

☒ **B** is incorrect because although the size of archives can be a concern, especially for longer retention periods, it is not the type of concern that will change over time or result in issues with deprecated technology. Because archives by nature do not change, size will not increase with data that is already archived, and additional storage can always be added, as needed, to handle longer retention requirements, as opposed to concerns over time with software versions and access.

☒ **D** is incorrect because archives typically are housed in less accessible means of storage, many times on tapes kept at secure external facilities. When the need for restoration arises, it may take some time for archives to be retrieved and restored. There is no need for archives to be immediately available, and the contract or SLA with a service provider should document the required or expected restoration times, ensuring they also will satisfy any regulatory requirements.

45. Which of the following data protection methodologies maintains the ability to connect back values to the original values?

    A. Tokenization

    B. Anonymization

    C. Obfuscation

    D. Dynamic mapping

    ☑ **A.** Tokenization replaces data fields with opaque handlers or descriptors. In the process, the original and sensitive information is removed from the data, and the token values can be mapped them back to the original values if needed.

    ☒ **B** is incorrect because anonymization removes indirect identifiers from data sets to protective sensitive information and prevent data from being matched up with an individual. However, the goal of anonymization is not to be able to map back to original data like is possible with tokenization.

    ☒ **C** is incorrect because obfuscation often replaces values with garbage or random data, and as such, it isn't possible to map back to the original values. Obfuscation is typically used to make data sets for development or non-production systems for testing that contain the format of production data but not the actual values.

    ☒ **D** is incorrect because dynamic mapping can refer to many things within a system or application, but in this instance it's provided as an erroneous choice.

46. Which of the following is not a commonly accepted strategy for data discovery?

    A. Labels

    B. Metadata

C. Signature hashing

D. Content analysis

☑ **C.** Data discovery is focused on the three main areas: labels, metadata, and content analysis. Signature hashing may be used for some of these methods for comparison and efficiency, but it would be used as a tool or process rather than one of the key strategies.

☒ **A** is incorrect because labels, which are applied to data for grouping or organization, are commonly used for the data discovery processes. The main shortcoming with using labels is that the process is dependent on the accurate and complete application of labels before the data is processed.

☒ **B** is incorrect because metadata, or data about data, is commonly used as a strategy for date discovery and classification. Metadata uses attributes such as type, creator, dates, and other identifying information about the data itself to make determinations for discovery.

☒ **D** is incorrect because content analysis, which is done against the actual data itself, is a main strategy for data discovery, even if it is the slowest and least accurate method. However, as tools become more mature and efficient, the use of content analysis is rapidly growing and becoming more accurate and useful.

47. Although the preservation and retention of data are the most important concepts that usually come to mind when you're considering archiving, what process is equally important to test regularly for the duration of the required retention period?

A. Recoverability

B. Portability

C. Encryption

D. Availability

☑ **A.** Over time, data that is archived can become inaccessible if an organization loses or deprecates the systems or technologies used to archive it, thus compromising its ability to restore that data. Regular tests should be done to ensure data can still be recovered, or the organization risks failing to meet regulatory requirements.

☒ **B** is incorrect because portability is the quality of being able to easily move between cloud providers. With data archives being static storage objects, portability is not a primary concern, nor should it be an impediment if a new hosting provider is needed, because the data types and formats should be universal and abstracted from the cloud provider.

☒ **C** is incorrect because encryption methods will still be available over time, as long as the keys are properly maintained and secured. This is independent of a specific cloud provider or specific archiving software or system.

☒ **D** is incorrect because availability is not a primary concern with archiving. Typically, offsite storage or storage services are used with archiving, in which case the immediate availability for restoration will not be possible, and some period of time, defined by regulation, is allowed for producing records and evidence.

48. You are reviewing the standard offerings from a prospective cloud provider, and one area of log collection promises full and complete access to operating system logs for all provisioned systems. Which cloud service category is this *MOST* likely referring to?

    A. Platform

    B. Desktop

    C. Software

    D. Infrastructure

    ☑ **D.** With Infrastructure as a Service (IaaS), the cloud customer is responsible for the provisioning, configuration, and support of operating systems and virtual machines. As such, the customer has full access to all systems and operating system logs, whereas with the other service categories, these items would not be provided.

    ☒ **A** is incorrect because with Platform as a Service (PaaS), the operating system is maintained by the cloud provider and is its responsibility, so chances are that full access to operating system logs will not be provided or even possible. A subset may be made available through certain tool sets or an SIEM solution, but direct and full access is typically not provided.

    ☒ **B** is incorrect because Desktop as a Service (DaaS) works much like SaaS, where the cloud provider is responsible for the overall system, platform, and software, and would not make full operating system logs available to the cloud customer, nor would the cloud provider necessarily provide a high level of value.

    ☒ **C** is incorrect because the operating system with Software as a Service (SaaS) is solely the responsibility of the cloud provider, who itself would retain full access to operating system logs. Because the cloud provider is solely responsible for the logs, there would be little need for the cloud customer to have access to them.

49. Which of the following will always serve as the starting point for the minimum period of data retention?

    A. Contract

    B. Regulation

    C. System resources

    D. Company policy

    ☑ **B.** Regulation will dictate, based on the type and content of data, the minimum period of data retention, as well as what events must be captured for retention. Regulation is specific to the type of data and the jurisdiction where it is located or consumed.

☒ **A** is incorrect because a contract will articulate and document data retention requirements between the cloud customer and the cloud provider; it will not serve as the basis for the actual policy dictating those requirements.

☒ **C** is incorrect because system resources would never be a factor for determining data retention requirements, as regulation would always supersede them, and it would be the responsibility of the cloud customer to ensure that sufficient system resources were allocated to support and meet retention requirements.

☒ **D** is incorrect because company policy forms the end basis for data retention, but the starting point will always be regulation. Company policies may always expand and build upon regulations, but regulations will always form the minimum starting basis for retention requirements.

50. Which type of masking would be appropriate for the creation of data sets for testing purposes, where the same structure and size are of importance?

   A. Dynamic

   B. Structured

   C. Tokenized

   D. Static

   ☑ **D.** Static masking is used to produce full data sets, with sensitive data removed, often for the purposes of testing or development, where the structure and size will need to resemble production data, just without the actual sensitive values.

   ☒ **A** is incorrect because dynamic masking is done between the data and application layers, and is meant for transaction purposes rather than the production of data sets.

   ☒ **B** is incorrect because "structured" refers to a type of storage used under Platform as a Service (PaaS). It is not a masking technique.

   ☒ **C** is incorrect because "tokenized" could refer to tokenization, where sensitive data is replaced by opaque handlers or descriptors, but with the ability to map back to the original values. However, this process would not be used for producing test data sets, where such a capability would be inappropriate and unnecessary.

3

Cloud Platform and Infrastructure Security Domain

Domain 3 is focused on the following topics:

- Physical aspects of a cloud environment
- Key components that make up a cloud environment
- Risks associated with cloud computing
- The design and planning for cloud-based security controls
- Auditing in a cloud environment
- Disaster recovery and business continuity in a cloud environment

Cloud platforms bring unique benefits to an organization and have many attractive capabilities for performance and scalability. They also remove the focus on hardware and instead focus on business requirements and measured service—all for a lower total cost versus running your own data center. However, cloud platforms also bring unique challenges and risks because of these very same factors. This chapter goes over those risks and challenges as well as how to address and mitigate them, and it covers the disaster recovery and business continuity requirements and benefits in a cloud environment.

1. Data centers have components that are either internal or external redundancies. Which of the following is considered an internal redundancy?

   A. Generators

   B. Power feeds

   C. Power distribution units

   D. Building access points

2. Limits within a cloud environment can be either hard limits or limits capable of adjusting to current demands and circumstances. Which of the following concepts encapsulates allowing a limit to adjust to current circumstances, without the actual limit value changing?

   A. Loaning

   B. Borrowing

   C. Adapting

   D. Scaling

3. When dealing with a cloud environment that has resource pooling and multitenancy, a cloud customer may want contractual assurances that sufficient resources to start and operate their services will always be available. What is this type of assurance called?

   A. Limit

   B. Reservation

   C. Share

   D. Guarantee

4. A BCDR plan has several different types of operations and major components. Which of the following is the most often overlooked part of the overall process, both in testing and in planning?

   A. Recovery of services

   B. Change management processes

   C. Staff availability and demands

   D. Restoration of services

5. What concept allows users or support staff to change some network configurations without having access to the actual networking hardware and administrative interfaces?

   A. Logical networks

   B. VLANs

   C. Broad network access

   D. Software-defined networking

6. Within a federated identity system, which entity takes the response from the identity provider and processes it to determine the authentication and authorization properties of the user?

   A. Service provider

   B. Service party

   C. Relying party

   D. Application provider

7. Which cloud storage method utilizes a key value to access data from an application or client?

   A. Object

   B. Volume

   C. Structured

   D. Unstructured

8. Which of the following is the most prominent potential problem point with object storage for systems that have high data reading and writing dependencies?

   A. Integrity of objects

   B. Replication of objects

   C. Size of objects

   D. Number of objects

9. When system resource utilization is experiencing heavy demand, possibly nearing the overall full capacity of the cloud environment, which of the following concepts will set the prioritization as to which virtual hosts receive the requested resources?

   A. Reservations

   B. Shares

   C. Limits

   D. Escrows

10. Which concept ensures that enough resources are available to the many tenants within a cloud environment and that a single system, service, or customer does not consume too many resources?

    A. Share

    B. Reservation

    C. Limit

    D. Cap

11. One of the most crucial metrics for a BCDR plan is how long it takes for services to be restored to a point of satisfaction for management. Which metric represents this point and value?

   A. RTO

   B. RPO

   C. RSL

   D. SRE

12. When resource limitations surpass the thresholds determined by the cloud provider and shares need to be invoked, which of the following is the driving factor for the determination of share allocations?

   A. Prioritization weighting

   B. Size of customer

   C. Number of users

   D. Costs of resources

13. Which metric is used to determine whether BCDR objectives have been met and measures the percentage of production-level restoration required for success?

   A. RTO

   B. RPO

   C. RSL

   D. SRE

14. Cloud environments are based entirely on virtual machines and virtual devices, and those images are also in need of storage within the environment. What type of storage is typically used for virtual images?

   A. Volume

   B. Structured

   C. Unstructured

   D. Object

15. An organization could have many reasons that are common throughout the industry to activate a BCDR situation. Which of the following is *NOT* a typical reason to activate a BCDR plan?

   A. Natural disaster

   B. Utility outage

   C. Staff loss

   D. Terrorist attack

16. What type of system is exposed to the public Internet but to maintain security is designed to perform just a specific function and has security controls and monitoring in place specifically focused on that capability?

    A. Honeypot

    B. Bastion

    C. WAF

    D. VPN

17. Which concept provides an acceptable level of assurance that an individual or entity is in fact whom they claim to be?

    A. Identification

    B. Authentication

    C. Authorization

    D. Integrity

18. A federated identity system is composed of three main components. Which of the following is *NOT* one of the three main components?

    A. Identity provider

    B. User

    C. Relying party

    D. API

19. Measured service is a very attractive aspect of cloud computing for an organization looking for BCDR solutions because it will keep costs down. Which of the following is also a key aspect of cloud computing that can make BCDR situations easier in a cloud environment than in a traditional data center?

    A. Broad network access

    B. Resource pooling

    C. Multitenancy

    D. Reversibility

20. With PaaS, which strategy is most commonly used for the deployment of operating system patches?

    A. Scripts

    B. Reimaging

    C. Customer administration

    D. APIs

21. During a system or application audit, which of the following populations will be the most important driver of the audit and testing?

    A. Regulators

    B. Management

    C. Shareholders

    D. Users

22. A primary focus during a BCDR situation is for systems and applications to meet an acceptable level of operations. Which value represents this status?

    A. RTO

    B. RPO

    C. RSL

    D. SRE

23. A variety of limits can be set within a cloud environment. Which of the following is *NOT* a unit where a limit can be set?

    A. Customer

    B. Application

    C. Virtual machine

    D. Hypervisor

24. Which of the following capabilities would *NOT* be covered by a reservation within a cloud environment?

    A. Running applications

    B. Starting virtual machines

    C. Auto-scaling

    D. Performing normal business operations

25. Without the ability to segregate networks physically within a cloud environment, what concept is heavily used for network isolation and segmentation?

    A. WAN

    B. VLAN

    C. LAN

    D. Firewalls

26. Under the guidance of industry-accepted best practices, which of the following is the correct frequency for BCDR plan testing?

    A. Annually

    B. Monthly

C. Quarterly

D. Bi-annually

27. Software-defined networking (SDN) is intended to separate different network capabilities and allow for the granting of granular configurations, permissions, and features to non-network staff or customers. Which network capability is separated from forwarding of traffic?

  A. Routing

  B. Firewalling

  C. Filtering

  D. IPS

28. Different storage paradigms within a cloud environment handle formatting, allocation, and security controls differently. What handles these aspects for volume storage?

  A. Operating system of host

  B. Hypervisor

  C. Management plane

  D. Storage host

29. Which aspect of cloud computing would be most negatively impacted by incurring vendor lock-in with a cloud provider?

  A. Interoperability

  B. Reversibility

  C. Portability

  D. Scalability

30. A denial of service (DoS) attack can potentially impact all customers within a cloud environment with the continued allocation of additional resources. Which of the following can be useful for a customer to protect themselves from a DoS attack against another customer?

  A. Limits

  B. Reservations

  C. Shares

  D. Borrows

31. What aspect of a Type 2 hypervisor involves additional security concerns that are not relevant with a Type 1 hypervisor?

  A. Reliance on a host operating system

  B. Proprietary software

  C. Programming languages

  D. Auditing

32. A common strategy employed when using cloud services for BCDR strategies is to only maintain images offline at the cloud provider, or to only have a minimal set of systems running until needed. With the strategy of only running a minimal level of systems until needed, which aspect of cloud computing would be most beneficial during an actual BCDR situation?

    A. Resource pooling

    B. Measured service

    C. Rapid elasticity

    D. Broad network access

33. With volume storage, a slice of storage space is allocated to a system to be used in whatever manner is necessary for that particular system and its requirements. What is this slice of storage referred to as?

    A. LAN

    B. LUN

    C. Partition

    D. Allocation

34. Although cloud storage systems will ultimately be consumed by cloud customers or users from a logical configuration, what are the two types of underlying physical storage systems most used with cloud computing?

    A. RAID and SAN

    B. SAN and iSCSI

    C. SCSI and RAID

    D. iSCSI and RAID

35. Although performing BCDR tests at regular intervals is a best practice to ensure processes and documentation are still relevant and efficient, which of the following represents a reason to conduct a BCDR review outside of the regular interval?

    A. Staff changes

    B. Application changes

    C. Regulatory changes

    D. Management changes

36. When an organization is considering the use of a cloud provider as part of its BCDR strategy, which of the following is most important to consider from a security perspective?

    A. Auditing

    B. Network access

    C. Jurisdiction

    D. Resource pooling

37. Why does the use of a Type 2 hypervisor typically incur more security concerns than a Type 1 hypervisor?

    A. A Type 2 hypervisor is always exposed to the public Internet for federated identity access.

    B. A Type 2 hypervisor allows users to directly perform some functions with their own access.

    C. A Type 2 hypervisor runs on top of an operating system and is dependent on the security of that OS for its own security.

    D. A Type 2 hypervisor is open source, so attackers can more easily find exploitable vulnerabilities.

38. When is a system hosted in a virtualized environment vulnerable but *NOT* vulnerable on a physical server?

    A. During patching

    B. During maintenance

    C. During change windows

    D. When the image is offline

1. C	**14.** D	**27.** C
2. B	**15.** C	**28.** A
3. B	**16.** B	**29.** C
4. D	**17.** B	**30.** B
5. D	**18.** D	**31.** A
6. C	**19.** A	**32.** C
7. A	**20.** B	**33.** B
8. B	**21.** A	**34.** A
9. B	**22.** B	**35.** B
10. C	**23.** D	**36.** C
11. A	**24.** C	**37.** C
12. A	**25.** B	**38.** D
13. C	**26.** A	

Comprehensive Answers and Explanations

1. Data centers have components that are either internal or external redundancies. Which of the following is considered an internal redundancy?

   A. Generators

   B. Power feeds

   C. Power distribution units

   D. Building access points

   ☑ **C.** Power distribution units are internal to a data center. They distribute power to racks, internal chillers, and any other internal systems that need direct power feeds. Because they are completely internal to the data center, they are considered an internal redundancy.

   ☒ **A** is incorrect because generators are external to a data center and provide electrical feeds in the event of a utility outage. Because they sit outside of the data center and feed power inward, they are considered an external redundancy.

   ☒ **B** is incorrect because power feeds come from external utilities or generators and send electrical power into the data center. Because they originate from outside the data center, they are considered external redundancies.

   ☒ **D** is incorrect because building access points provide staff access to internal layers of a data center from the outside. Because they provide external access to the data center, they are considered external redundancies.

2. Limits within a cloud environment can be either hard limits or limits capable of adjusting to current demands and circumstances. Which of the following concepts encapsulates allowing a limit to adjust to current circumstances, without the actual limit value changing?

   A. Loaning

   B. Borrowing

   C. Adapting

   D. Scaling

   ☑ **B.** Limits can be set as either hard or flexible within a cloud environment. When limits are flexible, rather than adjusting the actual limits when it is necessary to exceed them, the system allows customers or other systems to borrow resources, which are allocated to the customer or system in need. This maintains the actual limit in the system going forward, but allows for temporary expansion under certain circumstances.

   ☒ **A** is incorrect because the correct term is borrowing, not loaning.

☒ **C** is incorrect because the correct term is borrowing, not adapting.

☒ **D** is incorrect because the correct term is borrowing, not scaling.

3. When dealing with a cloud environment that has resource pooling and multitenancy, a cloud customer may want contractual assurances that sufficient resources to start and operate their services will always be available. What is this type of assurance called?

   A. Limit

   B. Reservation

   C. Share

   D. Guarantee

   ☑ **B.** A reservation is a minimum resource level guaranteed to a customer within a cloud environment. A reservation can pertain to the two main aspects of computing: memory and processing. With a reservation in place, a cloud customer is guaranteed by the cloud provider to always have at minimum the necessary resources available to power on and operate any of its services. In large cloud environments with numerous customers, this feature can be of particular importance in the case of denial of service attacks or high utilization of resources by other hosts and systems because it offers a guaranteed minimum level of operations to all customers.

   ☒ **A** is incorrect because limits are put in place to enforce the maximum allowable utilization of memory or processing by a cloud customer. These limits can be done at either the virtual machine level or a comprehensive level for a customer. They are meant to ensure that enormous cloud resources cannot be allocated to or consumed by a single host or customer to the detriment of other hosts and customers. Along with cloud computing features such as auto-scaling and on-demand self-service, limits can be either hard (or fixed) or flexible and allowed to change dynamically. Typically, when limits are allowed to change dynamically based on current conditions and consumption, it is done by "borrowing" additional resources rather through a change to the actual limits themselves.

   ☒ **C** is incorrect because the concept of shares within a cloud environment is used to mitigate and control customer requests for resource allocations in case the environment does not have the current capability to provide the needed resources. Shares work by prioritizing hosts within a cloud environment through a weighting system that is defined by the cloud provider. When periods of high utilization and allocation are reached, the system automatically uses the scoring of each host based on its share value to determine which hosts get access to the limited resources still available. The higher the value a particular host has, the more resources it will be allowed to utilize.

   ☒ **D** is incorrect because although the term guarantee sounds similar in concept to reservation, it is not the correct term being asked for by the question.

4. A BCDR plan has several different types of operations and major components. Which of the following is the most often overlooked part of the overall process, both in testing and in planning?

A. Recovery of services

B. Change management processes

C. Staff availability and demands

D. Restoration of services

☑ **D.** Once a BCDR event has concluded, and the regular data center and hosting resources are available again, it is crucial to conduct an orderly return to normal operations. Although BCDR plans tend to be very detailed and thoroughly tested for moving production operations to a recovery site, the same level of detail and testing is often not performed for returning services to normal operations. With this oversight, an organization can be left incurring substantial delays, costs, or even potentially downtime returning its data and services to their normal operating state.

☒ **A** is incorrect because the recovery of services during a disaster tends to be the overwhelming focus of any BCDR plan and testing, and is not something that would be overlooked at all.

☒ **B** is incorrect because most BCDR planning does a good job of ensuring that change management processes have been followed to ensure system consistency and documentation, and these processes are not typically overlooked during planning and testing.

☒ **C** is incorrect because the availability of staff and the demands placed upon them are tightly coupled with the restoration of services, and as such would not be overlooked.

5. What concept allows users or support staff to change some network configurations without having access to the actual networking hardware and administrative interfaces?

A. Logical networks

B. VLANs

C. Broad network access

D. Software-defined networking

☑ **D.** An important aspect of cloud computing is the use of software-defined networking (SDN). With SDN, the decisions concerning where traffic is filtered or sent and the actual forwarding of traffic are completely separate from each other. With cloud computing, this separation is important because it allows the administrators of the cloud network to quickly and dynamically adjust network flows and resources based on the current needs and demands of the cloud customers. With the separation from the actual network components, a cloud provider can build management tools that allow staffers using web portals or cloud administrative interfaces to make changes to the network without having to log into the actual network components or have the command knowledge of a network administrator to make changes. With the level of access provided and the types of resources available to control, a high level of security needs to be attached to any SDN implementation, with access tightly controlled and monitored regularly.

☒ **A** is incorrect because logical networks are a concept that involves the separation and segregation of network IP spaces within a larger physical network, but it does not pertain to the administration of networks or granting of administrative access.

☒ **B** is incorrect because virtual local area networks (VLANs) are the same concept as logical networks, where a network is broken up into different segments within a larger physical network, but it does not pertain to the administration of networks.

☒ **C** is incorrect because broad network access refers to cloud computing being available over the public Internet rather than using the internal or private networks typically associated with a traditional data center, but it does not pertain to the administration of networks.

6. Within a federated identity system, which entity takes the response from the identity provider and processes it to determine the authentication and authorization properties of the user?

   A. Service provider

   B. Service party

   C. Relying party

   D. Application provider

   ☑ **C.** During the authentication process, the identity provider sends certain predetermined attributes about the user to the relying party. The relying party then uses this information (name, location, job title, and so on) to determine the appropriate level and type of access to grant, or whether to grant access at all. The relying party, even in a federated system, makes this determination because it is tied to the actual application, and it makes the decisions based on the policies, requirements, or regulations of the data being accessed.

   ☒ **A** is incorrect because service provider, although it is often used in the same way as the term relying party, is not the correct term that is universally used in this case.

   ☒ **B** is incorrect because service party sounds similar to the term relying party but is not the correct term in this case.

   ☒ **D** is incorrect because application provider sounds similar to the term relying party but is not the correct term in this case.

7. Which cloud storage method utilizes a key value to access data from an application or client?

   A. Object

   B. Volume

C. Structured

D. Unstructured

☑ **A.** Object storage is hosted external from systems and applications and is accessed via a key value for each object that it stores. It is not organized in a directory or the hierarchical structure of a file system, but rather is a flat structure where each object is classified with an opaque key value.

☒ **B** is incorrect because volume storage uses the same traditional folders, directories, filenames, and structures as a file system on a regular computer or server. Although it could use filenames that look similar to key values, it is not stored or accessed in the same manner as object storage.

☒ **C** is incorrect because structured storage resembles a database paradigm, with defined structures, labels, and fields. It is not used for general object types, nor does it use key values in the same sense as object storage.

☒ **D** is incorrect because unstructured storage is used for supporting and auxiliary files in conjunction with structured storage, but it does not use key values in the same sense as object storage does.

8. Which of the following is the most prominent potential problem point with object storage for systems that have high data reading and writing dependencies?

A. Integrity of objects

B. Replication of objects

C. Size of objects

D. Number of objects

☑ **B.** Object storage systems are self-contained and external from a customer's servers or application servers. When objects are written to them, there is a potential for data consistency issues until the redundant servers have received the replicated data objects.

☒ **A** is incorrect because the integrity of objects is not a concern specifically related to applications that use high reading or writing dependencies.

☒ **C** is incorrect because the size of objects is not a specific concern pertinent to the question. However, the larger objects will take longer to fully replicate and could become an issue if a need to read arises soon after. However, with the root of the problem being replication, the best answer is specifically the replication of objects.

☒ **D** is incorrect because the number of objects is not a specific concern pertinent to the question. However, a larger number of objects will take longer to fully replicate and could become an issue if a need to read arises soon after. However, with the root of the problem being replication, the best answer is specifically the replication of objects.

9. When system resource utilization is experiencing heavy demand, possibly nearing the overall full capacity of the cloud environment, which of the following concepts will set the prioritization as to which virtual hosts receive the requested resources?

A. Reservations

B. Shares

C. Limits

D. Escrows

☑ **B.** The concept of shares within a cloud environment is used to mitigate and control customer requests for resource allocations in case the environment does not have the current capability to provide these resources. Shares work by prioritizing hosts within a cloud environment through a weighting system that is defined by the cloud provider. When periods of high utilization and allocation are reached, the system automatically uses the scoring of each host based on its share value to determine which hosts get access to the limited resources still available. The higher the value a particular host has, the more resources it will be allowed to utilize.

☒ **A** is incorrect because a reservation is a minimum resource level that is guaranteed to a customer within a cloud environment. A reservation can pertain to the two main aspects of computing: memory and processing. With a reservation in place, a cloud customer is guaranteed by the cloud provider to always have at minimum the necessary resources available to power on and operate any of its services. In large cloud environments with a large number of customers, this feature can be of particular importance in the case of denial of service attacks or high utilization of resources by other hosts and systems because it offers a guaranteed minimum level of operations to all customers.

☒ **C** is incorrect because limits are put in place to enforce maximum utilization of memory or processing by a cloud customer. These limits can either be done at the virtual machine level or a comprehensive level for a customer. They are meant to ensure that enormous cloud resources cannot be allocated or consumed by a single host or customer to the detriment of other hosts and customers. Along with cloud computing features such as auto-scaling and on-demand self-service, limits can be either hard (or fixed) or flexible and allowed to change dynamically. Typically, when limits are allowed to change dynamically based on current conditions and consumption, it is done by "borrowing" additional resources rather than through a change in the actual limits themselves.

☒ **D** is incorrect because escrows sounds similar to the term shares but is not the correct term in this case.

10. Which concept ensures that enough resources are available to the many tenants within a cloud environment and that a single system, service, or customer does not consume too many resources?

A. Share

B. Reservation

C. Limit

D. Cap

☑ **C.** Limits are put in place to enforce the maximum utilization of memory or processing by a cloud customer. These limits can either be done at the virtual machine level or a comprehensive level for a customer. They are meant to ensure that enormous cloud resources cannot be allocated or consumed by a single host or customer to the detriment of other hosts and customers. Along with cloud computing features such as auto-scaling and on-demand self-service, limits can be either hard (or fixed) or flexible and allowed to change dynamically. Typically, when limits are allowed to change dynamically based on current conditions and consumption, it is done by "borrowing" additional resources rather than making an actual change in the limits themselves.

☒ **A** is incorrect because the concept of shares within a cloud environment is used to mitigate and control customer requests for resource allocations in case the environment does not have the current capability to provide these resources. Shares work by prioritizing hosts within a cloud environment through a weighting system that is defined by the cloud provider. When periods of high utilization and allocation are reached, the system automatically uses the scoring of each host based on its share value to determine which hosts get access to the limited resources still available. The higher the value a particular host has, the more resources it will be allowed to utilize.

☒ **B** is incorrect because a reservation is a minimum resource level that is guaranteed to a customer within a cloud environment. A reservation can pertain to the two main aspects of computing: memory and processing. With a reservation in place, a cloud customer is guaranteed by the cloud provider to always have at minimum the necessary resources available to power on and operate any of its services. In large cloud environments with a large number of customers, this feature can be of particular importance in the case of denial of service attacks or high utilization of resources by other hosts and systems because it offers a guaranteed minimum level of operations to all customers.

☒ **D** is incorrect because although cap sounds similar to the term limits, it is not a correct term in this case.

11. One of the most crucial metrics for a BCDR plan is how long it takes for services to be restored to a point of satisfaction for management. Which metric represents this point and value?

    A. RTO

    B. RPO

    C. RSL

    D. SRE

    ☑ **A.** The recovery time objective (RTO) is a measurement of the amount of time it would take to recover operations in the event of a disaster to the point where management's objectives for BCDR are met.

☒ **B** is incorrect because the recovery point objective (RPO) is defined as the amount of data a company would need to maintain and recover in order to function at a level acceptable to management. This may or may not be a restoration to full operating capacity, depending on what management deems as crucial and essential.

☒ **C** is incorrect because the recovery service level (RSL) measures the percentage of the total typical production service level that needs to be restored to meet BCDR objectives in the case of a failure.

☒ **D** is incorrect because SRE is provided as an extraneous choice that is not pertinent to the question.

12. When resource limitations surpass the thresholds determined by the cloud provider and shares need to be invoked, which of the following is the driving factor for the determination of share allocations?

    A. Prioritization weighting

    B. Size of customer

    C. Number of users

    D. Costs of resources

    ☑ **A.** Systems and services within a cloud environment are assigned a prioritization value based on contractual requirements, level of services purchased, or other possible values. When limits are reached and resources need to be allocated, this prioritization weighting determines the order in which systems or services will receive requested resources.

    ☒ **B** is incorrect because the size of the customer is not pertinent to the prioritization weighting value, as it is dictated by the customer's contract and/or level of services purchased.

    ☒ **C** is incorrect because the number of users is not pertinent to the prioritization weighting value, as it is dictated by the customer's contract and/or level of services purchased.

    ☒ **D** is incorrect because the cost of resources is not pertinent to the prioritization weighting value, as it is dictated by the customer's contract and/or level of services purchased.

13. Which metric is used to determine whether BCDR objectives have been met and measures the percentage of production-level restoration required for success?

    A. RTO

    B. RPO

    C. RSL

    D. SRE

☑ **C.** The recovery service level (RSL) measures the percentage of the total typical production service level that needs to be restored to meet BCDR objectives in the case of a failure.

☒ **A** is incorrect because the recovery time objective (RTO) is a measurement of the amount of time it would take to recover operations in the event of a disaster to the point where management's objectives for BCDR are met.

☒ **B** is incorrect because the recovery point objective (RPO) is defined as the amount of data a company would need to maintain and recover in order to function at a level acceptable to management. This may or may not be a restoration to full operating capacity, depending on what management deems as crucial and essential.

☒ **D** is incorrect because SRE is provided as an extraneous choice that is not pertinent to the question.

14. Cloud environments are based entirely on virtual machines and virtual devices, and those images are also in need of storage within the environment. What type of storage is typically used for virtual images?

   A. Volume

   B. Structured

   C. Unstructured

   D. Object

☑ **D.** Object storage is hosted external from systems and applications, and is accessed via a key value for each object it stores. It is not organized in a directory or the hierarchical structure of a file system, but rather it has a flat structure where each object is classified with an opaque key value. Because it is an external and independent system, and not tied to specific customers, services, or servers, it is the correct place to store virtual images.

☒ **A** is incorrect because volume storage uses the same traditional folders, directories, filenames, and structures as a file system on a regular computer or server. Although it could use filenames that look similar to key values, it is not stored or accessed in the same manner as object storage. It is tied specifically to servers that are provisioned for customers and would not be an appropriate storage mechanism for virtual images.

☒ **B** is incorrect because structured storage resembles a database paradigm, with defined structures, labels, and fields. It is not used for general object types, nor does it use key values in the same sense as object storage. It is allocated to specific services and designed to meet their needs, and would not be an appropriate storage location for virtual images.

☒ **C** is incorrect because unstructured storage is used for supporting and auxiliary files in conjunction with structured storage, but it does not use key values in the same sense as object storage does. It is allocated to specific services and designed to meet their needs, and would not be an appropriate storage location for virtual images.

15. An organization could have many reasons that are common throughout the industry to activate a BCDR situation. Which of the following is *NOT* a typical reason to activate a BCDR plan?

A. Natural disaster

B. Utility outage

C. Staff loss

D. Terrorist attack

☑ **C.** BCDR situations involve widespread problems or disasters that typically impact an entire data center or enterprise. Loss of staff would not be an appropriate time to utilize a BCDR situation because it would not directly affect the systems and hosting, and the invocation of a BCDR situation is highly dependent on the appropriate staff being available and accessible.

☒ **A** is incorrect because a natural disaster is a prime consideration of BCDR strategies and would be a widespread event that could impact an entire data center.

☒ **B** is incorrect because a utility outage is a prime consideration of BCDR strategies and would be a widespread event that could impact an entire data center.

☒ **D** is incorrect because a terrorist attack is a prime consideration of BCDR strategies and would be a widespread event that could impact an entire data center.

16. What type of system is exposed to the public Internet but to maintain security is designed to perform just a specific function and has security controls and monitoring in place specifically focused on that capability?

A. Honeypot

B. Bastion

C. WAF

D. VPN

☑ **B.** A bastion host is a server that is fully exposed to the public Internet; it is extremely hardened to prevent attacks and is usually focused for one specific application or usage only. This singular focus allows for much more stringent security hardening and monitoring.

☒ **A** is incorrect because a honeypot is designed to resemble a production system with production data in order to entice attackers and monitor the methods they use to attempt to compromise it. This knowledge can then be used to augment or change security controls to meet the real threats the system or application is facing.

☒ **C** is incorrect because a web application firewall (WAF) is designed to filter incoming web traffic based on content and processes and then possibly take additional security measures against it, reject it, filter it, or many other types of operations that can be offloaded and done prior to reaching application servers.

D is incorrect because a virtual private network (VPN) is designed to provide a secure network tunnel into a protected network from the outside and enable systems administrative staff to perform their work duties or to access sensitive data in a more secure manner.

17. Which concept provides an acceptable level of assurance that an individual or entity is in fact whom they claim to be?

    A. Identification

    B. Authentication

    C. Authorization

    D. Integrity

    ☑ **B.** Authentication is the process by which one can be certain that the identification presented is true. By policy, this is done to an extent that a system can properly trust the access request.

    ☒ **A** is incorrect because identification is the process of singling out an entity—either a person or system/application—in a manner that makes that entity unique from any other identity. However, it does not provide a mechanism for verifying that identity.

    ☒ **C** is incorrect because authorization grants of the actual roles and entitlements appropriate for the user or system process to gain access to data and applications.

    ☒ **D** is incorrect because integrity pertains to the security concept of ensuring that data has not been modified by an unauthorized party, but it is not related to this specific question.

18. A federated identity system is composed of three main components. Which of the following is *NOT* one of the three main components?

    A. Identity provider

    B. User

    C. Relying party

    D. API

    ☑ **D.** A federated identity system is composed of users, an identity provider, and a relying party. Although API calls might be used in conjunction with some processes, they are not themselves a core component of a federated identity system.

    ☒ **A** is incorrect because an identity provider is a key component of a federated identity system. It performs authentication and provides authentication and authorization information about a user to the relying party.

    ☒ **B** is incorrect because a user is a key component of a federated identity system as the one requesting access, and it is the subject of the authentication and authorization data that is passed between the identity provider and relying party.

☒ **C** is incorrect because the relying party is a key component of a federated identity system. It accepts authentication and authorization information on a user for the identity provider, and then passes this onto the application for appropriate processing and access.

19. Measured service is a very attractive aspect of cloud computing for an organization looking for BCDR solutions because it will keep costs down. Which of the following is also a key aspect of cloud computing that can make BCDR situations easier in a cloud environment than in a traditional data center?

   A. Broad network access

   B. Resource pooling

   C. Multitenancy

   D. Reversibility

   ☑ **A.** Broad network access allows cloud services to be accessed from the public Internet and over a wide assortment of clients and devices. This is especially attractive during a possible BCDR situation because it would not require staff to travel to a data center location to execute the plan and would allow them to do so from anywhere they can get online.

   ☒ **B** is incorrect because resource pooling (the sharing of resources within a cloud environment among all the cloud customers) would not be a pertinent factor to a BCDR solution, nor would it directly impact the solution.

   ☒ **C** is incorrect because multitenancy (the hosting of many different cloud customers within the same cloud environment) would not be a pertinent factor to a BCDR solution, nor would it directly impact the solution.

   ☒ **D** is incorrect because reversibility (the ability to completely and quickly remove all data and components of a system from a cloud environment) would be an important factor during the final stages of a BCDR situation, but it is not the best answer to the question and the key points it addresses.

20. With PaaS, which strategy is most commonly used for the deployment of operating system patches?

   A. Scripts

   B. Reimaging

   C. Customer administration

   D. APIs

   ☑ **B.** With PaaS, the most common method for deploying operating system matches is through the use of new images for systems. PaaS provides a full application framework to deploy data and applications within, and it's maintained by the cloud provider. With a locked configuration that is centrally maintained, and the code and data being housed independent of the underlying system, using new images with patches installed and tested is the easier and most efficient way for distribution.

☒ **A** is incorrect because scripts are not typically used for operating system patches within a PaaS deployment model, as the use of new and tested images is the preferred approach.

☒ **C** is incorrect because the sole responsibility for maintaining the operating system within a PaaS environment lies with the cloud provider, and in most instances the cloud customer would not even have access or permissions to it.

☒ **D** is incorrect because APIs are used for services and components to communicate with each other and to exchange data. They would not be used (or appropriate to use) for operating system patches regardless of the cloud deployment model.

21. During a system or application audit, which of the following populations will be the most important driver of the audit and testing?

   A. Regulators

   B. Management

   C. Shareholders

   D. Users

   ☑ **A.** During almost all audit and testing processes, the main driver will be the regulators and the regulations to which the data is subjected. Regulations will drive most audits to ensure compliance, and they form the starting point for company security policies and requirements.

   ☒ **B** is incorrect because although management desires and demands will have a strong representation in audits and testing, the main focus will be on regulators and the regulations they are responsible for enforcing.

   ☒ **C** is incorrect because although shareholders' desires and demands will have a strong representation in audits and testing, the main focus will be on regulators and the regulations they are responsible for enforcing.

   ☒ **D** is incorrect because users will not form a major audience for the testing and auditing of systems, apart from the focus of protecting their data and privacy via regulation.

22. A primary focus during a BCDR situation is for systems and applications to meet an acceptable level of operations. Which value represents this status?

   A. RTO

   B. RPO

   C. RSL

   D. SRE

   ☑ **B.** The recovery point objective (RPO) is defined as the amount of data a company would need to maintain and recover in order to function at a level acceptable to management. This may or may not be a restoration to full operating capacity, depending on what management deems as crucial and essential.

☒ **A** is incorrect because the recovery time objective (RTO) is a measurement of the amount of time it would take to recover operations in the event of a disaster to the point where management's objectives for BCDR are met.

☒ **C** is incorrect because the recovery service level (RSL) measures the percentage of the total typical production service level that needs to be restored to meet BCDR objectives in the case of a failure.

☒ **D** is incorrect because SRE is provided as an extraneous choice that is not pertinent to the question.

23. A variety of limits can be set within a cloud environment. Which of the following is *NOT* a unit where a limit can be set?

   A. Customer

   B. Application

   C. Virtual machine

   D. Hypervisor

   ☑ **D.** Limits can be placed within a cloud environment on the granular level of customers, applications, or virtual machines. However, they cannot be placed on the level of the hypervisor. In a cloud environment, resources and virtual machines will be constantly moving around due to orchestration, so at any time it is impossible to predict what hypervisors resources may be on, or how long they will be utilizing a particular piece of hardware.

   ☒ **A** is incorrect because limits can be and commonly are set at the level of a particular customer.

   ☒ **B** is incorrect because limits can be and commonly are set at the level of a particular application.

   ☒ **C** is incorrect because limits can be and commonly are set at the level of a particular virtual machine.

24. Which of the following capabilities would *NOT* be covered by a reservation within a cloud environment?

   A. Running applications

   B. Starting virtual machines

   C. Auto-scaling

   D. Performing normal business operations

   ☑ **C.** With reservations, a cloud customer is guaranteed a minimal amount of resources to power on its virtual devices and perform a level of business operations. Auto-scaling involves the changing of allocated resources, usually by increasing them during high load, and as such would not be covered under a reservation.

☒ **A** is incorrect because running applications that are deployed in a cloud environment is a core component of reservations and the level granted to a particular cloud customer, system, or application.

☒ **B** is incorrect because starting virtual machines that are already established in a cloud environment is a core component of reservations and the level granted to a particular cloud customer, system, or application.

☒ **D** is incorrect because performing normal business operations in a cloud environment is a core component of reservations and the level granted to a particular cloud customer, system, or application.

25. Without the ability to segregate networks physically within a cloud environment, what concept is heavily used for network isolation and segmentation?

    A. WAN

    B. VLAN

    C. LAN

    D. Firewalls

    ☑ **B.** VLANs allow dedicated IP address spacing for servers that are in the same class or belong to the same application or customer, giving enhanced security to and isolation from other systems at the network level. VLANs are not dependent on physical network devices and as such can span across data centers regardless of where hardware is physically located; servers do not need to be in the same racks or even connected to the same switches or routers.

    ☒ **A** is incorrect because a wide area network (WAN) is a network that extends over a broad geographic area, but is not related to network isolation and segmentation.

    ☒ **C** is incorrect because a local area network (LAN) is used for connecting computers within a building or localized area, but is not related to network segmentation or isolation.

    ☒ **D** is incorrect because firewalls are used to deny or allow network traffic based on origination or destination IP address, protocol, and port, but are not used themselves for network isolation and segmentation.

26. Under the guidance of industry-accepted best practices, which of the following is the correct frequency for BCDR plan testing?

    A. Annually

    B. Monthly

    C. Quarterly

    D. Bi-annually

    ☑ **A.** Industry-accepted best practices, as well as many certification requirements, specify annual testing of BCDR plans.

☒ **B** is incorrect because industry-accepted best practices, as well as many certification requirements, specify annual testing of BCDR plans.

☒ **C** is incorrect because industry-accepted best practices, as well as many certification requirements, specify annual testing of BCDR plans.

☒ **D** is incorrect because industry-accepted best practices, as well as many certification requirements, specify annual testing of BCDR plans.

27. Software-defined networking (SDN) is intended to separate different network capabilities and allow for the granting of granular configurations, permissions, and features to non-network staff or customers. Which network capability is separated from forwarding of traffic?

    A. Routing

    B. Firewalling

    C. Filtering

    D. IPS

    ☑ **C.** SDN separates out the filtering of network traffic from the actual packet routing, allowing for a granular level of permissions and the ability to allow non-network admins to update some configurations without giving them actual access to network hardware or full access.

    ☒ **A** is incorrect because routing is the same as forwarding, and in this instance is not something delegated to non-network personnel.

    ☒ **B** is incorrect because firewalls are separate devices that perform specific security functions in regard to network traffic, but are not part of SDN.

    ☒ **D** is incorrect because an intrusion prevention system (IPS) is a separate device that allows for the filtering and blocking of specific traffic and content.

28. Different storage paradigms within a cloud environment handle formatting, allocation, and security controls differently. What handles these aspects for volume storage?

    A. Operating system of host

    B. Hypervisor

    C. Management plane

    D. Storage host

    ☑ **A.** Volume storage is allocated to a specific host and then mounted the same as a physical drive would be on a traditional server. At that point, the operating system is responsible for the formatting, provisioning, and security controls of the storage, the same as with a physical server.

    ☒ **B** is incorrect because the operating system of the host is responsible for the formatting, allocation, and security control of volume storage.

☒ **C** is incorrect because the operating system of the host is responsible for the formatting, allocation, and security control of volume storage.

☒ **D** is incorrect because the operating system of the host is responsible for the formatting, allocation, and security control of volume storage.

29. Which aspect of cloud computing would be most negatively impacted by incurring vendor lock-in with a cloud provider?

    A. Interoperability

    B. Reversibility

    C. Portability

    D. Scalability

    ☑ **C.** Portability is the ability for services and applications to easily move between different cloud providers. The more a customer relies on proprietary APIs or offerings of a specific cloud provider, the harder it will be later to move to a different cloud provider, thus causing the customer to incur vendor lock-in.

    ☒ **A** is incorrect because interoperability is the ability to reuse functions and components from applications for other purposes. Although it could be impacted by vendor lock-in through the reliance on proprietary APIs, portability is the better answer.

    ☒ **B** is incorrect because reversibility is the ability to quickly and easily remove all systems, services, and data from a cloud provider, and to ensure that these items have been removed in a timely manner. The reliance on proprietary APIs or other offerings would not have a significant impact on reversibility.

    ☒ **D** is incorrect because scalability is the ability to add or remove resources from a system or service, usually automatically and programmatically, to meet current demand. Although this could be impacted when moving to a new cloud environment that might work differently, the real problem is with portability, which in this case is the better answer.

30. A denial of service (DoS) attack can potentially impact all customers within a cloud environment with the continued allocation of additional resources. Which of the following can be useful for a customer to protect themselves from a DoS attack against another customer?

    A. Limits

    B. Reservations

    C. Shares

    D. Borrows

    ☑ **B.** A reservation is a minimum resource level guaranteed to a customer within a cloud environment. A reservation can pertain to the two main aspects of computing: memory and processing. With a reservation in place, a cloud customer is guaranteed by the cloud provider to always have at minimum the necessary resources available to power on and operate any of its services. In large cloud environments with a large number of customers, this feature can be of particular importance in the case of denial of service attacks or high utilization of resources by other hosts and systems because it offers a guaranteed minimum level of operations to all customers.

☒ **A** is incorrect because limits are put in place to enforce maximum utilization of memory or processing by a cloud customer. These limits can either be done at the virtual machine level or a comprehensive level for a customer. They are meant to ensure that enormous cloud resources cannot be allocated or consumed by a single host or customer to the detriment of other hosts and customers. Along with cloud computing features such as auto-scaling and on-demand self-service, limits can be either hard (or fixed) or flexible and allowed to change dynamically. Typically, when limits are allowed to change dynamically based on current conditions and consumption, it is done by "borrowing" additional resources rather than through a change in the actual limits themselves.

☒ **C** is incorrect because the concept of shares within a cloud environment is used to mitigate and control customer requests for resource allocations in case the environment does not have the current capability to provide these resources. Shares work by prioritizing hosts within a cloud environment through a weighting system that is defined by the cloud provider. When periods of high utilization and allocation are reached, the system automatically uses the scoring of each host based on its share value to determine which hosts get access to the limited resources still available. The higher the value a particular host has, the more resources it will be allowed to utilize.

☒ **D** is incorrect because borrows is a similar sounding term to shares, but it is not a correct term and isn't pertinent to the question.

31. What aspect of a Type 2 hypervisor involves additional security concerns that are not relevant with a Type 1 hypervisor?

   A. Reliance on a host operating system

   B. Proprietary software

   C. Programming languages

   D. Auditing

   ☑ **A.** A Type 2 hypervisor runs within a host operating system (versus a Type 1 hypervisor, which runs directly on the underlying physical hardware). Because of this, a Type 2 hypervisor has additional security concerns because the underlying operating system and its security become crucial to the hypervisor as well. If the underlying operating system is compromised, so too can the hosted hypervisor be easily compromised.

   ☒ **B** is incorrect because proprietary software is not a unique consideration to either a Type 1 or Type 2 hypervisor, and as such the security concerns would be the same.

   ☒ **C** is incorrect as programming languages used within hosted applications do not have any bearing on the hypervisor.

   ☒ **D** is incorrect because auditing itself is not a security concern, and compliance requirements would apply to both types of hypervisors.

32. A common strategy employed when using cloud services for BCDR strategies is to only maintain images offline at the cloud provider, or to only have a minimal set of systems running until needed. With the strategy of only running a minimal level of systems until needed, which aspect of cloud computing would be most beneficial during an actual BCDR situation?

   A. Resource pooling

   B. Measured service

   C. Rapid elasticity

   D. Broad network access

   ☑ **C.** When only a minimal level of resources is being run within a cloud environment, rapid elasticity could be very important as systems and traffic are brought online during a BCDR situation so that systems can automatically grow and adjust as needed.

   ☒ **A** is incorrect because resource pooling would not have a direct or significant impact on BCDR solutions, nor would it pertain to the strategy of having only limited resources online until needed.

   ☒ **B** is incorrect because measured service allows costs to remain low while only a minimal level of services are maintained. Once an organization is in an actual BCDR situation and its resource needs begin increasing, measured service becomes less of a benefit.

   ☒ **D** is incorrect because although broad network access would be a benefit for BCDR, as it would allow administrative staff to access systems from anywhere, it does not pertain specifically to the question in regard to maintaining a minimal level of services until needed.

33. With volume storage, a slice of storage space is allocated to a system to be used in whatever manner is necessary for that particular system and its requirements. What is this slice of storage referred to as?

   A. LAN

   B. LUN

   C. Partition

   D. Allocation

   ☑ **B.** A LUN is a logical unit number that is assigned to storage in a SAN environment to be accessed by controller hardware or software. It represents how storage is mapped and allocated to a particular system.

   ☒ **A** is incorrect because a local area network (LAN) does not pertain to storage systems at all.

   ☒ **C** is incorrect because a partition is related to storage and its allocation but is not pertinent to the question.

   ☒ **D** is incorrect because although allocation refers to the process of storage being given to a particular host, it is not the best answer to the question.

34. Although cloud storage systems will ultimately be consumed by cloud customers or users from a logical configuration, what are the two types of underlying physical storage systems most used with cloud computing?

A. RAID and SAN

B. SAN and iSCSI

C. SCSI and RAID

D. iSCSI and RAID

☑ **A.** Redundant array of independent disks (RAID) and storage area network (SAN) are the two main underlying types of physical storage systems used with cloud systems, and then shared and provisioned with the hypervisors, which then assign these physical storage systems to their hosted systems.

☒ **B** is incorrect because iSCSI is a communications protocol that allows SCSI commands to be sent over TCP, but it is not a storage system itself.

☒ **C** is incorrect because SCSI is a communications protocol used with physical hardware for controlling and accessing the storage.

☒ **D** is incorrect because iSCSI is a communications protocol that allows SCSI commands to be sent over TCP, but it is not a storage system itself.

35. Although performing BCDR tests at regular intervals is a best practice to ensure processes and documentation are still relevant and efficient, which of the following represents a reason to conduct a BCDR review outside of the regular interval?

A. Staff changes

B. Application changes

C. Regulatory changes

D. Management changes

☑ **B.** Any major application changes have the ability to fundamentally alter systems and configurations in a manner that will render a BCDR plan irrelevant or insufficient. Therefore, any time major application changes are made, a new BCDR test should be undertaken after a review to certify that it is still applicable and correct.

☒ **A** is incorrect because staffing changes will not directly impact systems or their configurations, and as such new testing or validation of a BCDR plan is unnecessary.

☒ **C** is incorrect because regulatory changes may lead to system or application changes, so they would only have an indirect impact on a BCDR plan. If major system changes are necessary, then the best answer applies to those changes, not the underlying regulatory changes.

☒ **D** is incorrect because management changes will not directly impact systems or their configurations, and as such new testing or validation of a BCDR plan is unnecessary.

36. When an organization is considering the use of a cloud provider as part of its BCDR strategy, which of the following is most important to consider from a security perspective?

A. Auditing

B. Network access

C. Jurisdiction

D. Resource pooling

☑ **C.** When an organization is choosing a cloud provider for a BCDR solution, jurisdiction becomes an important security consideration because it is almost certain the BCDR site will fall outside the jurisdiction of the main data-hosting facility. As such, it is imperative to ensure that any cloud solution is made with an understanding of jurisdictional and regulatory impacts to applications.

☒ **A** is incorrect because auditing will remain the same, with the same requirements, regardless of the BCDR location.

☒ **B** is incorrect because network access is not a major security concern with a different cloud provider, as all cloud providers will utilize broad network access. Although there may be some impact to the access methods or procedures, network access is not the best answer to the question.

☒ **D** is incorrect because resource pooling will not have an impact on an organization's BCDR strategy from a security perspective.

37. Why does the use of a Type 2 hypervisor typically incur more security concerns than a Type 1 hypervisor?

A. A Type 2 hypervisor is always exposed to the public Internet for federated identity access.

B. A Type 2 hypervisor allows users to directly perform some functions with their own access.

C. A Type 2 hypervisor runs on top of an operating system and is dependent on the security of that OS for its own security.

D. A Type 2 hypervisor is open source, so attackers can more easily find exploitable vulnerabilities.

☑ **C.** A Type 2 hypervisor runs on top of an operating system, unlike a Type 1 hypervisor, which runs directly on hardware. This makes the Type 2 hypervisor dependent on the operating system for its security.

☒ **A** is incorrect because hypervisors are never directly exposed to the public Internet, regardless of the type used.

☒ **B** is incorrect because users do not directly interact with hypervisors, regardless of the type used.

☒ **D** is incorrect because whether or not a hypervisor is open source is not related to the type of hypervisor used.

38. When is a system hosted in a virtualized environment vulnerable but *NOT* vulnerable on a physical server?

    A. During patching

    B. During maintenance

    C. During change windows

    D. When the image is offline

    ☑ **D.** When a physical server is powered off, it is not accessible to attackers. However, with a virtualized environment, even when it is powered off, the virtual image resides in storage, and if the storage system is compromised, the virtual image is vulnerable as well.

    ☒ **A** is incorrect because patching does not have a significant difference in vulnerability between a virtual environment and a physical environment.

    ☒ **B** is incorrect because maintenance patching does not have a significant difference in vulnerability between a virtual environment and a physical environment.

    ☒ **C** is incorrect because change windows do not have a significant difference in vulnerability between a virtual environment and a physical environment.

CHAPTER 4

Cloud Application Security Domain

Domain 4 is focused on the following topics:

- The knowledge needed when considering deploying applications in a cloud environment
- Common pitfalls with a cloud environment
- Security and functional testing of applications within a cloud
- The Software Development Life Cycle (SDLC) and how it relates to a cloud project
- Cloud-specific risks and threat models
- Supplemental security devices
- Federated identity systems
- Single sign-on and multifactor authentication

Cloud application development is rapidly increasing in popularity and prevalence. In order for an organization to make informed choices concerning its specific needs and requirements in regard to cloud computing, a well-educated Cloud Security Professional is needed who understands the most common challenges and issues with cloud development. Although many methodologies and approaches to security scanning and testing are similar between a cloud and traditional data center, due to the levels of access and controls in place by a cloud provider, these methodologies and approaches are not always feasible to the level required or expected by the cloud customer.

1. You have a new application that is about to be put into production and used by customers. Management would like to undertake an exhaustive test of the system by assessing the known controls and configurations as well as reviewing the source code and components. Which type of testing would this represent?

   A. SAST

   B. DAST

   C. Pen

   D. RASP

2. An employee of your company submitted a security ticket claiming that he was able to access areas of an application by going through certain functions that he should not be able to. What type of security vulnerability does this best illustrate?

   A. Missing function-level access control

   B. Security misconfiguration

   C. Sensitive data exposure

   D. Unvalidated redirects and forwards

3. Where would be the most appropriate location for an XML firewall within a system architecture?

   A. Between the presentation and application layers

   B. Between the application and data layers

   C. Between the firewalls and application servers

   D. Before the firewalls

4. When you are changing to a different data center for a disaster recovery scenario, which of the following could pose a challenge to the authentication systems over a geographic distance?

   A. Regulations

   B. Latency

   C. Redundancy

   D. Interoperability

5. Which type of testing involves externally attacking the security of a system but without actually attempting to alter systems or fully execute malicious actions?

   A. DAST

   B. SAST

   C. Pen

   D. RASP

6. A common strategy to mitigate costs when using a cloud solution for disaster recovery is to leave images offline at the DR provider and only turn them on when needed. Which of the following would be the least significant concern with this approach?

- **A.** Integrity
- **B.** Patching
- **C.** Confidentiality
- **D.** Reversibility

7. Which stage of the BCDR process takes into account the RPO and RTO requirements set forth by management and stakeholders?

- **A.** Gathering requirements
- **B.** Define scope
- **C.** Analyze
- **D.** Implement

8. Which of the following threats from the OWASP Top Ten is the most difficult for an organization to protect against?

- **A.** Advanced persistent threats
- **B.** Account hijacking
- **C.** Malicious insiders
- **D.** Denial of service

9. You have been tasked by management to run security tests against an application using the same toolsets and methodologies that a legitimate attacker would use, including actually attempting to leverage successful exploits. Which type of testing would this entail?

- **A.** Dynamic application security testing
- **B.** Penetration testing
- **C.** Simulation testing
- **D.** Static application security testing

10. Which of the following types of threats is focused on compromising the client rather than the server or application itself?

- **A.** Cross-site scripting
- **B.** Insecure direct object references
- **C.** Injection
- **D.** Cross-site request forgery

11. Which concept refers to the ability to validate and prove that a specific entity did not perform operations on a system?

    A. Repudiation

    B. Validation

    C. Integrity

    D. Authentication

12. Which of the following software applications is not a utility for managing code or system configurations?

    A. Puppet

    B. Chef

    C. Shibboleth

    D. GitHub

13. During an incident investigation from a suspected breach, it was discovered that some application code contained the names of underlying databases and systems that were able to be read by the attacker. What type of vulnerability does this best represent?

    A. Injection

    B. Sensitive data exposure

    C. Security misconfigurations

    D. Insecure direct object references

14. What standard is used between different entities within a federated system to exchange information about authentication and user attributes?

    A. SAML

    B. XML

    C. HTML

    D. TLS

15. Which concept is often used to isolate and separate information or processes within an environment for either security concerns or regulatory requirements?

    A. Virtualization

    B. Segregation

    C. Sandboxing

    D. Honeypots

16. Which type of threat is often used in conjunction with phishing attempts and is often viewed as greatly increasing the likeliness of success?

    A. Unvalidated redirects and forwards

    B. Cross-site request forgery

C. Cross-site scripting

D. Insecure direct object references

17. What is the primary security mechanism used to protect SOAP and REST APIs?

   A. Firewalls

   B. XML firewalls

   C. Encryption

   D. WAFs

18. Which type of testing tends to produce the best and most comprehensive results for discovering system vulnerabilities?

   A. Static

   B. Dynamic

   C. Pen

   D. Vulnerability

19. Which of the following represents the *R* component of the DREAD threat risk modeling system?

   A. Reproducibility

   B. Repudiation

   C. Redundancy

   D. Reversibility

20. During a periodic or specific testing of a BCDR plan, which of the following pairs of objectives is the main metric used for the overall evaluation of the plan?

   A. RPO and SRE

   B. RSL and RTO

   C. RTO and RPO

   D. ARO and RSL

21. Which of the following options would be possible, in conjunction with a USB drive, to fulfill an application's multifactor authentication requirements?

   A. RFID chip card

   B. Password

   C. RSA token

   D. Access card

22. Which of the following types of organizations is most likely to make use of open source software technologies?

    A. Government agencies

    B. Corporations

    C. Universities

    D. Military

23. Which component consumes assertions from identity providers and makes a determination as to whether to grant access, and at what level, if applicable to a user?

    A. Service party

    B. Application provider

    C. Service broker

    D. Relying party

24. Which of the following choices represents the *D* component of the STRIDE threat model from OWASP?

    A. Data loss

    B. Data breach

    C. Denial of service

    D. Disclosure

25. Many organizations will have different environments for development versus production, even using different cloud providers or different systems between the two. Which of the following would be the *BEST* reason to have both production systems and development systems hosted within the same cloud environment?

    A. Operating systems

    B. VPN access

    C. Storage systems

    D. APIs

26. It was discovered that an attacker was able to send properly formatted SQL code through your web application in order to obtain the entire schema of the underlying database. What type of attack does this best represent?

    A. Injection

    B. Sensitive data exposure

    C. Security misconfiguration

    D. Insecure direct object references

27. Your application has been a continued target for SQL injection attempts. Which of the following technologies would be best used to combat the likeliness of a successful SQL injection exploit from occurring?

   A. XML accelerator

   B. WAF

   C. Sandbox

   D. Firewall

28. A federated identity system is composed of two main components. Which of the following pairs represents the correct two components?

   A. Identity provider and relying party

   B. Authentication provider and service provider

   C. Identity provider and relying provider

   D. Single sign-on and application

29. Which concept involves the ability for a system to respond to attack methods being used against it and automatically alter security configurations and countermeasures to compensate for them?

   A. DAST

   B. Pen

   C. RASP

   D. SAST

30. What type of testing runs known attacks and signatures against a system to determine a risk rating based upon discovered weaknesses?

   A. Vulnerability scanning

   B. Pen testing

   C. Baseline scanning

   D. Compliance scanning

31. With cloud systems making exclusive use of broad network access, which technology is commonly used for support personnel to access systems for maintenance and administration?

   A. IPSec

   B. TLS

   C. SSH

   D. VPN

32. What type of device is often leveraged to assist legacy applications that may not have the programmatic capability to process assertions from modern web services?

   A. Web application firewall

   B. XML accelerator

   C. Relying party

   D. XML firewall

33. At which phase of the SDLC process should security begin participating?

   A. Requirements gathering

   B. Requirements analysis

   C. Design

   D. Testing

34. Which of the following is *NOT* part of the OWASP Top Ten list of critical web application security risks?

   A. Injection

   B. Sensitive data exposure

   C. Insecure direct object references

   D. User ID and password authentication schemes

35. What type of identity system allows trust and verifications between the authentication systems of multiple organizations?

   A. Federated

   B. Collaborative

   C. Integrated

   D. Bidirectional

36. It is vital during the initial requirements gathering for a new project or application to include all the pertinent stakeholders who will both drive the requirements and determine whether the critical success factors have been achieved. Which of the following would *NOT* be a key stakeholder to include during these initial stages?

   A. Developers

   B. Management

   C. Security

   D. Users

37. The Simple Object Access Protocol (SOAP) allows programs from different environments or platforms to communicate seamlessly with each other over HTTP. If you are using SOAP, which data format are you using for information exchange?

A. SAML

B. XML

C. JSON

D. HTML

38. Single sign-on systems work by authenticating users from a centralized location or using a centralized method, and then allowing applications that trust the system to grant those users access. What would be passed between the authentication system and the applications to grant a user access?

A. Ticket

B. Certificate

C. Credential

D. Token

1. A	**14.** A	**27.** B
2. A	**15.** C	**28.** A
3. C	**16.** A	**29.** C
4. B	**17.** C	**30.** A
5. A	**18.** A	**31.** D
6. D	**19.** A	**32.** B
7. A	**20.** C	**33.** A
8. C	**21.** B	**34.** D
9. B	**22.** C	**35.** A
10. A	**23.** D	**36.** A
11. A	**24.** C	**37.** B
12. C	**25.** D	**38.** D
13. D	**26.** A	

Comprehensive Answers and Explanations

1. You have a new application that is about to be put into production and used by customers. Management would like to undertake an exhaustive test of the system by assessing the known controls and configurations as well as reviewing the source code and components. Which type of testing would this represent?

   A. SAST

   B. DAST

   C. Pen

   D. RASP

   ☑ **A.** Static application security testing (SAST) assesses both the source code and components of an application. It is done as a "white-box" test, as those performing the tests have full access to the actual source code and configuration documentation of the application. Tests are done against an offline system.

   ☒ **B** is incorrect because dynamic application security testing (DAST) is run as a "black-box" test, where those performing the test have no internal or particular knowledge of a system and must discover everything they know about it through the use of utilities.

   ☒ **C** is incorrect because pen testing is also done as a "black-box" test, but using the same tools and methodologies that an attacker would use in order to evaluate the security of the application. Pen testing is designed to assess vulnerabilities in various types of real-world scenarios.

   ☒ **D** is incorrect because runtime application self-protection (RASP) is used to test against systems that have the ability to detect attacks and threats, and then to automatically adjust their security settings or other configurations to compensate for and mitigate these attacks and threats. RASP is designed to be done in real time on live systems.

2. An employee of your company submitted a security ticket claiming that he was able to access areas of an application by going through certain functions that he should not be able to. What type of security vulnerability does this best illustrate?

   A. Missing function-level access control

   B. Security misconfiguration

   C. Sensitive data exposure

   D. Unvalidated redirects and forwards

   ☑ **A.** Many applications will do authorization checks and assign access rights when a user first accesses the application. As the user traverses the application and accesses different functions, if the application does not verify authorization for each function, it is possible for the user to be able to elevate access, either intentionally or accidentally. The application should verify authorization as a user accesses each new function or piece of data.

☒ **B** is incorrect because security misconfiguration refers to a system where baselines were not correctly applied, unauthorized changes were made, or security patches and updates from the vendor were not applied.

☒ **C** is incorrect because sensitive data exposure occurs when protected data, such as PII or credit card information, is not properly encrypted or masked, and is thus susceptible to attackers. This exposure refers to specific data within the application and is not directly related to specific functions of the application.

☒ **D** is incorrect because unvalidated redirects and forwards occur when an application allows external links or redirects but does not properly validate or secure them. This enables an attacker to potentially redirect users through a legitimate and secure application to an external site for phishing attempts or other malware attacks. This site will appear to be safe and legitimate to the users because it originated from within a trusted application.

3. Where would be the most appropriate location for an XML firewall within a system architecture?

   A. Between the presentation and application layers

   B. Between the application and data layers

   C. Between the firewalls and application servers

   D. Before the firewalls

   ☑ **C.** An XML firewall validates XML data before it reaches an application server. The appliance can perform validation as well as control what users or services are allowed to access specific XML functions of an application. Positioning the XML firewall between the firewalls and applications allows for initial network filtering based on origination and destination of packets before the content analysis of the appliance is performed and before the traffic is allowed to reach the application servers.

   ☒ **A** is incorrect because the validation and scrutiny of XML data will need to be done before the request reaches the application from the outside. If the data can reach even the presentation layer, then application access is allowed, which could let in malformed or dangerous data.

   ☒ **B** is incorrect because the data would have already reached the application servers and been consumed by them before accessing the data layer, which would allow potentially malformed or dangerous XML data into the application and through processing prior to being scrutinized.

   ☒ **D** is incorrect because a system would want network validation done before content validation. A firewall can block or allow specific traffic from legitimate origins as a first line of defense at a much lower overhead processing cost compared to the content analysis required by an XML firewall.

4. When you are changing to a different data center for a disaster recovery scenario, which of the following could pose a challenge to the authentication systems over a geographic distance?

   A. Regulations

   B. Latency

   C. Redundancy

   D. Interoperability

   ☑ **B.** Authentication systems, as a security check, enforce limited time requirements for authentication tokens and any checks to be performed and validated. If it takes longer than the allowed time, the request will be considered stale and invalid, and it will likely loop back to try the process again. If a large geographic distance exists and network latency occurs, it is possible on some systems, if they have short validity periods, for authentications to fail and for system access to be denied.

   ☒ **A** is incorrect because regulations are always a concern, especially over a large geographic distance, where some variations are almost guaranteed. However, this is not the best answer here because it is not specific to authentication systems and their operational use.

   ☒ **C** is incorrect because redundancy is not something that will be impacted by geographic distance between data centers. Systems can have redundancy implemented in a variety of ways, regardless of where they are actually hosted or the distance between them.

   ☒ **D** is incorrect because interoperability will be a global issue across the entire enterprise, not one specifically impacting authentication systems. With most modern authentication systems, interoperability is also not a primary concern because these systems are specifically designed to be multiplatform and flexible.

5. Which type of testing involves externally attacking the security of a system but without actually attempting to alter systems or fully execute malicious actions?

   A. DAST

   B. SAST

   C. Pen

   D. RASP

   ☑ **A.** Dynamic application security testing (DAST) is run as a "black-box" test where those running the test have no internal or particular knowledge of the system and must discover everything they know about it through the use of utilities. DAST does not attempt to fully execute malicious actions in the same manner as pen testing does.

   ☒ **B** is incorrect because static application security testing (SAST) assesses both the source code and components of an application. It is done as a "white-box" test, as those performing the tests have full access to the actual source code and configuration documentation of the application. Also, tests are done against an offline system.

⊠ **C** is incorrect because pen testing is also done as a "black-box" test but using the same tools and methodologies that an attacker would use in order to evaluate the security of the application. It is designed to test vulnerabilities in various types of real-world scenarios and to actually execute exploits.

⊠ **D** is incorrect because runtime application self-protection (RASP) involves testing against systems that have the ability to detect attacks and threats as well as to automatically adjust their security settings or other configurations to compensate for and mitigate them. RASP is designed to be done in real time on live systems.

6. A common strategy to mitigate costs when using a cloud solution for disaster recovery is to leave images offline at the DR provider and only turn them on when needed. Which of the following would be the least significant concern with this approach?

   A. Integrity

   B. Patching

   C. Confidentiality

   D. Reversibility

   ☑ **D.** With images at a disaster recovery (DR) site, reversibility is still a concern, but in almost all cases it should be trivial to quickly delete them and remove them from the system, if needed. Although still a concern in any cloud deployment, of the possible choices, reversibility would be the least concern for a DR focus.

   ⊠ **A** is incorrect because the integrity of images is always a primary concern within a cloud environment. Unlike with physical servers, images when offline can still be accessed via a compromised system and potentially altered or compromised.

   ⊠ **B** is incorrect because patching would be a great concern when images are kept offline. The patching process would need to be augmented to guarantee that images were brought online and patched to the same level as current production systems to maintain consistency.

   ⊠ **C** is incorrect because confidentiality is a primary concern even with images that are offline. In an offline state, the images still reside as files within the storage of the cloud provider, and as such, a compromised management plane or hypervisor, as well as the storage system itself, could expose those files to access and copying.

7. Which stage of the BCDR process takes into account the RPO and RTO requirements set forth by management and stakeholders?

   A. Gathering requirements

   B. Define scope

   C. Analyze

   D. Implement

☑ **A.** When you are gathering initial requirements for a business continuity and disaster recovery (BCDR) process, the recovery point objective (RPO) and recovery time objective (RTO) will be the two primary factors that drive all your decisions and planning. There are many ways to accomplish continuity and disaster recovery, but the requirements for the point and time are the ultimate drivers that determine which solutions will meet management objectives.

☒ **B** is incorrect because the scope-defining stage involves taking the requirements and determining the extent of the project or application. By this point, the RPO and RTO would already need to be defined and used as a guide to establish the requirements overall.

☒ **C** is incorrect because the analyze stage involves taking the project requirements and translating them into an actionable project plan, complete with timelines and specific ordering and objectives. This would occur well after the RPO and RTO have been documented and integrated.

☒ **D** is incorrect because the implementation stage involves the actual execution of the project. This is after all planning has been completed and documented.

8. Which of the following threats from the OWASP Top Ten is the most difficult for an organization to protect against?

   A. Advanced persistent threats

   B. Account hijacking

   C. Malicious insiders

   D. Denial of service

   ☑ **C.** Malicious insiders are individuals with trusted and valid access to a system or application who then misuse that access for malicious ends. This can include stealing data, using it for their own purposes, selling it, or granting others unauthorized access to it.

   ☒ **A** is incorrect because advanced persistent threats involve users establishing a presence within an application or system and then using that access over a period of time to access data or processes to steal information. The attacker needs to first establish access to the system, either through phishing and other social engineering tactics or through traditional system compromises and vulnerabilities. In those cases, security personnel and administrators can utilize countermeasures to minimize the chances of compromise.

   ☒ **B** is incorrect because account hijacking involves either a shared account being abused or someone gaining access to another's account. Account hijacking can be minimized by policies that prevent or forbid account sharing, as well as through technological measures such as requiring multifactor authentication.

   ☒ **D** is incorrect because denial of service (DoS) does not actually involve the compromise of a system or application, but is rather focused on availability. Many different approaches are available for preventing or minimizing the impact of DoS attacks against a system.

9. You have been tasked by management to run security tests against an application using the same toolsets and methodologies that a legitimate attacker would use, including actually attempting to leverage successful exploits. Which type of testing would this entail?

A. Dynamic application security testing

B. Penetration testing

C. Simulation testing

D. Static application security testing

☑ **B.** Penetration (or pen) testing is done as a "black-box" test but using the same tools and methodologies an attacker would use in order to evaluate the security of the application. It is designed to test vulnerabilities with various types of real-world scenarios and to actually execute exploits.

☒ **A** is incorrect because dynamic application security testing (DAST) is run as a "black-box" test where those running the test have no internal or particular knowledge of the system and must discover everything they know about it through the use of utilities. DAST does not attempt to fully execute malicious actions in the same manner as pen testing does.

☒ **C** is incorrect because simulation testing is not a type of security testing that is a part of the CCSP or a standard type in general. It is simply provided as an erroneous option.

☒ **D** is incorrect because static application security testing (SAST) assesses both the source code and components of an application. It is done as a "white-box" test, and those running the tests have full access to the actual source code and configuration documentation of the application. Also, tests are done against an offline system.

10. Which of the following types of threats is focused on compromising the client rather than the server or application itself?

A. Cross-site scripting

B. Insecure direct object references

C. Injection

D. Cross-site request forgery

☑ **A.** Cross-site scripting (XSS) is an attack where a malicious actor is able to send untrusted data to a user's browser without it going through any validation or sanitization processes, or perhaps the code is not properly escaped from processing by the browser. The code is then executed on the user's browser with their own access and permissions, thus allowing an attacker to redirect the user's web traffic, steal data from their session, or potentially access information on the user's own computer that their browser has the ability to access.

☒ **B** is incorrect because insecure direct object references occur when a developer has in their code a reference to something on the application side, such as a database key, the directory structure of the application, configuration information about the hosting system, or any other information that pertains to the workings of the application that should not be exposed to users or the network.

☒ **C** is incorrect because an injection attack is where a malicious actor sends commands or other arbitrary data through input and data fields with the intent of having the application or system execute the code as part of its normal processing and queries. This can trick an application into exposing data that is not intended or authorized to be exposed, or it could potentially allow an attacker to gain insight into configurations or security controls.

☒ **D** is incorrect because a cross-site request forgery attack forces an authenticated client that a user has open to send forged requests under the user's own credentials to execute commands and requests that the application thinks are coming from a trusted client and user.

11. Which concept refers to the ability to validate and prove that a specific entity did not perform operations on a system?

   A. Repudiation

   B. Validation

   C. Integrity

   D. Authentication

   ☑ **A.** Repudiation relates to the ability to prove that a specific user or entity did not perform specific functions or access specific data within a system or application. With comprehensive logging, any transaction on a system is open to dispute or challenge by a user, who can claim they never performed the type of transaction the system says they did or challenge the data contained on the system.

   ☒ **B** is incorrect because validation often refers to ensuring that data inputs are in the correct format and within acceptable parameters. It does not pertain to verifying the specific source or maintaining documentation that can later be used to prove it.

   ☒ **C** is incorrect because integrity relates to the assurance that data has not been altered, created, or deleted by unauthorized parties or processes. It is not related to proving that a specific entity performed an operation.

   ☒ **D** is incorrect because authentication involves the ability to prove an identity to a system or service to satisfy the particular requirements to meet that burden of proof. It is not related to proving that a specific entity conducted an operation on a service.

12. Which of the following software applications is not a utility for managing code or system configurations?

   A. Puppet

   B. Chef

   C. Shibboleth

   D. GitHub

☑ **C.** Shibboleth is an open source, federated identity system that is widely used by universities, nonprofits, government agencies, and other resource- or technology-related organizations.

☒ **A** is incorrect because puppet is an open source software package that is used to maintain configurations on different types of systems and operates via an agent installed on each system.

☒ **B** is incorrect because Chef is a software package for deploying and configuring servers in a manner where configuration is treated like code and deployed to servers for execution.

☒ **D** is incorrect because GitHub is a very widely used software platform that provides a code repository for collaborative development, including branching and versioning capabilities.

13. During an incident investigation from a suspected breach, it was discovered that some application code contained the names of underlying databases and systems that were able to be read by the attacker. What type of vulnerability does this best represent?

    A. Injection

    B. Sensitive data exposure

    C. Security misconfigurations

    D. Insecure direct object references

    ☑ **D.** Insecure direct object references occur when a developer has in their code a reference to something on the application side such as a database key, the directory structure of the application, configuration information about the hosting system, or any other information that pertains to the workings of the application that should not be exposed to users or the network.

    ☒ **A** is incorrect because an injection attack is where a malicious actor sends commands or other arbitrary data through input and data fields with the intent of having the application or system execute the code as part of its normal processing and queries. This can trick an application into exposing data that is not intended or authorized to be exposed, or potentially allow an attacker to gain insight into configurations or security controls.

    ☒ **B** is incorrect because sensitive data exposure relates to web applications regularly utilizing sensitive user data, such as credit cards, authentication credentials, personally identifiable information (PII), and financial information. If this information is not properly protected through encryption and secure transport mechanisms, it can quickly become an easy target for attackers. Web applications must enforce strong encryption and security controls on the application side, but also require secure methods of communication with browsers and other clients that are used for accessing the information.

☒ **C** is incorrect because security misconfigurations occur when applications and systems are not properly configured or maintained in a secure manner. This can be due to a shortcoming in security baselines or configurations, unauthorized changes to system configurations, or a failure to patch and upgrade systems as security patches are released by the vendor. Security misconfigurations also include not changing the default configurations or credentials that come with an application prior to its use and deployment.

14. What standard is used between different entities within a federated system to exchange information about authentication and user attributes?

   A. SAML

   B. XML

   C. HTML

   D. TLS

   ☑ **A.** The Security Assertion Markup Language (SAML) is an open standard for exchanging information for authentication and authorization between an identity provider and a relying party. SAML provides information to ensure that authentication has been completed successfully. It also provides the identification for the identity provider and organization as well as a set of attributes about the user to be given to the relying party.

   ☒ **B** is incorrect because XML is similar to SAML in structure and format, but is not used for exchanging information with a federated system. XML is a standard format for encoding and exchanging information, but it is not used specifically for authentication and authorization.

   ☒ **C** is incorrect because HTML is used for encoding web pages to be consumed by clients such as web browsers. It is not a protocol or specification for exchanging information in the same manner as XML or SAML.

   ☒ **D** is incorrect because TLS is specifically for facilitating secure communication between two parties, including negotiating the connection and then actually encrypting and protecting packets as they are transmitted between the two parties. It is heavily used within federated systems, but is not the protocol used for actually passing information between the two parties. It just secures the information.

15. Which concept is often used to isolate and separate information or processes within an environment for either security concerns or regulatory requirements?

   A. Virtualization

   B. Segregation

   C. Sandboxing

   D. Honeypots

☑ **C.** Sandboxing involves the segregation and isolation of information or processes from others within the same system or application, typically for security concerns. Sandboxing typically is used for data isolation, such as keeping different communities and populations of users with similar data isolated from each other. The need for sandboxing can be due to internal reasons, such as policies, or it can come from external sources, such as regulatory or legal requirements.

☒ **A** is incorrect because virtualization involves hosting multiple different systems under the same physical hardware. The hosts are run under the supervision and control of a hypervisor instead of given direct access to the underlying hardware. Virtualization is not specifically used for separation of systems or information for security or regulatory requirements.

☒ **B** is incorrect because segregation is a general concept that relates to the topic of the question but is not an official term or concept used within computing. It is provided as an erroneous answer.

☒ **D** is incorrect because honeypots are special systems designed to appear in configuration and data as production systems, but they are kept isolated and use fake data for the purposes of enticing attackers to them. This allows an organization to learn about the types of attacks being employed against their systems and to determine additional or different security approaches for their actual systems.

16. Which type of threat is often used in conjunction with phishing attempts and is often viewed as greatly increasing the likeliness of success?

    A. Unvalidated redirects and forwards

    B. Cross-site request forgery

    C. Cross-site scripting

    D. Insecure direct object references

☑ **A.** Unvalidated redirects and forwards occur when an application allows external links or redirects but does not properly validate or secure them. This allows an attacker to potentially redirect users through a legitimate and secure application to an external site for phishing attempts or other malware attacks. The site will appear to be safe and legitimate to the user because it originated from within a trusted application.

☒ **B** is incorrect because a cross-site request forgery attack forces an authenticated client that a user has open to send forged requests under the user's own credentials to execute commands and requests that the application thinks are coming from a trusted client and user.

☒ **C** is incorrect because cross-site scripting is an attack where a malicious actor is able to send untrusted data to a user's browser without going through any validation or sanitization processes, or perhaps the code is not properly escaped from processing by the browser. The code is then executed on the user's browser with their own access and permissions, thus allowing an attacker to redirect their web traffic, steal data from their session, or potentially access information on the user's own computer that their browser has the ability to access.

☒ **D** is incorrect because insecure direct object references occur when a developer has in their code a reference to something on the application side, such as a database key, the directory structure of the application, configuration information about the hosting system, or any other information that pertains to the workings of the application that should not be exposed to users or the network.

17. What is the primary security mechanism used to protect SOAP and REST APIs?

   A. Firewalls

   B. XML firewalls

   C. Encryption

   D. WAFs

   ☑ **C.** The SOAP and REST APIs do not have built-in security mechanisms and must rely on external mechanisms. The primary means to protect both APIs is through the use of encryption, typically through the use of TLS to secure the transmission of data across the networks between the clients and services.

   ☒ **A** is incorrect because although firewalls may be used with some APIs to limit and control access to them, it does not provide as thorough security as encryption, nor does it secure the data transmissions from the APIs at all.

   ☒ **B** is incorrect because XML firewalls are used to validate and control XML flowing into a system. They may be used with APIs for additional security and XML validation offloading, but they will not secure the data transmissions across the network from the APIs.

   ☒ **D** is incorrect because a web application firewall (WAF) will enable extensive filtering and security checks on the content of data packets flowing between API services, but they will not secure the actual data transmissions in any way.

18. Which type of testing tends to produce the best and most comprehensive results for discovering system vulnerabilities?

   A. Static

   B. Dynamic

   C. Pen

   D. Vulnerability

   ☑ **A.** Static application security testing (SAST) tests both the source code and components of an application. It is done as a "white-box" test, as those running the tests have full access to the actual source code and configuration documentation of the application. Also, tests are done against an offline system. SAST is considered the most comprehensive type of testing due to the knowledge of the systems and access to source code by the testers.

   ☒ **B** is incorrect because dynamic application security testing (DAST) is run as a "black-box" test where those running the test have no internal or particular knowledge of the system and must discover everything they know about it through the use of utilities. DAST does not attempt to fully execute malicious actions in the same manner as pen testing.

☒ **C** is incorrect because pen testing is done as a "black-box" test, but using the same tools and methodologies that an attacker would use in order to evaluate the security of the application. Pen testing is designed to assess vulnerabilities with various types of real-world scenarios and to actually execute exploits.

☒ **D** is incorrect because vulnerability scanning is done using a predefined set of signatures and parameters to evaluate a system and give a risk rating based on the findings. Vulnerability scanning does not involve extensive knowledge of a system or go beyond the preconfigured tests that are run for compliance.

19. Which of the following represents the *R* component of the DREAD threat risk modeling system?

   A. Reproducibility

   B. Repudiation

   C. Redundancy

   D. Reversibility

   ☑ **A.** Reproducibility is the measure of how easy it is to reproduce an exploit. On the low end, a value of 0 signifies a near impossibility of exploit, even with administrative access. This would likely occur where other defensive measures prevent access or exploit. On the high end, a value of 10 signifies an easy exploit, such as simply accessing the application with a client, without needing authentication or other methods. Any value in the middle will be subjective and determined based on the particulars of the application, as well as any other mitigating factors from other defensive mechanisms.

   ☒ **B** is incorrect because the *R* component of the DREAD threat risk model is reproducibility, not repudiation.

   ☒ **C** is incorrect because the *R* component of the DREAD threat risk model is reproducibility, not redundancy.

   ☒ **D** is incorrect because the *R* component of the DREAD threat risk model is reproducibility, not reversibility.

20. During a periodic or specific testing of a BCDR plan, which of the following pairs of objectives is the main metric used for the overall evaluation of the plan?

   A. RPO and SRE

   B. RSL and RTO

   C. RTO and RPO

   D. ARO and RSL

☑ **C.** During a BCDR test, the recovery time objective (RTO) and the recovery point objective (RPO) are the two main objectives that are tested and evaluated. The RPO is defined by management as the point where a successful restore of an environment will have occurred, and the RTO represents the acceptable amount of time required to do so.

☒ **A** is incorrect because the RPO and RTO are the key metrics and considerations of a BCDR test.

☒ **B** is incorrect because the RPO and RTO are the key metrics and considerations of a BCDR test.

☒ **D** is incorrect because the RPO and RTO are the key metrics and considerations of a BCDR test.

21. Which of the following options would be possible, in conjunction with a USB drive, to fulfill an application's multifactor authentication requirements?

   A. RFID chip card

   B. Password

   C. RSA token

   D. Access card

☑ **B.** A USB thumb drive represents something that a user possesses. Because a password is something that a user knows, it would be an appropriate factor to use with a USB drive for multifactor authentication.

☒ **A** is incorrect because a USB thumb drive represents something that a user has or possesses, which is also the same category as an RFID chip card. As such, an RFID chip card would not be appropriate to use to fulfill multifactor authentication requirements because it comes from the same class of credentials.

☒ **C** is incorrect because a USB thumb drive represents something that a user has or possesses, which is also the same category as an RSA token. As such, an RSA token would not be appropriate to use to fulfill multifactor authentication requirements because it comes from the same class of credentials.

☒ **D** is incorrect because a USB thumb drive represents something that a user has or possesses, which is also the same category as an access card. As such, an access card would not be appropriate to use to fulfill multifactor authentication requirements because it comes from the same class of credentials.

22. Which of the following types of organizations is most likely to make use of open source software technologies?

   A. Government agencies

   B. Corporations

   C. Universities

   D. Military

☑ **C.** Universities make extensive use of open source technologies, especially compared to other types of organizations. There are multiple reasons why this is the case. One reason is that the open and research-oriented nature of universities makes them more accepting of open source technologies. Another reason is the more stringent budgetary realities that many universities face.

☒ **A** is incorrect because government agencies for the most part do not make extensive use of open source technologies, in many instances due to audit and support requirements by law or regulation.

☒ **B** is incorrect because corporations do not typically make extensive use of open source technologies and tend to defer to proprietary software that comes with support.

☒ **D** is incorrect because the military tends to use proprietary software that comes with support—especially software that is written specifically for its unique needs and requirements.

23. Which component consumes assertions from identity providers and makes a determination as to whether to grant access, and at what level, if applicable to a user?

    A. Service party

    B. Application provider

    C. Service broker

    D. Relying party

    ☑ **D.** A relying party consumes security assertions from identity providers and then makes decisions as to whether to grant access and at what level. The decisions can be based on anything about the user that is presented in the attributes from the identity provider, such as status, organization, and location.

    ☒ **A** is incorrect because service party is a similar sounding term to relying party, but it is not the correct term.

    ☒ **B** is incorrect because application provider is not a term associated with a federated identity system.

    ☒ **C** is incorrect because a service broker is a different concept that is not related to the components of a federated identity system.

24. Which of the following choices represents the *D* component of the STRIDE threat model from OWASP?

    A. Data loss

    B. Data breach

    C. Denial of service

    D. Disclosure

☑ **C.** The *D* component of the STRIDE threat model refers to denial of service. Any application is a possible target of a denial of service attack. From the application side, the developers should minimize how many operations are performed for unauthenticated users. This will keep the application running as quickly as possible and using the least amount of system resources to help minimize the impact of any such attacks. The use of front-end caching technologies can also minimize the impact of attacks because they will remove many queries from the actual application servers.

☒ **A** is incorrect because the *D* component of the STRIDE threat model refers to denial of service, not data loss.

☒ **B** is incorrect because the *D* component of the STRIDE threat model refers to denial of service, not data breach.

☒ **D** is incorrect because the *D* component of the STRIDE threat model refers to denial of service, not disclosure.

25. Many organizations will have different environments for development versus production, even using different cloud providers or different systems between the two. Which of the following would be the *BEST* reason to have both production systems and development systems hosted within the same cloud environment?

    A. Operating systems

    B. VPN access

    C. Storage systems

    D. APIs

    ☑ **D.** Cloud providers have their own suite of APIs that are offered and maintained within their environments and are available to customers. Having both production and development systems hosted within the same cloud provider will ensure that the same APIs are available and used throughout the system, thus lessening the possibility of problems originating when code is moved into a new environment for production release.

    ☒ **A** is incorrect because operating systems will typically be widely available across cloud environments and not specifically dependent on the environment.

    ☒ **B** is incorrect because VPNs are widely used through cloud environments, and the same capabilities should be available regardless of environment. Also, a VPN will generally not have a direct impact on the availability or functioning of an application.

    ☒ **C** is incorrect because storage systems among the various cloud providers could have differences, but overall they should operate and appear consistent to the applications and systems hosted within them. They should not pose a significant burden due to a move between providers unless a specific proprietary storage system that is unique to a cloud provider is used.

26. It was discovered that an attacker was able to send properly formatted SQL code through your web application in order to obtain the entire schema of the underlying database. What type of attack does this best represent?

   A. Injection

   B. Sensitive data exposure

   C. Security misconfiguration

   D. Insecure direct object references

   ☑ **A.** An injection attack is where a malicious actor sends commands or other arbitrary data through input and data fields with the intent of having the application or system execute the code as part of its normal processing and queries. This can trick an application into exposing data that is not intended or authorized, or it can potentially allow an attacker to gain insight into configurations or security controls.

   ☒ **B** is incorrect because sensitive data exposure refers to how many web applications regularly utilize sensitive user data, such as credit cards, authentication credentials, personally identifiable information (PII), and financial information. If this information is not properly protected through encryption and secure transport mechanisms, it can quickly become an easy target for attackers. Web applications must enforce strong encryption and security controls on the application side, but also secure methods of communication are also required with browsers and other clients that are used to access the information. With sensitive information, applications should ideally perform checks against browsers to ensure they meet security standards based on the versions and protocols supported.

   ☒ **C** is incorrect because security misconfiguration occurs when applications and systems are not properly configured or maintained in a secure manner. This can be due to a shortcoming in security baselines or configurations, unauthorized changes to system configurations, or a failure to patch and upgrade systems as security patches are released by the vendor. Security misconfiguration also includes not changing the default configurations or credentials that come with an application prior to its use and deployment.

   ☒ **D** is incorrect because insecure direct object references occur when a developer has in their code a reference to something on the application side such as a database key, the directory structure of the application, configuration information about the hosting system, or any other information that pertains to the workings of the application that should not be exposed to users or the network.

27. Your application has been a continued target for SQL injection attempts. Which of the following technologies would be best used to combat the likeliness of a successful SQL injection exploit from occurring?

   A. XML accelerator

   B. WAF

C. Sandbox

D. Firewall

☑ **B.** A web application firewall (WAF) is an appliance or plug-in that parses and filters HTTP traffic from a browser or client and applies a set of rules before the traffic is allowed to proceed to the actual application server. The most common uses for a WAF are to find and block SQL injection and cross-site scripting attacks before they reach an application.

☒ **A** is incorrect because an XML accelerator is an appliance designed to offload the processing of XML from the actual applications and systems and instead leverage optimized and dedicated appliances designed just for that purpose. In most instances, especially for a heavily used application, an XML accelerator can drastically improve system performance and provide possible security benefits as well because the XML processing is done on a dedicated resource, away from the actual application. This allows for the parsing and verification of inputs and values before the actual application code is hit, much in the same way as an XML firewall.

☒ **C** is incorrect because a sandbox is a concept for segregating systems within a network from each other for security, regulatory, or testing requirements.

☒ **D** is incorrect because a firewall is used to control network-level access based on the origination and destination IP address as well as the ports and protocols used. A firewall does not provide the ability to inspect the actual traffic for content, such as a SQL injection attempt.

28. A federated identity system is composed of two main components. Which of the following pairs represents the correct two components?

A. Identity provider and relying party

B. Authentication provider and service provider

C. Identity provider and relying provider

D. Single sign-on and application

☑ **A.** The two components that comprise a federated identity system are the identity provider, which handles the authentication and release of attributes about a user, and the relying party, which accepts the authentication and consumes the attributes about the user, typically then making them available to an application or service.

☒ **B** is incorrect because although authentication provider and service provider sound similar to the correct terms, and in some cases are used in the same manner as the official terms, they are not correct in this case.

☒ **C** is incorrect because only identity provider is a correct term for one component. The other component is the relying party; it consumes authentication tokens and attributes and does not serve as a provider of them.

☒ **D** is incorrect because although single sign-on and application do describe to some extent the most widespread use of a federated identity system, these terms are not universal and are not correct in this case.

29. Which concept involves the ability for a system to respond to attack methods being used against it and automatically alter security configurations and countermeasures to compensate for them?

A. DAST

B. Pen

C. RASP

D. SAST

☑ **C.** Runtime application self-protection (RASP) involves testing against systems that have the capability to detect attacks and threats and to automatically adjust their security settings or other configurations to compensate for and mitigate these attacks and threats. RASP is designed to be done in real time on live systems.

☒ **A** is incorrect because dynamic application security testing (DAST) is run as a "black-box" test where those running the test have no internal or particular knowledge of the system and must discover everything they know about it through the use of utilities. DAST does not attempt to fully execute malicious actions in the same manner as pen testing.

☒ **B** is incorrect because pen testing is done as a "black-box" test, but using the same tools and methodologies that an attacker would use in order to evaluate the security of the application. Pen testing is designed to assess vulnerabilities with various types of real-world scenarios and to actually execute exploits.

☒ **D** is incorrect because static application security testing (SAST) tests both the source code and the components of an application. It is done as a "white-box" test, as those running the tests have full access to the actual source code and configuration documentation of the application. Also, tests are run against an offline system.

30. What type of testing runs known attacks and signatures against a system to determine a risk rating based upon discovered weaknesses?

A. Vulnerability scanning

B. Pen testing

C. Baseline scanning

D. Compliance scanning

☑ **A.** Vulnerability scanning is done using a predefined set of signatures and parameters to evaluate a system and give a risk rating based on its findings. It does not have extensive knowledge of a system or go beyond the preconfigured tests that it runs for compliance.

☒ **B** is incorrect because pen testing is done as a "black-box" test, but using the same tools and methodologies that an attacker would use in order to evaluate the security of the application. Pen testing is designed to access vulnerabilities with various types of real-world scenarios and to actually execute exploits.

☒ **C** is incorrect because baseline scanning is done to confirm that servers and systems have appropriately and correctly applied baseline configuration requirements. Baseline scanning does not test vulnerabilities specifically; instead, it is solely focused on ensuring baseline compliance and flagging any deviations for remediation.

☒ **D** is incorrect because compliance scanning can refer to either baseline scanning or scanning to ensure that server configurations and policies are in place to meet regulatory requirements. It is essentially the same as baseline scanning in most cases because the regulatory requirements and corporate policies will form the basis of the baselines.

31. With cloud systems making exclusive use of broad network access, which technology is commonly used for support personnel to access systems for maintenance and administration?

   A. IPSec

   B. TLS

   C. SSH

   D. VPN

   ☑ **D.** A virtual private network (VPN) is used to create a secure network tunnel from outside of a cloud environment into the internal networks, and in many instances it's used to access trusted zones that are not accessible to the public. VPNs are crucial for systems support personnel and administrators to maintain and configure servers.

   ☒ **A** is incorrect because Internet Protocol Security (IPSec) is used to encrypt packets at the network layer between two hosts. It would not be used to provide the type of access that is being described in the question.

   ☒ **B** is incorrect because TLS is an encryption method that would likely be used in conjunction with a VPN, but it does not inherently present the same types of capabilities or features that administrators would use to connect from the outside into a secure internal network.

   ☒ **C** is incorrect because SSH is used for Secure Shell access to some operating systems and could be used in conjunction with a VPN, but it would not provide the network-level access into a secure zone in the same manner as a VPN.

32. What type of device is often leveraged to assist legacy applications that may not have the programmatic capability to process assertions from modern web services?

   A. Web application firewall

   B. XML accelerator

   C. Relying party

   D. XML firewall

☑ **B.** XML accelerators are appliances designed to offload the processing of XML from the actual applications and systems and instead leverage optimized and dedicated appliances designed just for that purpose. In most instances, especially for a heavily used application, an XML accelerator can drastically improve system performance and provide possible security benefits as well because the XML processing is done on a dedicated resource, away from the actual application. This allows for the parsing and verification of inputs and values before the actual application code is hit, much in the same way as an XML firewall. This is particularly useful in situations where enterprise applications might not be designed or equipped to handle the typical XML assertions and web services traffic that cloud applications often use, and it can provide for integration without the need for complete application changes or coding.

☒ **A** is incorrect because a web application firewall (WAF) is designed for parsing incoming web requests for security concerns or filtering based on many different aspects of the requests. Although a WAF could be used for some validation of XML code, it would not be helpful in processing XML or assisting applications in doing so.

☒ **C** is incorrect because a relying party is part of a federated identity system and consumes security assertions from an identity provider and then processes the attributes contained within them. A relying party is not used to process XML for applications or to validate it.

☒ **D** is incorrect because XML firewalls are commonly used to validate incoming XML code before it reaches the actual application. They are typically deployed in line between the firewall and application server, and as such, traffic will pass through them before hitting the application. An XML firewall can validate data that is incoming, as well as provide granular controls for what systems and users can access the XML interfaces.

33. At which phase of the SDLC process should security begin participating?

   A. Requirements gathering

   B. Requirements analysis

   C. Design

   D. Testing

☑ **A.** Because the requirements-gathering phase is the earliest phase, when the crucial decisions will be made that will drive and dictate every phase thereafter, it is vital to include security from this earliest point. By including security from the beginning, an organization can ensure that proper security controls and designs are being implemented, thus lessening the change of having to redo parts of the project later or incurring significant loss of time or money addressing security concerns.

☒ **B** is incorrect because the requirements analysis occurs after vital early decisions have been already made, which should include security.

☒ **C** is incorrect because the design phase occurs after requirements have been defined and many key decisions have been made; it is too far along to include security.

☒ **D** is incorrect because the testing phase occurs after the project has been defined and implemented. Although including security in testing is certainly vital, it is far too late in the process for security to be involved and it drastically increases the likelihood of security gaps occurring and additional time and money being necessary to address those gaps.

34. Which of the following is *NOT* part of the OWASP Top Ten list of critical web application security risks?

- **A.** Injection
- **B.** Sensitive data exposure
- **C.** Insecure direct object references
- **D.** User ID and password authentication schemes

☑ **D.** User ID and password authentication schemes are not a specific component of the OWASP Top Ten list of critical web application security risks. Many other components will incorporate threats to authentication schemes and systems, but the list does not treat them as their own entity.

☒ **A** is incorrect because injection is a specific component of the list. An injection attack is where a malicious actor sends commands or other arbitrary data through input and data fields with the intent of having the application or system execute the code as part of its normal processing and queries. This can trick an application into exposing data that is not intended or authorized, or potentially allow an attacker to gain insight into configurations or security controls.

☒ **B** is incorrect because sensitive data exposure is a specific component of the list. Sensitive data exposure occurs when protected information, such as PII or credit card information, is not properly encrypted or masked, and is thus susceptible to attackers. This refers to specific data within the application and is not directly related to specific functions of the application.

☒ **C** is incorrect because insecure direct object references are a specific component of the list. Insecure direct object references occur when a developer has in their code a reference to something on the application side, such as a database key, the directory structure of the application, configuration information about the hosting system, or any other information that pertains to the workings of the application that should not be exposed to users or the network.

35. What type of identity system allows trust and verifications between the authentication systems of multiple organizations?

- **A.** Federated
- **B.** Collaborative
- **C.** Integrated
- **D.** Bidirectional

☑ **A.** Federated identity systems work by allowing an identity provider at a user's organization to be trusted by relying parties connected to applications and services for authentication and then providing appropriate authorization based on attributes released from the identity provider.

☒ **B** is incorrect because federated is the correct term for the question, not collaborative.

☒ **C** is incorrect because federated is the correct term for the question, not integrated.

☒ **D** is incorrect because federated is the correct term for the question, not bidirectional.

36. It is vital during the initial requirements gathering for a new project or application to include all the pertinent stakeholders who will both drive the requirements and determine whether the critical success factors have been achieved. Which of the following would *NOT* be a key stakeholder to include during these initial stages?

   A. Developers

   B. Management

   C. Security

   D. Users

   ☑ **A.** During the requirements-gathering stage, developers are not typically included. Before a project reaches the developers, a detailed plan must be developed to define the project, what constitutes success, and what the specific requirements are before developers are consulted. In many instances, the specific requirements of the project may even define who the developers will be based on skillsets, expertise, and chosen technologies and budgets.

   ☒ **B** is incorrect because management will be the key driver of any project and must always be included at all stages, but especially at the initial stages of requirements gathering and project scoping.

   ☒ **C** is incorrect because security should always be included from the very beginning stages of any project and development planning to ensure things are done in a secure manner. Without the early involvement of security, the risk is greatly increased of substantial extra costs or having to redo parts of the project later.

   ☒ **D** is incorrect because the involvement of the ultimate users of the system, or users of similar or previous systems, can give invaluable insight into a development project and will be the determinants of the ultimate success or failure of the project.

37. The Simple Object Access Protocol (SOAP) allows programs from different environments or platforms to communicate seamlessly with each other over HTTP. If you are using SOAP, which data format are you using for information exchange?

   A. SAML

   B. XML

   C. JSON

   D. HTML

☑ **B.** The SOAP protocol exclusively uses the Extensible Markup Language (XML) for its data encoding and information exchange.

☒ **A** is incorrect because the Security Assertion Markup Language (SAML) is used for federated identity systems to exchange authentication/authorization information and attributes about a user, but it is not used with the SOAP protocol.

☒ **C** is incorrect because although JavaScript Object Notation (JSON) is a widely used human-readable data format, it is not used by the SOAP protocol.

☒ **D** is incorrect because although the Hypertext Markup Language (HTML) is used for websites and web applications to encode data for web browsers to interpret, it is not used by the SOAP protocol.

38. Single sign-on systems work by authenticating users from a centralized location or using a centralized method, and then allowing applications that trust the system to grant those users access. What would be passed between the authentication system and the applications to grant a user access?

A. Ticket

B. Certificate

C. Credential

D. Token

☑ **D.** Single sign-on systems use tokens to pass authentication information between systems that can be trusted to allow the user access and to confirm their identity.

☒ **A** is incorrect because although tickets are used with many different types of systems, this is not the correct answer to the question.

☒ **B** is incorrect because although certificates may be used with some systems for authentication, they are not then passed to other systems once authenticated.

☒ **C** is incorrect because credentials are used to verify a user at the authentication source but are not passed between systems.

Operations Domain

Domain 5 is focused on the following topics:

- The planning and design processes for a cloud data center
- How to implement, run, and manage both the physical and logical aspects of a data center
- How to secure and harden servers, networks, and storage systems
- How to develop and implement baselines
- How to conduct risk assessments of cloud systems
- The ITIL service components for managing and complying with regulations
- How to secure and collect digital evidence from a cloud environment

The operations domain is focused on how to plan, design, run, manage, and operate both the logical and physical components of a cloud data center. We will cover the key components of each layer—including servers, network devices, and storage systems—and what makes them unique to a cloud data center versus a traditional data center. We will also investigate the risk assessment process for a system and how it relates to cloud systems, as well as how forensic evidence is collected and the unique challenges and considerations it presents in a cloud environment.

1. Which TLS protocol is responsible for performing authentication between parties and determining encryption algorithms?

   A. Record

   B. Negotiation

   C. Handshake

   D. Transmission

2. You are designing a new data center, and management considers it imperative that best practices are followed for the cabling layout and design, especially considering the complexity of modern data centers. Which standard would you look to in fulfilling this requirement?

   A. BISCI

   B. IDCA

   C. NFPA

   D. Uptime Institute

3. At which layer does the IPSec protocol operate to encrypt and protect communications between two parties?

   A. Network

   B. Application

   C. Transport

   D. Data link

4. Which set of standards contains the publication titled "National Electric Code" and serves as guidance for complex and high-capacity electrical systems, including safety and emergency cutoff procedures and requirements?

   A. IDCA

   B. NFPA

   C. BISCI

   D. Uptime Institute

5. To optimize the auto-scaling capabilities of a cloud deployment, when would the optimal time be to apply baselines to systems?

   A. Immediately after enabling a virtual machine

   B. Before penetration testing is done

   C. Immediately prior to putting the system into production

   D. Before the image is created

6. What does the TLS protocol use for authentication between two parties?

   A. Certificates

   B. Tickets

   C. Tokens

   D. SAML

7. The traditional approach to data center design is to use a tiered topology for layers of redundancy. Which organization publishes this widely used standard and collection of best practices?

   A. Uptime Institute

   B. IDCA

   C. NPFA

   D. BISCI

8. DHCP is heavily used within cloud environments to maintain network configurations in a centralized manner. Which of the following is *NOT* a network configuration that plays a role with DHCP?

   A. IP address

   B. Hostname

   C. MAC address

   D. Gateway

9. Which component of the ITIL framework includes dependency checks?

   A. Change management

   B. Continuity management

   C. Release management

   D. Availability management

10. Which process is used to properly maintain balanced resources across a cloud environment and to respond to changing needs from conditions due to auto-scaling?

    A. DCOM

    B. Distributed optimization

    C. Dynamic optimization

    D. Elasticity

11. Which TLS protocol handles the secure communications between parties, specifically the send/receive operations?

    A. Handshake

    B. Transmission

    C. Negotiation

    D. Record

12. DNSSEC relies on digital signatures and allows a client lookup to validate a DNS resolution back to its authoritative source. What is this process called?

   A. Zone signing

   B. Authentication

   C. Realm signing

   D. Domain signing

13. A host-based IDS can suffer from security vulnerabilities if the host itself is compromised. Which of the following concepts can be best used to mitigate risk with an HIDS?

   A. Administrative privileges

   B. Read-only storage

   C. Baselines

   D. Encryption

14. Clusters can bring many benefits to a computing environment, both for administrators and users. Which of the following is *NOT* something that will be increased through the use of clustering?

   A. Availability

   B. Redundancy

   C. Integrity

   D. Failover

15. Which of the following is commonly used by cloud providers to assure customers about security practices or to entice new customers to their services?

   A. Audits

   B. Baselines

   C. Vulnerability assessments

   D. Certifications

16. Within a cloud environment, what is the most widely used protocol for communication with storage devices?

   A. SATA

   B. SCSI

   C. WAN

   D. iSCSI

17. Which of the following is *NOT* one of the types of unexpected events that continuity management deals with?

   A. Incidents

   B. Changes

C. Outages

D. Disaster

18. Which type of assessment is based on data and numbers rather than on documentation and observation?

A. Qualitative

B. Numeric

C. Quantitative

D. Metric

19. What does the risk assessment–related acronym SLE stand for?

A. Single loss expectancy

B. System loss emergency

C. Service loss emergency

D. Service loss expectancy

20. Which of the following core concepts of cloud computing is *NOT* something that orchestration would play a role in?

A. Auto-scaling

B. Portability

C. Customer billing

D. Provisioning

21. Monitoring is essential in a cloud environment to ensure that SLA requirements from all the tenants will be met satisfactorily. Which of the following groupings represents the common four essential metrics?

A. CPU, disk, memory, network

B. Disk, network, CPU, bandwidth

C. Memory, network, users, disk

D. Users, network, memory, CPU

22. Which of the following is *NOT* a core component of an operational management plan for a cloud environment?

A. Scheduling

B. Maintenance

C. Orchestration

D. Integration

23. Which of the following is a major concern with cloud storage communications over iSCSI that must be addressed through additional technologies?

    A. Confidentiality

    B. Integrity

    C. Availability

    D. Provisioning

24. Which risk response involves the use of insurance as a possible strategy for an organization?

    A. Acceptance

    B. Avoidance

    C. Transference

    D. Mitigation

25. During the assessment phase of a risk evaluation, what are the two types of tests that are performed?

    A. Internal and external

    B. Technical and managerial

    C. Physical and logical

    D. Qualitative and quantitative

26. The single loss expectancy (SLE) takes into consideration the value of the asset and the exposure factor. What is the exposure factor?

    A. Loss due to successful exploit, as a percentage

    B. Estimated number of times a threat will be successful

    C. Loss due to successful exploit, as a dollar amount

    D. Number of times the asset was successfully exploited in the previous year

27. Which of the following technologies is commonly used to learn about the methods or sources attackers are using against a system in order to find better configurations or security strategies to use for protection?

    A. Firewall

    B. WAF

    C. Honeypot

    D. IDS

28. Which quality of a SIEM solution allows administrators to find broad attacks against an infrastructure that may go unnoticed if they're only looking at a single host?

    A. Correlation

    B. Aggregation

C. Monitoring

D. Consolidation

29. The use of baseline images, especially with the auto-scaling capabilities of cloud environments, is crucial for secure operations. What is the first step undertaken when creating a new baseline image?

   A. Clean the operating system install.

   B. Update all software on the install.

   C. Disable or remove all nonessential services.

   D. Bring patching up the latest level.

30. In order to maintain proper utilization and balancing of resources within a cloud environment, distributed resource scheduling (DRS) is heavily used. What resources is DRS *NOT* used with?

   A. Virtual machines

   B. Physical servers

   C. Storage solutions

   D. Clusters

31. What concept is used for network segregation and isolation within a cloud environment?

   A. VPN

   B. LAN

   C. VLAN

   D. Cabling

32. Which of the following is *NOT* a capability of the TLS record protocol?

   A. Sending data

   B. Holding an open communications channel

   C. Authenticating connections

   D. Receiving data

33. Firewalls are used to control access to networks based on origin, ports, destination, and protocols used. Which of the following is *NOT* a typical origin or destination designation used?

   A. VLAN

   B. Physical network

   C. IP address

   D. IP range

34. Which of the following is a very common complaint concerning the use of an IDS?

   A. False positives

   B. Latency

   C. Incorrect blocking

   D. Dropping packets

35. Which component of ITIL involves the constant evaluation of the correctness of the level of provisioned resources?

   A. Availability management

   B. Capacity management

   C. Continuity management

   D. Configuration management

36. Which of the following can add significant costs to an organization following a successful exploit?

   A. Regulations

   B. Interoperability

   C. Measured service

   D. Availability

37. Which type of cloud deployment requires the least amount of involvement from the cloud provider to make logs available to the cloud customer?

   A. PaaS

   B. IaaS

   C. SaaS

   D. DaaS

38. Although traditionally data centers have relied on a tiered topology for layers of redundancy, which organization publishes the Infinity Paradigm, which shifts away from a tiered topology in favor of a macro-level approach?

   A. Uptime Institute

   B. BISCI

   C. IDCA

   D. NFPA

1. C	**14.** C	**27.** C
2. A	**15.** D	**28.** B
3. A	**16.** D	**29.** A
4. B	**17.** B	**30.** B
5. D	**18.** C	**31.** C
6. A	**19.** A	**32.** C
7. A	**20.** B	**33.** B
8. B	**21.** A	**34.** A
9. A	**22.** D	**35.** B
10. C	**23.** A	**36.** A
11. D	**24.** C	**37.** B
12. A	**25.** D	**38.** C
13. B	**26.** A	

Comprehensive Answers and Explanations

1. Which TLS protocol is responsible for performing authentication between parties and determining encryption algorithms?

   A. Record

   B. Negotiation

   C. Handshake

   D. Transmission

   ☑ **C.** The handshake protocol of TLS negotiates and establishes the connection between two parties and enables the secure communications channel that will then handle secure data transmission. The protocol exchanges all information needed to authenticate and negotiate the encryption algorithms to be used as well as to create the session ID for the transaction.

   ☒ **A** is incorrect because the record protocol of TLS entails the encryption and authentication of the actual packets used for transmission of data over the secure channel, but it's only capable of the actual transmission and is not involved with the establishing or negotiation of the connection.

   ☒ **B** is incorrect because negotiation is a component of the handshake protocol, but it's only one portion of it and is not a protocol by itself.

   ☒ **D** is incorrect because the transmission of data is a component of the record protocol but is not a protocol of TLS by itself.

2. You are designing a new data center, and management considers it imperative that best practices are followed for the cabling layout and design, especially considering the complexity of modern data centers. Which standard would you look to in fulfilling this requirement?

   A. BISCI

   B. IDCA

   C. NFPA

   D. Uptime Institute

   ☑ **A.** Building Industry Consulting Services International (BISCI) issues certifications and develops standards in the area of complex cabling for data systems. Their standards are focused on cabling design and setups and includes specifications on power, energy, efficiency, and hot/cold aisle setups.

   ☒ **B** is incorrect because the International Data Center Authority (IDCA) established the Infinity Paradigm, which is intended to be a comprehensive data center design and operations framework. The Infinity Paradigm differs from other standards by shifting away from a tiered architecture and instead embracing a macro-level approach, where the entire data center is considered as a whole.

☒ **C** is incorrect because the National Fire Protection Association (NFPA) publishes a large collection of standards regarding fire protection for almost any type of facility, although it does offer ones specifically focused on data centers.

☒ **D** is incorrect because the Uptime Institute publishes the most widely used standard for data center design based on a tiered-topology approach. This standard has four tiers, each progressively adding layers and requirements for redundancy and fault tolerance.

3. At which layer does the IPSec protocol operate to encrypt and protect communications between two parties?

   A. Network

   B. Application

   C. Transport

   D. Data link

   ☑ **A.** IPSec works at the network layer of the OSI model. The network layer provides the actual routing and switching for packets and data transmission between nodes.

   ☒ **B** is incorrect because the application layer provides application and end-user processes, such as file transfers, web browsing, and e-mail.

   ☒ **C** is incorrect because the transport layer provides data transmissions similar to what IPSec is used for, but it operates at a higher level with more capabilities than are used for IPSec.

   ☒ **D** is incorrect because the data-link layer provides packet encoding and decoding as well as handles errors from the physical layer, but it does not contain the routing and forwarding capabilities necessary for IPSec.

4. Which set of standards contains the publication titled "National Electric Code" and serves as guidance for complex and high-capacity electrical systems, including safety and emergency cutoff procedures and requirements?

   A. IDCA

   B. NFPA

   C. BISCI

   D. Uptime Institute

   ☑ **B.** The National Fire Protection Association (NFPA) publishes a large collection of standards regarding fire protection for almost any type of facility, and does offer ones specifically focused on data centers. These standards cover the overall electrical systems within data centers, including emergency procedures and requirements for the immediate cutting of power in case of an emergency.

   ☒ **A** is incorrect because the International Data Center Authority (IDCA) established the Infinity Paradigm, which is intended to be a comprehensive data center design and operations framework. The Infinity Paradigm differs from other standards by shifting away from a tiered architecture and instead embracing a macro-level approach, where the entire data center is considered as a whole.

☒ **C** is incorrect because Building Industry Consulting Services International (BISCI) issues certifications and develops standards in the area of complex cabling for data systems. The standards are focused on cabling design and setups, and includes specifications on power, energy, efficiency, and hot/cold aisle setups.

☒ **D** is incorrect because the Uptime Institute publishes the most widely used standard for data center design based on a tiered topology approach. This standard has four tiers, each progressively adding layers and requirements for redundancy and fault tolerance.

5. To optimize the auto-scaling capabilities of a cloud deployment, when would the optimal time be to apply baselines to systems?

   A. Immediately after enabling a virtual machine

   B. Before penetration testing is done

   C. Immediately prior to putting the system into production

   D. Before the image is created

   ☑ **D.** The optimal time for the application of baselines for use with auto-scaling is before the image that will be used in production is created. With auto-scaling, you want the systems ready to be used with minimal additional configurations as soon as they are enabled within the cloud. Applying baselines, along with verifying them before the image to be used is created, will alleviate the need to do so after a new virtual machine is powered on and will increase its immediate availability.

   ☒ **A** is incorrect because applying baselines after a virtual machine is brought online would dramatically delay the availability of the new system and create additional work and processing before it can be used. This would negate the intended goal and purposes of auto-scaling.

   ☒ **B** is incorrect because penetration testing would not be done immediately upon new systems being enabled via auto-scaling. Certainly penetration testing against the image before it is created and finalized for use with auto-scaling is desirable, but the correct time is not immediately after a system is enabled.

   ☒ **C** is incorrect because performing baseline applications after a new virtual machine is enabled would negate the benefits and speed of auto-scaling, and with the use of an image for all new systems, it would create redundant work versus a baseline application before the image is finalized.

6. What does the TLS protocol use for authentication between two parties?

   A. Certificates

   B. Tickets

C. Tokens

D. SAML

   ☑ **A.** The TLS protocol uses X.509 certificates for authentication between the two parties that are negotiating a secure communications channel. The same certificates that are used for authentication are also used for the encryption of the communications channel.

   ☒ **B** is incorrect because tickets are not used with the TLS protocol but rather are commonly used with other systems such as Kerberos.

   ☒ **C** is incorrect because tokens are not used with TLS but rather are commonly used with other systems such as multifactor authentication schemes.

   ☒ **D** is incorrect because the Security Assertion Markup Language (SAML) is commonly used for exchanging authentication and authorization information between two parties, but it is not used with TLS.

7. The traditional approach to data center design is to use a tiered topology for layers of redundancy. Which organization publishes this widely used standard and collection of best practices?

A. Uptime Institute

B. IDCA

C. NPFA

D. BISCI

   ☑ **A.** The Uptime Institute publishes the most widely used standard for data center design based on a tiered-topology approach. This standard has four tiers, each progressively adding layers and requirements for redundancy and fault tolerance.

   ☒ **B** is incorrect because the International Data Center Authority (IDCA) established the Infinity Paradigm, which is intended to be a comprehensive data center design and operations framework. The Infinity Paradigm differs from other standards by shifting away from a tiered architecture and instead embraces a macro-level approach where the entire data center is considered as a whole.

   ☒ **C** is incorrect because the National Fire Protection Association (NFPA) publishes a large collection of standards regarding fire protection for almost any type of facility, and it does offer ones specifically focused on data centers. These standards cover the overall electrical systems within data centers, including emergency procedures and requirements for the immediate cutting of power in case of an emergency.

   ☒ **D** is incorrect because Building Industry Consulting Services International (BISCI) issues certifications and develops standards in the area of complex cabling for data systems. The standards are focused on cabling design and setups includes specifications on power, energy, efficiency, and hot/cold aisle setups.

8. DHCP is heavily used within cloud environments to maintain network configurations in a centralized manner. Which of the following is *NOT* a network configuration that plays a role with DHCP?

   A. IP address

   B. Hostname

   C. MAC address

   D. Gateway

   ☑ **B.** Hostname resolution is provided via the Domain Name System (DNS) and is not provided as part of the network configuration for a specific server.

   ☒ **A** is incorrect because the IP address is one of the core network configuration items provided via DHCP to a server.

   ☒ **C** is incorrect because the MAC address is what the DHCP servers use to track and maintain network configuration settings for a host.

   ☒ **D** is incorrect because a gateway address would be assigned by a DHCP server as part of the network configuration given to the host.

9. Which component of the ITIL framework includes dependency checks?

   A. Change management

   B. Continuity management

   C. Release management

   D. Availability management

   ☑ **A.** The change management process oversees the entire implementation and release of changes to a production environment, including management approvals, notifications, and testing/validation. As part of the approval process, a dependency check is done to validate the scope of potential impact and to ensure that a proper validation plan is fully in place.

   ☒ **B** is incorrect because continuity management is focused on planning for the successful restoration of systems or services after an unexpected outage, incident, or disaster.

   ☒ **C** is incorrect because release management is focused on the actual execution of a production release, including validation. The main focus is on properly mapping out all steps required for a release and then configuring and deploying it. Although dependency validations will be part of a release management process, they are performed after the checks will have been done as part of the change management process.

   ☒ **D** is incorrect because availability management is focused on making sure system resources, processes, personnel, and toolsets are properly allocated and secured to meet SLA requirements for performance.

10. Which process is used to properly maintain balanced resources across a cloud environment and to respond to changing needs from conditions due to auto-scaling?

    A. DCOM

    B. Distributed optimization

    C. Dynamic optimization

    D. Elasticity

    ☑ **C.** Dynamic optimization is the process through which the cloud environment is constantly maintained to ensure that resources are available when and where needed and that physical nodes do not become overloaded or near capacity while others are underutilized.

    ☒ **A** is incorrect because DCOM refers to the Distributed Component Object Model, which is a set of Microsoft interfaces and services that can be requested by systems throughout a network.

    ☒ **B** is incorrect because distributed optimization is a distractor term that sounds similar to the correct answer.

    ☒ **D** is incorrect because elasticity refers to the ability of a cloud environment to resize resources to meet current demand, either through increasing or decreasing them; however, dynamic optimization is the more correct answer in this case because it refers to analysis and determination, not just the ability to adjust resource levels.

11. Which TLS protocol handles the secure communications between parties, specifically the send/receive operations?

    A. Handshake

    B. Transmission

    C. Negotiation

    D. Record

    ☑ **D.** The TLS record protocol handles the actual transmission of secure information over the encrypted channel. It only handles the sending and receiving of secure data and relies on the handshake protocol for all information necessary to handle the transmission.

    ☒ **A** is incorrect because the handshake protocol of TLS negotiates and establishes the connection between two parties and enables the secure communications channel that will then handle secure data transmission. The protocol exchanges all information needed to authenticate and negotiate the encryption algorithms to be used as well as to create the session ID for the transaction.

    ☒ **B** is incorrect because although transmission is certainly a key function of TLS and the record protocol, it is not the name of a protocol itself.

    ☒ **C** is incorrect because negotiation is a component of the handshake protocol; it is not the name of a protocol itself.

12. DNSSEC relies on digital signatures and allows a client lookup to validate a DNS resolution back to its authoritative source. What is this process called?

A. Zone signing

B. Authentication

C. Realm signing

D. Domain signing

☑ **A.** Zone signing is the process of a client using digital signatures to validate a DNS resolution request back to the authoritative source.

☒ **B** is incorrect because authentication is not a component of either DNS or DNSSEC.

☒ **C** is incorrect because realm signing is provided as a similar term to zone signing but is not an applicable term here, nor is it pertinent to DNSSEC.

☒ **D** is incorrect because domain signing is provided as a similar term to zone signing but is not an applicable term here, nor is it pertinent to DNSSEC.

13. A host-based IDS can suffer from security vulnerabilities if the host itself is compromised. Which of the following concepts can be best used to mitigate risk with an HIDS?

A. Administrative privileges

B. Read-only storage

C. Baselines

D. Encryption

☑ **B.** A common strategy for mitigating the corruption of a host-based IDS due to the host itself being compromised is to store the signatures and configurations for the HIDS in read-only storage. In this case, if the host is compromised, the configurations and signatures are still protected and cannot be modified by the attacker.

☒ **A** is incorrect because although administrative privileges are important to the protection of any system, if a malicious actor is able to compromise a host and obtain access, it is very likely he will be able to elevate privileges and overcome administrative controls.

☒ **C** is incorrect because although baselines are crucial to ensuring that systems meet expected configurations and that policies are enforced, if a system is compromised, the settings applied at the time of the baselines are susceptible to alteration or overriding by the attacker.

☒ **D** is incorrect because encryption is not used to protect an HIDS. In fact, encryption is actually a big impediment to HIDS analyzing traffic because it won't be able to read the encrypted packets.

14. Clusters can bring many benefits to a computing environment, both for administrators and users. Which of the following is *NOT* something that will be increased through the use of clustering?

A. Availability

B. Redundancy

C. Integrity

D. Failover

☑ **C.** Integrity, being the assurance that files have not been modified or altered through unauthorized means, is not something that the use of clustering would increase. Instead, clustering is focused on availability and redundancy.

☒ **A** is incorrect because availability is a key feature and goal of clustering because it eliminates having a single point of failure within systems.

☒ **B** is incorrect because redundancy is a key component and goal of clustering because it enables multiple systems to be available to service requests if needed.

☒ **D** is incorrect because failover is a key concept of clustering and is the most common configuration with active and passive nodes of a system.

15. Which of the following is commonly used by cloud providers to assure customers about security practices or to entice new customers to their services?

A. Audits

B. Baselines

C. Vulnerability assessments

D. Certifications

☑ **D.** With cloud environments being proprietary and serving many different customers, having a method for assuring customers or prospective customers as to the security of the environment is necessary. A primary method of providing this assurance is through the use of reputable certifications that are recognized throughout the industry and have well-known standards.

☒ **A** is incorrect because although audits serve a prominent role in the evaluation of security practices of a cloud provider, they are unlikely to ever be seen by a cloud customer because they contained detailed information on vulnerabilities and practices.

☒ **B** is incorrect because although baselines form the basis for securing systems, they are also highly subjective to the particular host and its intended purpose. With IaaS implementations, the baselines are the responsibility of the cloud customer.

Also, with PaaS and SaaS implementations, baselines serve as the starting point for security and would ultimately need audits or certifications to be meaningful to and trusted by customers.

☒ **C** is incorrect because vulnerability assessments are only a piece of the overall security assurance puzzle, and they are not appropriate to share with customers or potential customers. They can play a role in audits and certifications, though.

16. Within a cloud environment, what is the most widely used protocol for communication with storage devices?

    A. SATA

    B. SCSI

    C. WAN

    D. iSCSI

    ☑ **D.** iSCSI is widely used for communication with storage devices within a cloud environment. It provides the ability to use SCSI commands over the TCP protocol. It allows systems to use block-level storage that behaves the same as a SAN attached to a physical server would but works with the logical and networked nature of a cloud environment.

    ☒ **A** is incorrect because SATA is a computer bus interface that connects systems to physical storage devices such as hard drives. Within a cloud environment, this would not be possible because all systems are virtualized.

    ☒ **B** is incorrect because SCSI is a standard for connecting peripherals such as hard drives to computers. With the virtualized nature of cloud computing, this would not be pertinent or even possible.

    ☒ **C** is incorrect because a wide area network (WAN) is a private network that extends across large geographical regions. It is not specifically related to storage devices or communication with them, nor is it specifically related to cloud computing and storage.

17. Which of the following is *NOT* one of the types of unexpected events that continuity management deals with?

    A. Incidents

    B. Changes

    C. Outages

    D. Disaster

    ☑ **B.** Continuity management deals with unexpected events and the restoration of services as quickly as possible. Changes are not unexpected because they are planned and approved, and as such are covered by change management, not continuity management.

    ☒ **A** is incorrect because incidents, which are defined as events that disrupt the delivery of services, are a key concern and consideration of continuity management.

☒ **C** is incorrect because outages, and the expedient restoration of services, are a key component of continuing management. An outage is any unexpected or unplanned loss of systems, services, or communications.

☒ **D** is incorrect because a disaster is an outage caused by the loss of physical assets or facilities, such as those caused by fires, natural disasters, and other similar types of events, versus simple hardware failures or outages.

18. Which type of assessment is based on data and numbers rather than on documentation and observation?

   A. Qualitative

   B. Numeric

   C. Quantitative

   D. Metric

   ☑ **C.** Quantitative assessments are data driven and assign numerical values for various metrics to perform comparisons. Prominent calculations used with quantitative assessments are the single loss expectancy (SLE), annualized rate of occurrence (ARO), and annualized loss expectancy (ALE).

   ☒ **A** is incorrect because qualitative assessments are done with nonnumeric data and are descriptive in nature. They typically involve reviews of documentation and interviews with system maintainers, developers, and security personnel. Many times, qualitative assessments are done when an organization lacks the time, money, or sophistication to conduct a quantitative assessment.

   ☒ **B** is incorrect because although numeric sounds similar to quantitative and encapsulates key aspects of that assessment type, it is not an official term for a type of assessment.

   ☒ **D** is incorrect because although metric is a type of value and measure used with quantitative assessments, it is not a type of assessment itself.

19. What does the risk assessment–related acronym SLE stand for?

   A. Single loss expectancy

   B. System loss emergency

   C. Service loss emergency

   D. Service loss expectancy

   ☑ **A.** The acronym SLE stands for single loss expectancy. The SLE is defined as the difference between the original value of an asset and the remaining value of the asset after a single successful exploit. It is calculated by multiplying the asset value in dollars by the exposure factor, which is the loss due to a successful exploit as a percentage.

   ☒ **B** is incorrect because the acronym SLE stands for single loss expectancy and not system loss emergency.

☒ **C** is incorrect because the acronym SLE stands for single loss expectancy and not service loss emergency.

☒ **D** is incorrect because the acronym SLE stands for single loss expectancy and not service loss expectancy.

20. Which of the following core concepts of cloud computing is *NOT* something that orchestration would play a role in?

    A. Auto-scaling

    B. Portability

    C. Customer billing

    D. Provisioning

    ☑ **B.** Portability is the ability for a cloud customer to move data and services easily among various cloud providers. It allows an organization to avoid vendor lock-in and to be able to always shop for more competitive pricing or better feature offerings among cloud providers. Orchestration within a cloud environment does not play a role in the portability of a service.

    ☒ **A** is incorrect because auto-scaling is a major utilizer of orchestration within a cloud environment because resources can be changed programmatically to meet current demand for services without the need for staff intervention.

    ☒ **C** is incorrect because orchestration handles many of the customer billing operations within a cloud environment. Because automatic processes handle the provisioning of services and resources within the environment, orchestration will automatically update billing for the cloud customer as part of measured service offerings.

    ☒ **D** is incorrect because the provisioning of resources throughout the cloud environment is handled almost entirely through orchestration as well as automatic and programmatic processes.

21. Monitoring is essential in a cloud environment to ensure that SLA requirements from all the tenants will be met satisfactorily. Which of the following groupings represents the common four essential metrics?

    A. CPU, disk, memory, network

    B. Disk, network, CPU, bandwidth

    C. Memory, network, users, disk

    D. Users, network, memory, CPU

    ☑ **A.** CPU, disk, memory, and network resources are the key components of what a cloud customer purchases from a cloud provider. They are also the main focus of SLA requirements between the cloud customer and cloud provider. As such, the four metrics are very closely monitored within a cloud environment for many important uses.

☒ **B** is incorrect because bandwidth is similar to networking and is not a key metric. In this case, disk would replace bandwidth to arrive at the correct answer.

☒ **C** is incorrect because users would not be a metric under SLA requirements or impact billing as a sole metric. In this case, CPU would replace users to arrive at the correct answer.

☒ **D** is incorrect because users would not be a metric under SLA requirements or impact billing as a sole metric. In this case, disk would replace users to arrive at the correct answer.

22. Which of the following is *NOT* a core component of an operational management plan for a cloud environment?

   A. Scheduling

   B. Maintenance

   C. Orchestration

   D. Integration

☑ **D.** Integration is a concept that is covered within the processes of a management plan to fulfill customer needs, but by itself it's not a core component of a cloud management plan that would be implemented and maintained by the cloud provider.

☒ **A** is incorrect because scheduling is a core component of a management plan for a cloud provider. With a cloud environment hosting many different tenants and services, it is highly unlikely that there will ever be a time when all systems can tolerate interruptions for system maintenance. The cloud provider will have to take into account the needs and requirements from their tenants for any maintenance that entails downtime or degradation in services, with comprehensive communication being absolutely essential.

☒ **B** is incorrect because maintenance is a major concern within a cloud environment due to multitenancy and the uptime requirements of modern services. With cloud services being virtualized, it is usual practice to move around virtual machines so that work on the underlying physical systems can be performed without any impact to customers. The one major concern within a cloud relates to self-service provisioning and auto-scaling. The cloud provider needs to ensure at any time when physical servers are offline for maintenance that the cloud provider has enough resources available to handle contingencies.

☒ **C** is incorrect because orchestration is a major component of a cloud management plan. It relates to the automation processes used for provisioning, auto-scaling, billing, and reporting. Orchestration is a top concern within a cloud environment because almost all customer and user services depend on it being available, with customers able to make changes at any time.

23. Which of the following is a major concern with cloud storage communications over iSCSI that must be addressed through additional technologies?

   A. Confidentiality

   B. Integrity

   C. Availability

   D. Provisioning

   ☑ **A.** iSCSI allows for the use of SCSI commands over a TCP network, and is vital for storage communications with a completely virtualized environment like a cloud. However, iSCSI does not have the ability to do encryption or secure communications by itself, and must rely on an external technology or configuration to secure the actual transmission and communications and ensure confidentiality is maintained.

   ☒ **B** is incorrect because integrity, as far as ensuring storage operations are complete and verified, is provided as a capability of iSCSI, the same as if the storage were physically connected. The protocol ensures that read and write operations are completed successfully and the data presented is correct from its source.

   ☒ **C** is incorrect because availability is a factor of the overall environment, and not one specifically related to iSCSI. Also, iSCSI does not present unique concerns as it relates to availability.

   ☒ **D** is incorrect because provisioning is not a concern as it relates to iSCSI at all and only pertains to other operational concerns within the cloud environment.

24. Which risk response involves the use of insurance as a possible strategy for an organization?

   A. Acceptance

   B. Avoidance

   C. Transference

   D. Mitigation

   ☑ **C.** Risk transference involves having another entity assume the risk on behalf of the organization. Although not all risk and liability can be transferred to another party, one common strategy is the use of insurance to alleviate financial risk from exploits. However, although this may help alleviate certain financial risks to an organization such as fines and direct payments, it cannot mitigate financial risks from loss of reputation or public scrutiny.

   ☒ **A** is incorrect because risk acceptance is when an organization decides to not mitigate a risk, but instead accept it and deal with any consequences should they occur. This is typically only done with low-level risks, and ones where the organization has undertaken a comprehensive analysis and determined the costs of having the risk exploited are lower than the costs to prevent it from happening.

☒ **B** is incorrect because risk avoidance typically involves the disabling of services or functions so that those vulnerable are not exposed or accessible. This is typically the least desirable option for addressing risk, as it means degradation of services or loss of business in most cases.

☒ **D** is incorrect because mitigation involves fixing the exploit or putting in place appropriate countermeasures to prevent the exploit. This is the most common approach to handling risk and vulnerabilities.

25. During the assessment phase of a risk evaluation, what are the two types of tests that are performed?

   A. Internal and external

   B. Technical and managerial

   C. Physical and logical

   D. Qualitative and quantitative

   ☑ **D.** The two types of tests performed during a risk assessment are qualitative and quantitative. Qualitative tests involve a review of system and process documentation as well as interviews with developers, systems staff, and security personnel. Quantitative assessments are data driven and use measurable factors that can have mathematical comparisons done on them.

   ☒ **A** is incorrect because internal and external are typical types of audits that are performed but are not types of risk assessment tests.

   ☒ **B** is incorrect because technical and managerial, although types of operations and evaluations, are not risk assessment tests.

   ☒ **C** is incorrect because physical and logical are types of systems and controls but are not risk assessment test types.

26. The single loss expectancy (SLE) takes into consideration the value of the asset and the exposure factor. What is the exposure factor?

   A. Loss due to successful exploit, as a percentage

   B. Estimated number of times a threat will be successful

   C. Loss due to successful exploit, as a dollar amount

   D. Number of times the asset was successfully exploited in the previous year

   ☑ **A.** To calculate the single loss expectancy (SLE) value, you multiply the value of the asset by the exposure factor. The exposure factor is defined as the loss due to a successful exploit as a percentage. The product of the two values will give the expected loss in value for a single successful exploit.

   ☒ **B** is incorrect because the estimated number of times a threat will be successful, which actually pertains to an estimate for a single year-long period, is actually the definition of the annualized rate of occurrence (ARO).

☒ **C** is incorrect because loss due to a successful exploit, as a dollar amount, is essentially the same as the single loss expectancy value itself.

☒ **D** is incorrect because the number of times an asset was successfully exploited in the previous year is not a value that is used in any of the quantitative risk assessment calculations.

27. Which of the following technologies is commonly used to learn about the methods or sources attackers are using against a system in order to find better configurations or security strategies to use for protection?

   A. Firewall

   B. WAF

   C. Honeypot

   D. IDS

   ☑ **C.** A honeypot is a system, isolated away from the production systems, that is designed to appear to an attacker to be a legitimate part of a production system and, as such, contain production data. It is intended to lure attackers into breaching it rather than the actual production systems. Through extensive monitoring and data collection, administrators can learn about the types of attacks being used against their systems and use that information to improve their own security and countermeasures.

   ☒ **A** is incorrect because a firewall can be used to allow or deny network communications between two systems based on IP address, port, or protocol. It is based on predefined variables and is not used in the same sense as a honeypot to learn about attack methods and improve security.

   ☒ **B** is incorrect because a web application firewall (WAF) is an application-based firewall that can be used to block a more extensive set of conditions present with web-based applications (for example, XSS and SQL injection attacks). It is designed to block on the application layer in the same way a traditional firewall blocks on the network layer. Unlike a honeypot, it is not intended to be used to entice attackers in order to learn about their methods.

   ☒ **D** is incorrect because an IDS monitors traffic to already existing systems and applications across the network, and it alerts staff to any suspicious-looking traffic. Although an IDS can be used to glean information about attack methods and threats facing an application, honeypot is the best answer in this case because that is its intended purpose.

28. Which quality of a SIEM solution allows administrators to find broad attacks against an infrastructure that may go unnoticed if they're only looking at a single host?

   A. Correlation

   B. Aggregation

C. Monitoring

D. Consolidation

☑ **B.** A SIEM solution pulls together and aggregates logs from any or all devices across an enterprise, including servers, security systems, storage systems, and network devices. With aggregation, searches from a single interface can be done against the entire enterprise, which could reveal attacks that are hitting many devices. Some attacks might not hit individual devices with enough attempts or techniques to trigger an alert from security systems. However, looking at the aggregate may show a very different picture and allow security administrators to detect attacks that otherwise might go unnoticed.

☒ **A** is incorrect because correlation refers to the ability to look at logs from different kinds of devices and tie together attacks or attempts as they move through the enterprise. Although correlation is similar to aggregation in that it looks at more than one type of device, it is not the best answer in this case.

☒ **C** is incorrect because monitoring refers to a SIEM solution having the ability to detect event data signatures from predefined parameters and alert administrators to them. This works much like an IDS would on network traffic, but it can cover a far broader and heterogeneous range of devices.

☒ **D** is incorrect because although consolidation is a similar term to aggregation, it is not the official term used.

29. The use of baseline images, especially with the auto-scaling capabilities of cloud environments, is crucial for secure operations. What is the first step undertaken when creating a new baseline image?

A. Clean the operating system install.

B. Update all software on the install.

C. Disable or remove all nonessential services.

D. Bring patching up the latest level.

☑ **A.** In order to create a new baseline image, it is crucial that you start with a clean operating system install. This ensures that you are starting from a base image with known configuration settings and defaults in place. Starting with an image that has been in use or modified increases the likelihood that configuration or policy changes have been put in place that will end up on the image you are trying to create (possibly without you realizing that they were carried over), thus impacting security, or at the very least leading to an unintended configuration.

☒ **B** is incorrect because you would not update all software on a baseline image until after you perform a clean install and have evaluated each software package for the correct version and feature set to be included with the image. Updating software without a clean install, or without analyzing which versions and features are necessary and required, can lead to inadvertent configurations or services on the final image.

☒ **C** is incorrect because disabling or removing all nonessential services is crucial. This would be done after a clean, default install was performed and a known state was achieved on the system.

☒ **D** is incorrect because bringing patching up the latest level is crucial, but only when applied to a clean installation where the patching can be properly tracked and verified.

30. In order to maintain proper utilization and balancing of resources within a cloud environment, distributed resource scheduling (DRS) is heavily used. What resources is DRS *NOT* used with?

A. Virtual machines

B. Physical servers

C. Storage solutions

D. Clusters

☑ **B.** Distributed resource scheduling (DRS) balances virtual computing workloads over an environment to ensure that all are properly balanced on the underlying physical servers. DRS looks at the physical servers to determine load and balance, but it does not have the capability to change configurations or alter the physical servers. Due to their physical nature, they cannot be migrated in the way virtual resources can.

☒ **A** is incorrect because virtual servers are one of the key components of a cloud environment that DRS monitors and moves to maintain balance and available resources. As physical servers' loads and demands change, virtual machines can be moved among them to maintain proper balance and distribution of processes and resources.

☒ **C** is incorrect because storage solutions within a cloud environment are constantly monitored as part of DRS to ensure adequate storage is available between physical hosts. As storage demands change, DRS will balance and migrate storage among physical locations to maintain the proper use of resources.

☒ **D** is incorrect because clusters, and the virtual components that comprise their systems and storage, are constantly monitored by DRS to ensure proper balancing and availability of resources. Although a cluster is special in regard to its redundant nature, the underlying storage and virtual machines still must be maintained by the cloud environment and balanced with other similar systems.

31. What concept is used for network segregation and isolation within a cloud environment?

A. VPN

B. LAN

C. VLAN

D. Cabling

☑ **C.** A virtual local area network (VLAN) is used for separating networks logically within a physical network. This is crucial to cloud computing because the physical segregation of networks and systems is not possible; everything must be done virtually. VLANs can be used to separate zones and types of servers, or for any other type of segregation necessary for security or operations. VLANs can also span physical hosts, which is crucial in a cloud environment where hosts are constantly changing or migrating among physical assets.

☒ **A** is incorrect because a VPN is used for creating a secure communications channel from a device into a network. It is not a concept that allows for network segregation and isolation. A VPN is crucial to working with isolated and segregated networks in a secure manner, but it does not facilitate the separation itself.

☒ **B** is incorrect because a local area network (LAN) relates to networked devices within a limited area. Although this area can be something as large as a university or even a company, it does not relate directly to a cloud environment and its wider distributed nature.

☒ **D** is incorrect because cabling within a cloud environment would not be used to segregate network traffic—nor would any other physical means, due to the nature of virtualization and resource pooling.

32. Which of the following is *NOT* a capability of the TLS record protocol?

A. Sending data

B. Holding an open communications channel

C. Authenticating connections

D. Receiving data

☑ **C.** The TLS record protocol handles the actual transmission of packets between two systems; it does not handle any of the capabilities beyond that, such as authentication of connections (which is handled by the TLS handshake protocol).

☒ **A** is incorrect because sending data is a primary function performed by the limited record protocol.

☒ **B** is incorrect because holding open a communications channel for the transmission of packets is a primary function performed by the limited record protocol.

☒ **D** is incorrect because receiving data is a primary function performed by the limited record protocol.

33. Firewalls are used to control access to networks based on origin, ports, destination, and protocols used. Which of the following is *NOT* a typical origin or destination designation used?

A. VLAN

B. Physical network

C. IP address

D. IP range

☑ **B.** Firewalls are aware of the source and destination addresses of packets, as well as the ports and protocols used. They do not have the ability to distinguish what is a physical network versus a logical network, as that would depend on other variables such as IP blocks or ranges. Also, with a network that isn't local, there would be no way for a firewall to make a physical-versus-logical determination.

☒ **A** is incorrect because a VLAN, and the parameters that define it via IP blocks and ranges, would be a variable a firewall could use to make a determination to allow or reject traffic.

☒ **C** is incorrect because an IP address would provide a single source or destination address that a firewall could utilize to determine whether to allow or deny packets.

☒ **D** is incorrect because an IP range would provide a group of IP addresses to be used as a source or destination address that a firewall could utilize to determine whether to allow or deny packets.

34. Which of the following is a very common complaint concerning the use of an IDS?

A. False positives

B. Latency

C. Incorrect blocking

D. Dropping packets

☑ **A.** With an IDS watching network traffic, the likeliness of generating false positives—and in some cases an enormous number of false positives—is very likely. An IDS requires ongoing tuning to eliminate false positives. However, if false positives are totally eliminated, it is very likely you will miss actual alerts to real threats and attacks.

☒ **B** is incorrect because an IDS is a passive device on a network and should not impact the transmission of packets between systems as they flow through the IDS for inspection.

☒ **C** is incorrect because an IDS is only used to inspect and alert on suspicious traffic. It does not have the ability actually block traffic.

☒ **D** is incorrect because an IDS is a passive device on a network and is not involved with the routing or blocking of packets, which could lead to packets being dropped or lost.

35. Which component of ITIL involves the constant evaluation of the correctness of the level of provisioned resources?

   A. Availability management

   B. Capacity management

   C. Continuity management

   D. Configuration management

   ☑ **B.** Capacity management involves the evaluation of the resources provisioned and available within a cloud environment to ensure that the proper levels are maintained and that the system is not over- or underbuilt for what is necessary to meet demands.

   ☒ **A** is incorrect because availability management is focused on resources being available to users and services when they are needed; it's primarily concerned with uptime and accessibility from the correct locations.

   ☒ **C** is incorrect because continuity management is focused on the restoration of services and continuity of operations following an unexpected outage or disaster.

   ☒ **D** is incorrect because configuration management is focused on tracking all devices and services within the enterprise and maintaining information on their provisioning and level of resources.

36. Which of the following can add significant costs to an organization following a successful exploit?

   A. Regulations

   B. Interoperability

   C. Measured service

   D. Availability

   ☑ **A.** Regulations often carry with them specific penalties or sanctions for any violations or exposures from exploits. These are above and beyond the costs for an organization to restore operations. In cases with sensitive and protected data, the costs can be substantial from the regulations themselves as well as exposure to any civil liability beyond the regulations.

   ☒ **B** is incorrect because interoperability refers to the ability to reuse components or services from one application for another. It would not have a direct impact or add additional costs after a successful exploit.

   ☒ **C** is incorrect because measured service refers to cloud customers incurring costs and billing for only those services they consume, and for the duration they are consuming them. A successful exploit of a system would not have any lasting ramifications for measured service.

   ☒ **D** is incorrect because although availability might be impacted during a successful exploit and its remediation, it will have not have a long-lasting impact beyond the restoration of services.

37. Which type of cloud deployment requires the least amount of involvement from the cloud provider to make logs available to the cloud customer?

    A. PaaS

    B. IaaS

    C. SaaS

    D. DaaS

    ☑ **B.** Within Infrastructure as a Service (IaaS), the cloud customer is responsible for managing its own systems and virtual appliances. Therefore, with full administrative access, the customer would by default have access to all event data and logs from its systems. The only involvement necessary from the cloud provider would be when logs from an infrastructure level, outside the control of the cloud customer, are required.

    ☒ **A** is incorrect because Platform as a Service (PaaS) is maintained from the application down by the cloud provider, and typically without the cloud customer having any type of administrative access. With PaaS, the event data often needs to be exposed by the cloud provider in order for the cloud customer to access it.

    ☒ **C** is incorrect because Software as a Service (SaaS) is completely closed and the application entirely maintained by the cloud provider. Any access to event or log data will need to be facilitated by the cloud provider.

    ☒ **D** is incorrect because Desktop as a Service (DaaS) is completely closed and the application entirely maintained by the cloud provider. Any access to event or log data will need to be facilitated by the cloud provider.

38. Although traditionally data centers have relied on a tiered topology for layers of redundancy, which organization publishes the Infinity Paradigm, which shifts away from a tiered topology in favor of a macro-level approach?

    A. Uptime Institute

    B. BISCI

    C. IDCA

    D. NFPA

    ☑ **C.** The International Data Center Authority (IDCA) established the Infinity Paradigm, which is intended to be a comprehensive data center design and operations framework. The Infinity Paradigm differs from other standards by shifting away from a tiered architecture and instead embracing a macro-level approach where the entire data center is considered as a whole.

☒ **A** is incorrect because the Uptime Institute publishes the most widely used standard for data center design based on a tiered-topology approach. This standard has four tiers, each progressively adding layers and requirements for redundancy and fault tolerance.

☒ **B** is incorrect because Building Industry Consulting Services International (BISCI) issues certifications in the area of complex cabling for data systems and develops standards for them. The standard is focused on cabling design and setups, and it also includes specifications on power, energy, efficiency, and hot/cold aisle setups.

☒ **D** is incorrect because the National Fire Protection Association (NFPA) publishes a large collection of standards regarding fire protection for almost any type of facility, including data centers.

6

Legal and Compliance Domain

Domain 6 is focused on the following topics:

- Legal risks and controls relating to cloud computing
- eDiscovery and forensic requirements
- Laws pertaining to PII
- Audit types
- Audit processes in a cloud environment
- Risk management as it pertains to the cloud
- Outsourcing to a cloud and overseeing the contract

Cloud computing presents many unique challenges on the legal and policy fronts because it often crosses jurisdictional lines that will have different rules and regulations as to data privacy and protection. Although auditing all IT systems is a very critical and sensitive process, a cloud environment presents unique challenges and requirements for auditing because cloud customers will not have full access to systems or processes in the same manner they would in a traditional data center. Risk management also poses unique challenges in a cloud because it expands the realm of operations and systems for an organization, and the realities of a cloud environment introduce additional risks and complexities, especially with multitenancy.

1. The nature of cloud computing and how it operates make complying with data discovery and disclosure orders more difficult. Which of the following concepts provides the biggest challenge in regard to data collection, pursuant to a legal order?

   A. Portability

   B. Multitenancy

   C. Reversibility

   D. Auto-scaling

2. Which security concept pertains to protecting sensitive information from disclosure but also ensuring it is accessible to the appropriate parties?

   A. Confidentiality

   B. Integrity

   C. Availability

   D. Privacy

3. With cloud computing crossing many jurisdictional boundaries, it is a virtual certainty that conflicts will arise between differing regulations. What is the major impediment to resolving conflicts between multiple jurisdictions to form an overall policy?

   A. Language differences

   B. Technologies used

   C. Licensing issues

   D. Lack of international authority

4. Which of the following regulations originates from a professional or industry organization, rather than from a legal or governmental authority?

   A. PCI DSS

   B. FISMA

   C. HIPAA

   D. SOX

5. What is a very common method of verifying the integrity of a file that has been downloaded from a site or vendor distribution, to ensure it has not been modified during transmission?

   A. File size

   B. Checksum

   C. Filename

   D. Metadata

6. The Safe Harbor program was developed to bridge the gap in privacy regulations between two different jurisdictions. Which two jurisdictions are involved in the program?

   A. The United States and Japan

   B. Russia and the European Union

   C. The United States and the European Union

   D. The European Union and Japan

7. Regulatory frameworks can come from a variety of jurisdictions, both legal and professional. Which of the following regulatory frameworks pertains to the handling of credit card transactions?

   A. PCI DSS

   B. FISMA

   C. HIPAA

   D. FIPS 140-2

8. Audits are regularly undertaken by an organization in both internal and external formats, to ensure regulatory or corporate policy compliance, among many other potential factors. Which of the following is *NOT* something evaluated as part of an internal audit?

   A. Efficiency

   B. Regulations

   C. Design plans

   D. Costs

9. What principle must always been included with an SOC 2 report?

   A. Confidentiality

   B. Security

   C. Privacy

   D. Processing integrity

10. What will determine the responsibilities for both the cloud provider and the cloud customer in the event of litigation impacting a system or service?

    A. Contract

    B. SLA

    C. Regulation

    D. SOW

11. The first step with an internal information security management system (ISMS) involves defining an organization's security policies. After security policies have been defined, what is the next step in the process?

    A. Risk assessment

    B. Scope definition

    C. Implement controls

    D. Continual improvement

12. Without direct access by customers to the underlying infrastructure of a cloud environment, coupled with their limited knowledge of many operations and configurations, what can be used for customers to gain assurance of security controls and implementations?

    A. SLAs

    B. Contracts

    C. Regulations

    D. Certifications

13. Cloud environments pose many unique challenges for a data custodian to properly adhere to policies and the use of data. What poses the biggest challenge for a data custodian with a PaaS implementation, over and above the same concerns with IaaS?

    A. Access to systems

    B. Knowledge of systems

    C. Data classification rules

    D. Contractual requirements

14. During the lessons learned phase of an audit, reducing duplication is key for lowering both costs and time involved for staff with audits. Which of the following will prevent elimination of duplication in many instances?

    A. Corporate policies

    B. Vendor recommendations

    C. Regulations

    D. Stakeholders

15. The ISO/IEC 27001:2013 security standard contains 14 different domains that cover virtually all areas of IT operations and procedures. Which of the following is *NOT* one of the domains listed in the standard?

    A. Legal

    B. Management

    C. Assets

    D. Supplier Relationships

16. What is the process that requires searching, identifying, collecting, and securing electronic data or records for use within criminal or civil legal matters?

    A. Disclosure

    B. Subpoena

    C. Retention

    D. eDiscovery

17. What vehicle will delineate the responsibilities for compliance and data collection pursuant to an eDiscovery request?

    A. SLA

    B. Contract

    C. Regulation

    D. SOW

18. Which type of report is considered for "general" use and does not contain any sensitive information?

    A. SOC 1

    B. SAS-70

    C. SOC 3

    D. SOC 2

19. Which of the following would *NOT* be used as input toward the gap analysis aspect of an audit?

    A. Customer feedback

    B. Stakeholder interviews

    C. Documentation review

    D. Audit testing

20. Data is used by many different roles within an organization. Although all roles have the responsibility for protecting the data and conforming to any policies governing its use or access, which role is specifically responsible for determining the appropriate controls to be applied as well as appropriate use?

    A. Data custodian

    B. Data owner

    C. Data originator

    D. Database administrator

21. Many processes are substantially different between fulfilling an eDiscovery request in a cloud environment versus a traditional data center. Which of the following concepts is a major factor within a cloud environment?

 A. Broad network access

 B. Measured service

 C. Elasticity

 D. On-demand self-service

22. Which type of PII will often have public disclosure requirements for any compromise of personal data?

 A. Contractual

 B. Jurisdictional

 C. Regulated

 D. Sensitive

23. Which of the following laws is highly related to the preservation and retention of electronic records?

 A. HIPAA

 B. Safe Harbor

 C. SOX

 D. GLBA

24. During an SOC 2 audit, the change management policies and procedures of an organization are evaluated. Which principle of the SOC 2 audit includes this evaluation?

 A. Security

 B. Privacy

 C. Processing integrity

 D. Availability

25. Which of the following is *NOT* one of the steps involved in the audit plan?

 A. Define objectives

 B. Remediation

 C. Define scope

 D. Lessons learned

26. ISO/IEC 27018 was developed to establish standards for privacy involving cloud computing. One of its key components specifies the type and frequency of audits. Which of the following represents the type and frequency of audits established under the standard?

   A. Independent, yearly

   B. Internal, every six months

   C. Independent, every six months

   D. Internal, yearly

27. Which step of the audit plan determines how many staff will need to be allocated on behalf of the organization and the auditors to conduct a successful audit?

   A. Define scope

   B. Lessons learned

   C. Define objectives

   D. Conduct the audit

28. Many jurisdictions around the world have comprehensive regulations regarding privacy and data protection. Which jurisdiction lacks an overall comprehensive policy that covers its entire jurisdictional area?

   A. United States

   B. European Union

   C. Russia

   D. Japan

29. An audit scope statement defines the entire process and procedures to be used while conducting of an audit. Which of the following items is *NOT* something that would be found in an audit scope statement?

   A. Exclusions

   B. Costs

   C. Certifications

   D. Reports

30. Which of the following laws pertains to the protection and confidentiality of PII, related specifically to financial institutions?

   A. HIPAA

   B. SOX

   C. Safe Harbor

   D. GLBA

1. B	**11.** B	**21.** B
2. A	**12.** D	**22.** C
3. D	**13.** B	**23.** C
4. A	**14.** C	**24.** A
5. B	**15.** A	**25.** B
6. C	**16.** D	**26.** A
7. A	**17.** B	**27.** C
8. B	**18.** C	**28.** A
9. B	**19.** A	**29.** B
10. A	**20.** B	**30.** D

Comprehensive Answers and Explanations

1. The nature of cloud computing and how it operates make complying with data discovery and disclosure orders more difficult. Which of the following concepts provides the biggest challenge in regard to data collection, pursuant to a legal order?

   A. Portability

   B. Multitenancy

   C. Reversibility

   D. Auto-scaling

   ☑ **B.** In a traditional data center, where an organization owns and controls all systems, data, and physical equipment, it is very easy to isolate and duplicate anything necessary. Within a cloud environment, with multitenancy and many customers sharing the same resources, it isn't practical for the cloud provider to make easy snapshots or isolate physical storage systems or servers. Different collection methods are necessary in a cloud environment, which often are more labor or cost intensive, and with additional complexity involved.

   ☒ **A** is incorrect because portability refers to the ability for a system, service, or application to move with ease between different cloud providers. It gives additional flexibility to a cloud customer and prevents vendor lock-in, which would eliminate a cloud customer from seeking competition and constantly shopping for cheaper services or better support.

   ☒ **C** is incorrect because reversibility refers to the ability of a cloud customer to easily remove their data, systems, and applications from a cloud provider, with certainty that it has been securely and completely removed. The requirements for removal, including methods and timelines, should be covered by the contract between the cloud customer and cloud provider.

   ☒ **D** is incorrect because auto-scaling pertains to a cloud environment's ability to programmatically adjust the necessary resources to meet current demand, either by adding or removing allocated resources.

2. Which security concept pertains to protecting sensitive information from disclosure but also ensuring it is accessible to the appropriate parties?

   A. Confidentiality

   B. Integrity

   C. Availability

   D. Privacy

☑ **A.** Confidentiality pertains to the protection of sensitive information from disclosure to unauthorized parties, either through accidental disclosure or by the actions of malicious actors. It has a second component that is related to ensuring that data is available to authorized parties and provisioned for appropriate access.

☒ **B** is incorrect because integrity refers to ensuring that data has not been corrupted or altered through unauthorized or inappropriate actions. It is solely focused on the format and correctness of the data, and may be used in conjunction with confidentiality in some instances. However, data is not required to be protected or to be sensitive in nature for integrity to be a necessary concern.

☒ **C** is incorrect because availability pertains to data being accessible when necessary and in a secure manner. It may involve sensitive data or can be completely open and public for dissemination, but with necessary requirements for access and availability for crucial operations.

☒ **D** is incorrect because privacy is considered a subset of confidentiality, as it is focused on personal data and the right or ability to control how it is collected or used, as well as the ability to have it removed from a system or application when desired or no long necessary for use.

3. With cloud computing crossing many jurisdictional boundaries, it is a virtual certainty that conflicts will arise between differing regulations. What is the major impediment to resolving conflicts between multiple jurisdictions to form an overall policy?

   A. Language differences

   B. Technologies used

   C. Licensing issues

   D. Lack of international authority

   ☑ **D.** The biggest problem with resolving jurisdictional conflicts is the lack of an international authority. Each jurisdiction, typically along national lines, establishes its own regulations and laws pertaining to data protection. When conflicts between jurisdictions arise, it is incumbent upon those jurisdictions to work out the issue. Typically, no centralized authority exists at the international level that can be used to resolve potential conflicts or to mediate.

   ☒ **A** is incorrect because language differences would not be a significant impediment. Although it is quite likely that you could encounter language differences when dealing across borders with different locales, these are easily overcome with translators, or even computer programs that can handle translations well.

☒ **B** is incorrect because the technologies used would not serve as a hindrance to regulations compliance in any significant way that is unique to multiple jurisdictions. Technologies always need to match compliance requirements to an acceptable standard, so hosting across multiple jurisdictions is not a unique circumstance in this regard.

☒ **C** is incorrect because licensing issues are also not unique across jurisdictions, nor do they directly play into issues with regulatory compliance. They are more central to contractual issues.

4. Which of the following regulations originates from a professional or industry organization, rather than from a legal or governmental authority?

   A. PCI DSS

   B. FISMA

   C. HIPAA

   D. SOX

   ☑ **A.** The Payment Card Industry Data Security Standard (PCI DSS) was first implemented in 2004 and was designed by the major credit card brands to ensure that a minimal level of security standards was being used by merchants when processing credit card payments and utilizing their networks. It was implemented by industry groups and companies rather than a legal or governmental authority.

   ☒ **B** is incorrect because the Federal Information Security Management Act (FISMA) was signed into law in 2002 in the United States and pertains to the security of federal government IT systems and outlines requirements for agency security programs.

   ☒ **C** is incorrect because the Health Insurance Portability and Accountability Act (HIPAA) was implemented by the United States in 1996 and provides security for the privacy and protection of personal medical records.

   ☒ **D** is incorrect because the Sarbanes–Oxley Act (SOX) became law in the United States in 2002 and sets requirements for publicly traded companies and public accounting firms in regard to disclosure and recordkeeping.

5. What is a very common method of verifying the integrity of a file that has been downloaded from a site or vendor distribution, to ensure it has not been modified during transmission?

   A. File size

   B. Checksum

   C. Filename

   D. Metadata

☑ **B.** A checksum is the output of an algorithm processing a cryptographic hashing function against a piece of data or a file. The same algorithm can be run against a file at another time and compared to the original, known, true value to determine if the file has been altered at all from its original and correct state. Using a checksum is an easy and quick way to determine if a file has been altered or tampered with in any way.

☒ **A** is incorrect because file size would not be a reliable method for determining if a file has been altered at all, as modifications can be made that would not alter the size of a file yet could substantially change the contents of the data.

☒ **C** is incorrect because filenames can easily be changed at any time, and there is no way to know if the filename presented is the correct or original value.

☒ **D** is incorrect because metadata represents attributes of the data itself and can easily be manipulated, altered, or forged.

6. The Safe Harbor program was developed to bridge the gap in privacy regulations between two different jurisdictions. Which two jurisdictions are involved in the program?

   A. The United States and Japan

   B. Russia and the European Union

   C. The United States and the European Union

   D. The European Union and Japan

   ☑ **C.** The Safe Harbor program was designed by the US Department of Commerce as a voluntary set of regulations that a company can use to meet the stricter privacy and data protection requirements of the European Union, and thus allow United States companies to comply with contractual and regulatory requirements necessary to doing business within EU borders.

   ☒ **A** is incorrect because the Safe Harbor program pertains to the United States and the European Union, not the United States and Japan.

   ☒ **B** is incorrect because the Safe Harbor program pertains to the United States and the European Union, not Russia and the European Union.

   ☒ **D** is incorrect because the Safe Harbor program pertains to the United States and the European Union, not the European Union and Japan.

7. Regulatory frameworks can come from a variety of jurisdictions, both legal and professional. Which of the following regulatory frameworks pertains to the handling of credit card transactions?

   A. PCI DSS

   B. FISMA

C. HIPAA

D. FIPS 140-2

☑ **A.** The Payment Card Industry Data Security Standard (PCI DSS) is a regulatory framework developed by the major credit card brands, designed to set minimum standards for merchants to follow when processing and transmitting data across their networks and interacting with their payment systems.

☒ **B** is incorrect because the Federal Information Security Management Act (FISMA) is a United States government law that pertains to the protection and security of systems used by government agencies and their contractors.

☒ **C** is incorrect because the Health Insurance Portability and Accountability Act (HIPAA) is a United States government law that pertains to the protection of medical records and personal privacy related to them.

☒ **D** is incorrect because the FIPS 140-2 standards were developed by the government of the United States and pertain to the certification of cryptographic modules used within systems.

8. Audits are regularly undertaken by an organization in both internal and external formats, to ensure regulatory or corporate policy compliance, among many other potential factors. Which of the following is *NOT* something evaluated as part of an internal audit?

A. Efficiency

B. Regulations

C. Design plans

D. Costs

☑ **B.** Compliance with regulations is considered an external audit. It is done by an independent third party that does not have any stake or financial interests in the organization undergoing the audit. Most regulations have specific requirements as to the type of audit, and in some cases who the appropriate auditors should be selected from as well.

☒ **A** is incorrect because efficiency—specifically, operational efficiency—is a key component of internal audits that is done to improve business processes and streamline operations.

☒ **C** is incorrect because design plans are something that would be evaluated as part of an internal audit, with a goal of assisting in efficiency and determining appropriate level of resources needed.

☒ **D** is incorrect because costs are not a factor in regulatory compliance audits at all and are instead a component of internal audits, typically with an eye toward any changes that can be made to reduce overall operating costs.

9. What principle must always been included with an SOC 2 report?

   A. Confidentiality

   B. Security

   C. Privacy

   D. Processing integrity

   ☑ **B.** The SOC 2 reports are composed of five principles: confidentiality, processing integrity, availability, privacy, and security. If a principle other than security is desired, the security principle must also be included, as it is required for all reports.

   ☒ **A** is incorrect because confidentiality is a principle of the SOC 2 reports that pertains to the protection of sensitive information and compliance with any regulations required to be applied to it, but it is not a required principle to be included in all reports.

   ☒ **C** is incorrect because privacy is a principle of the SOC 2 reports that pertains to the protection of personal information to meet an organization's privacy policy, as well as any applicable regulations, but it is not a required principle of all SOC 2 reports.

   ☒ **D** is incorrect because processing integrity is a principle of the SOC 2 reports that pertains to ensuring that only authorized parties can manipulate data, and only do so in an appropriate manner, but it is not required as a principle with all reports.

10. What will determine the responsibilities for both the cloud provider and the cloud customer in the event of litigation impacting a system or service?

    A. Contract

    B. SLA

    C. Regulation

    D. SOW

    ☑ **A.** In the event of any litigation, either against the cloud customer's systems or services or against the cloud provider, the contract should clearly document the responsibilities and duties of each party as far as communication and compliance.

    ☒ **B** is incorrect because the service level agreement (SLA) will specify specific operational thresholds and performance metrics, but would not be the appropriate document for litigation responsibilities.

    ☒ **C** is incorrect because regulations will dictate minimum standards for security and configurations, but will not determine the responsibilities or duties on behalf of the cloud provider or cloud customer in regard to compliance with litigation.

    ☒ **D** is incorrect because a statement of work (SOW) will document the specific work items and tasks necessary to turn a contract into an actual implementation, but will not document or dictate duties or responsibilities for compliance with litigation.

11. The first step with an internal information security management system (ISMS) involves defining an organization's security policies. After security policies have been defined, what is the next step in the process?

   A. Risk assessment

   B. Scope definition

   C. Implement controls

   D. Continual improvement

   ☑ **B.** After the formulation of security policies, the next step is to define the scope of the ISMS efforts, which will define and drive all future activities and determine what is to be included and to what extent.

   ☒ **A** is incorrect because the risk assessment occurs after the defining of security polices and determining the scope. The risk assessment is then used to determine how to approach the known risks with an eye toward regulatory compliance or management expectations.

   ☒ **C** is incorrect because controls are implemented after the risk assessment has been completed and the scope and need for control have been appropriately determined. Implementing controls prior the completion of the risk assessment increases the likelihood of controls that do not meet objectives or that incur additional costs or gaps in compliance.

   ☒ **D** is incorrect because continual improvement is the last component, after the ISMS has been properly determined and implemented, with an eye toward ongoing operations and adherence to regulatory compliance, for both new and existing regulations.

12. Without direct access by customers to the underlying infrastructure of a cloud environment, coupled with their limited knowledge of many operations and configurations, what can be used for customers to gain assurance of security controls and implementations?

   A. SLAs

   B. Contracts

   C. Regulations

   D. Certifications

   ☑ **D.** With a cloud customer having very limited insight into the configuration and operational practices of a cloud provider, certifications are often used to provide assurances that standards are being met, as well as specifics in regard to minimum settings and protection standards. With certification programs publishing publicly available standards and frameworks, having an independently verified audit to show adherence can provide a cloud customer with confidence in the cloud provider's practices; this can also serve as a means of compliance with their own regulations.

☒ **A** is incorrect because service level agreements (SLAs) are intended to outline performance metrics and expectations for support and implementations; it would not be used as a means to gain assurances concerning security implementations and configurations.

☒ **B** is incorrect because contracts document the broad parameters and high-level points of a business relationship. They formalize regulations and expectations between the cloud customer and the cloud provider, but do not serve to provide assurance or validation for specific configurations, but only the requirement to do so.

☒ **C** is incorrect because regulations will dictate specific requirements for configurations and minimum standards, but will not provide assurance of their implementation in the way that certifications will. In fact, in many instances, certifications are designed specifically to comply with regulations.

13. Cloud environments pose many unique challenges for a data custodian to properly adhere to policies and the use of data. What poses the biggest challenge for a data custodian with a PaaS implementation, over and above the same concerns with IaaS?

A. Access to systems

B. Knowledge of systems

C. Data classification rules

D. Contractual requirements

☑ **B.** In order for a data custodian to do his job with a high degree of confidence, he needs to have extensive knowledge of systems and configurations, including the security controls in place and how they are implemented. With a cloud implementation, the depth of knowledge is going to be much shallower than it would be with a traditional data center, where full control is likely. This is even more of a struggle within a cloud when PaaS is used and the cloud provider is responsible for the majority of the system configurations and administration.

☒ **A** is incorrect because although access to systems does pose a challenge, especially with the much more limited access available in a PaaS implementation, it does not pose the same level of challenge as knowledge of the systems and the underlying infrastructure.

☒ **C** is incorrect because data classification rules will be universal regardless of the particular hosting model used. Whether the data is hosted under IaaS or PaaS will not make any difference in classification rules.

☒ **D** is incorrect because contractual requirements would not have any impact on the challenges a data custodian faces, nor are there any differences between IaaS and PaaS hosting deployments.

14. During the lessons learned phase of an audit, reducing duplication is key for lowering both costs and time involved for staff with audits. Which of the following will prevent elimination of duplication in many instances?

   A. Corporate policies

   B. Vendor recommendations

   C. Regulations

   D. Stakeholders

   ☑ **C.** Although many areas of duplication are possible to eliminate with a thorough evaluation after audits have been completed, requirements that come from regulations will prevent the total elimination of duplication. Regulations have specific audit requirements that must be fulfilled, and will typically not allow substitution of other audit results, or the acceptance of equivalences. Regulations typically require specific audits, sometimes even performed by specific auditors, that must be satisfactory completed.

   ☒ **A** is incorrect because corporate policies can always be adjusted to allow for the elimination of duplication with audits. Because the company controls its own policies, it also has control over the modification of them, or the acceptance of similar audits to fulfill requirements.

   ☒ **B** is incorrect because vendor recommendations will not directly play into audits. Auditors may use best practice recommendations from vendors as input into their own testing plans and methodologies, but that decision is subjective and always open to modification.

   ☒ **D** is incorrect because stakeholders will not often have direct influence on audits and how they are conducted, beyond perhaps mandating specific certifications or standards that should be followed. However, stakeholders can always allow for modifications, whereas regulations will not be flexible in most instances for individual organizations.

15. The ISO/IEC 27001:2013 security standard contains 14 different domains that cover virtually all areas of IT operations and procedures. Which of the following is *NOT* one of the domains listed in the standard?

   A. Legal

   B. Management

   C. Assets

   D. Supplier Relationships

   ☑ **A.** The ISO/IEC 27001:2013 security standard contains 14 different domains, but legal is not one that's specifically mentioned. However, even though legal is not specifically mentioned, like many other concepts, it can be found throughout many of the other domains to varying degrees.

☒ **B** is incorrect because management is one of the 14 individual domains contained in the ISO/IEC 27001:2013 standard.

☒ **C** is in correct because assets is one of the 14 individual domains contained in the ISO/IEC 27001:2013 standard.

☒ **D** is incorrect because supplier relationships is one of the 14 individual domains contained in the ISO/IEC 27001:2013 standard.

16. What is the process that requires searching, identifying, collecting, and securing electronic data or records for use within criminal or civil legal matters?

   A. Disclosure

   B. Subpoena

   C. Retention

   D. eDiscovery

   ☑ **D.** eDiscovery is the process that requires searching, identifying, collecting, and securing electronic data or records, typically to be used for criminal or civil legal matters. It is similar to the discovery process typically used for evidence collection or document production in the course of a legal inquiry, just specifically focused on electronic records and the particular needs and processes required for them.

   ☒ **A** is incorrect because although disclosure could pertain to handing over the evidence to the requesting authority pursuant to their eDiscovery order, it is not an official term used here.

   ☒ **B** is incorrect because a subpoena is a legal mechanism to compel the production and turning over of records, but it's a more general term that isn't specific to electronic evidence. It would, however, serve as the official legal way of compelling an eDiscovery process.

   ☒ **C** is incorrect because retention refers to storing and archiving of data for a period of time to meet regulations or policies.

17. What vehicle will delineate the responsibilities for compliance and data collection pursuant to an eDiscovery request?

   A. SLA

   B. Contract

   C. Regulation

   D. SOW

   ☑ **B.** When dealing with possible eDiscovery in a cloud environment, where responsibilities are a shared between the cloud customer and cloud provider, it is essential for the contract to outline responsibilities and the requirements for their completion, including time requirements.

☒ **A** is incorrect because a service level agreement (SLA) is used to determine if contractual obligations are being met, based on agreed-upon metrics and requirements.

☒ **C** is incorrect because regulations play a key role in the scope and requirements of an eDiscovery order; they are not a factor in how information is collected or the specific responsibilities for its collection.

☒ **D** is incorrect because a statement of work (SOW) defines the actual work to implement contractual requirements as well as the scope, but it does not relate to compliance with an eDiscovery order.

18. Which type of report is considered for "general" use and does not contain any sensitive information.

   A. SOC 1

   B. SAS-70

   C. SOC 3

   D. SOC 2

   ☑ **C.** SOC 3 reports are very similar in approach and substance to SOC 2 reports, but they are designed for general use and do not contain any sensitive information.

   ☒ **A** is incorrect because SOC 1 reports are designed for restricted use, and only for internal staff, current customers, or auditors on behalf of regulators.

   ☒ **B** is incorrect because SAS-70 reports are actually deprecated at this time, but even when in widespread use, they were considered restricted-use reports and were similar to SOC 1 reports.

   ☒ **D** is incorrect because SOC 2 reports, although more broad in substance and duration than SOC 1 reports, are still considered "restricted use" and not for public dissemination.

19. Which of the following would *NOT* be used as input toward the gap analysis aspect of an audit?

   A. Customer feedback

   B. Stakeholder interviews

   C. Documentation review

   D. Audit testing

   ☑ **A.** Customer feedback, although very important to an organization, would not be a factor in a gap analysis, because it would not have any impact on security configurations or their deviations from policy or baselines.

   ☒ **B** is incorrect because stakeholder interviews form an important part of an audit review and the gathering of information on processes, decisions, and implementation policies.

☒ **C** is incorrect because documentation review is a key component of an audit and gap analysis because it forms the basis for policies and regulations, as well as the specific implementations that an organization feels are prudent and should be in place.

☒ **D** is incorrect because actual audit testing is perhaps the most important part of an audit because it determines whether the configurations and controls in place actually match those documented in policy or regulation and should be in place.

20. Data is used by many different roles within an organization. Although all roles have the responsibility for protecting the data and conforming to any policies governing its use or access, which role is specifically responsible for determining the appropriate controls to be applied as well as appropriate use?

   A. Data custodian

   B. Data owner

   C. Data originator

   D. Database administrator

   ☑ **B.** The data owner is responsible for determining the appropriate controls for data, as well as ensuring they are applied and enforced. The data owner sets the policy for the use of the data, taking into account any regulations and policies, and then oversees that the data is used appropriately within those rules.

   ☒ **A** is incorrect because the data custodian works with the data owner on appropriate use and processing of data. This is a technical role rather than a managerial role.

   ☒ **C** is incorrect because data originator is the role that creates the data, through a variety of means or processes, but is not responsible for overseeing or enforcing policy on its protection or appropriate use.

   ☒ **D** is incorrect because database administrator is a purely technical role that has a duty to follow and enforce policy but does not determine controls or appropriate use.

21. Many processes are substantially different between fulfilling an eDiscovery request in a cloud environment versus a traditional data center. Which of the following concepts is a major factor within a cloud environment?

   A. Broad network access

   B. Measured service

   C. Elasticity

   D. On-demand self-service

   ☑ **B.** Measured service is a cloud concept in which a cloud customer only pays for the resources they are actively using and have allocated. This becomes an important concept when dealing with eDiscovery orders because substantial disk space may be needed to make copies of data or to preserve it, pursuant to the order. During the time the disk is being used, an organization could potentially incur substantial extra costs from the cloud provider, unless accommodations have been made via the contract.

☒ **A** is incorrect because broad network access pertains to the ability to access cloud resources of the public Internet, through a variety of different devices or clients. It would not have a significant impact on the fulfillment of an eDiscovery order.

☒ **C** is incorrect because elasticity pertains to the ability for a cloud environment to adjust resources as needed to meet the current demands of a service or system, either in an increasing or decreasing capacity. This is typically done via automated means and would not be a significant factor in the successful fulfillment of an eDiscovery order.

☒ **D** is incorrect because on-demand self-service pertains to the ability of a cloud customer to automatically request and provision resources within a cloud environment, without having to involve the staff of the cloud provider. Although this may factor into the ability of a cloud customer to allocate additional resources to accommodate an eDiscovery order fulfillment, it would not be a substantial factor in it.

22. Which type of PII will often have public disclosure requirements for any compromise of personal data?

   A. Contractual

   B. Jurisdictional

   C. Regulated

   D. Sensitive

   ☑ **C. Regulated** PII is data that is protected via law or regulation and carries with it the enforcement of the jurisdiction governing its use and protection. Most regulations also stipulate disclosure requirements that an organization must follow for the unauthorized or inappropriate release or compromise of PII information to the affected individuals.

   ☒ **A** is incorrect because contractual PII is data that has mandated protection requirements based solely on the contract between the cloud customer and cloud provider. This may have disclosure requirements as part of it, but not with the same force or requirements as regulated PII.

   ☒ **B** is incorrect because jurisdictional is not a type of PII protection. Regulated PII is applied at the jurisdiction level and is the most appropriate answer.

   ☒ **D** is incorrect because "sensitive" typically refers to data that has particular protection requirements or would be of high value for someone to obtain. However, it is not a specific type of PII, nor are there any specific and direct requirements for its use and protection.

23. Which of the following laws is highly related to the preservation and retention of electronic records?

A. HIPAA

B. Safe Harbor

C. SOX

D. GLBA

☑ **C.** The Sarbanes–Oxley Act (SOX) of 2002 pertains to the records publicly traded companies, accounting firms, and many other types of organizations must retain. It specifies not only the type of records that must be preserved but also the duration of retention.

☒ **A** is incorrect because the Health Insurance Portability and Accountability Act (HIPAA) of 1996 pertains to the protection of patient privacy and medical records. It is not focused on the preservation or retention of electronic records.

☒ **B** is incorrect because the Safe Harbor program was developed by the United States Department of Commerce as a way for US companies to bridge the privacy laws between the United States and the European Union and comply with the more strict requirements.

☒ **D** is incorrect because the Gramm–Leach–Bliley Act (GLBA) of 1999 is focused on how financial institutions handle the private information of individuals. It is not specifically focused on records retention or preservation.

24. During an SOC 2 audit, the change management policies and procedures of an organization are evaluated. Which principle of the SOC 2 audit includes this evaluation?

A. Security

B. Privacy

C. Processing integrity

D. Availability

☑ **A.** The change management policies and practices of an organization are included as part of the security principle of the SOC 2 report. The change management principle pertains to how an organization determines what changes are needed as well as how they are approved, implemented, tested, and verified. The goal is to ensure that all changes are done in a methodical and controlled manner, with appropriate approvals and safeguards to prevent unauthorized changes.

☒ **B** is incorrect because the privacy principle does not have subcomponents. It is focused on how an organization uses, collects, and stores personal and private information, and it does so in a manner that conforms to the organization's stated policy privacy as well as any pertinent regulations, laws, or standards requirements.

☒ **C** is incorrect because the processing integrity principle does not have subcomponents. It is focused on how an organization's systems process information, and it does so in a manner that is accurate, verified, and done only by authorized parties.

☒ **D** is incorrect because the availability principle focuses on how a system has requirements and expectations for uptime and accessibility, and it is able to meet those requirements within parameters set by contract or expectation.

25. Which of the following is *NOT* one of the steps involved in the audit plan?

   A. Define objectives

   B. Remediation

   C. Define scope

   D. Lessons learned

   ☑ **B.** Remediation of any findings or deficiencies is handled after the completion of an audit, but is not a part of the actual audit. Although strategies for remediation are often discussed with auditors to ensure that steps taken will satisfy the deficiency, the actual remediation of them is not part of the audit itself.

   ☒ **A** is incorrect because defining objectives is the first step in the formulation of the audit plan. The objectives take into account policies and regulations, as well as the risk acceptance level desired, in order to form the outline of the overall audit, including the purpose of the audit.

   ☒ **C** is incorrect because defining the scope of the audit occurs after the defining of objectives. The scope includes what exactly will be included in the audit, as well as how things will be tested. It serves as the official map for the audit and all the steps and processes that must be completed as part of it.

   ☒ **D** is incorrect because the lessons learned analysis is performed after the audit has been conducted. It represents the opportunity to review the audit and the steps taken to accomplish it, including the scope, and serves to refine future audits and processes.

26. ISO/IEC 27018 was developed to establish standards for privacy involving cloud computing. One of its key components specifies the type and frequency of audits. Which of the following represents the type and frequency of audits established under the standard?

   A. Independent, yearly

   B. Internal, every six months

   C. Independent, every six months

   D. Internal, yearly

   ☑ **A.** Under the ISO/IEC 27018 standards, audits should be completed by an independent entity that does not have any financial or management stake in the organization or application, and should be done at least yearly.

☒ **B** is incorrect because the audits must be done by an independent entity, at least on a yearly basis, not internally every six months.

☒ **C** is incorrect because the audits must be done by an independent entity, at least on a yearly basis, not every six months.

☒ **D** is incorrect because the audits must be done by an independent entity, at least on a yearly basis, not internally.

27. Which step of the audit plan determines how many staff will need to be allocated on behalf of the organization and the auditors to conduct a successful audit?

    A. Define scope

    B. Lessons learned

    C. Define objectives

    D. Conduct the audit

    ☑ **C.** During the defining objectives stage of an audit, the policies and regulations to be audited against are determined, as well as the risk acceptance of the organization in regard to them. As part of this process, the number of staff needed to complete the audit is determined, both on the part of the auditors and on the organization being audited.

    ☒ **A** is incorrect because defining the scope of the audit occurs after the defining of objectives. The scope includes what exactly will be included in the audit, as well as how things will be tested. It serves as the official map for the audit and all the steps and processes that must be completed as part of it.

    ☒ **B** is incorrect because the lessons learned analysis is performed after the audit has been conducted. It represents the opportunity to review the audit and the steps taken to accomplish it, including the scope, and serves to refine future audits and processes.

    ☒ **D** is incorrect because the actual conducting of the audit entails testing of controls against policies and expected configurations to determine any gaps or "findings."

28. Many jurisdictions around the world have comprehensive regulations regarding privacy and data protection. Which jurisdiction lacks an overall comprehensive policy that covers its entire jurisdictional area?

    A. United States

    B. European Union

    C. Russia

    D. Japan

☑ **A.** The United States lacks an overall comprehensive privacy regulation for data protection. Although various regulations pertain to specific types of data or institutions, there is no single, comprehensive regulation for personal information or privacy protection.

☒ **B** is incorrect because the European Union has long been one of the top drivers of data privacy and personal protection. It issued Directive 95/45 EC in 1995, which established data privacy as a human right.

☒ **C** is incorrect because Russia put into effect Russian Law 526-FZ in 2015, which requires all data and processing for personal information on Russian citizens to be done by systems and applications that physically reside and are hosted within the borders of the Russian Federation.

☒ **D** is incorrect because Germany is part of the European Union, and as such, it is covered under the privacy policies and regulations the EU has issued.

29. An audit scope statement defines the entire process and procedures to be used while conducting of an audit. Which of the following items is *NOT* something that would be found in an audit scope statement?

   A. Exclusions

   B. Costs

   C. Certifications

   D. Reports

☑ **B.** The costs of the audit are not something that is included in an audit scope statement. They would be determined by contract separately. Although the intended scope of the audit will likely have an impact on costs, they are not included in the audit scope statement.

☒ **A** is incorrect because any exclusions to the audit—either systems, applications, or services, as well as any particular features that are not to be included—would be a core component of the audit scope statement.

☒ **C** is incorrect because any required certifications on the part of the auditors or the organization would be a core component of the audit scope statement.

☒ **D** is incorrect because the final reports, including format, are defined as part of the audit scope statement. Also included is the audience for the dissemination of the reports upon completion of the audit.

30. Which of the following laws pertains to the protection and confidentiality of PII, related specifically to financial institutions?

A. HIPAA

B. SOX

C. Safe Harbor

D. GLBA

☑ **D.** The Gramm–Leach–Bliley Act (GLBA) of 1999 is focused on how financial institutions handle the private information of individuals.

☒ **A** is incorrect because the Health Insurance Portability and Accountability Act (HIPAA) of 1996 pertains to the protection of patient privacy and medical records, not to financial institutions.

☒ **B** is incorrect because the Sarbanes–Oxley Act (SOX) of 2002 pertains to the records that publicly traded companies, accounting firms, and many other types of organizations must retain. It specifies not only the type of records that must be preserved but also the duration of retention.

☒ **C** is incorrect because the Safe Harbor program was developed by the United States Department of Commerce as a way for US companies to bridge the privacy laws between the United States and the European Union and comply with the more strict requirements.

Pre-assessment Test

This pre-assessment test is designed to help you prepare to study for the CCSP Certified Cloud Security Professional examination. You should take this test to identify the areas where you should focus your study and preparation.

The pre-assessment test includes 48 questions that are similar in style and format to the questions on the exam. As you prepare to take this test, try to simulate the actual exam conditions as closely as possible. Go to a quiet place and be sure that you will not be interrupted for the full length of time it will take to complete the test. You should give yourself one hour and 30 minutes. Do not use any reference materials or other assistance while taking the pre-assessment—remember, the idea is to help you determine what areas you need to focus on during your preparation for the actual exam.

The pre-assessment test contains questions divided in proportion to the CCSP exam. Here is a breakdown of the exam content:

Domain	Exam Weight	Number of Pre-assessment Questions
1: Architectural Concepts and Design Requirements	19 percent	9
2: Cloud Data Security	20 percent	10
3: Cloud Platform and Infrastructure Security	19 percent	9
4: Cloud Application Security	15 percent	7
5: Operations	15 percent	7
6: Legal and Compliance	12 percent	6

Complete the entire pre-assessment test before checking your results. Once you have finished, use both the "Quick Answer Key" and the "Comprehensive Answers and Explanations" sections to score your test. Use the table in the "Analyzing Your Results" section to determine how well you performed. The objective map at the end of the appendix will help you identify those areas that require the most attention while you prepare for the exam.

Are you ready? Set your clock for one hour and 30 minutes and begin!

1. Which cloud service category is most associated with auto-scaling offerings for a cloud customer?

   A. IaaS

   B. PaaS

   C. SaaS

   D. DaaS

2. Which of the following is *NOT* considered one of the core building-block technologies of cloud computing and services offered by cloud providers?

   A. CPU

   B. Memory

   C. Operating systems

   D. Storage

3. If an organization desires to utilize multiple cloud providers for the purposes of redundancy and disaster recovery strategies, which cloud deployment model would be the most appropriate?

   A. Hybrid

   B. Private

   C. Public

   D. Community

4. Which of the following strategies to ensure data deletion and unrecoverability is the most likely to be available within a cloud environment?

   A. Degaussing

   B. Cryptographic erasure

   C. Overwriting

   D. Shredding

5. Which key aspect of cloud computing allows the cloud customer to administer their configurations or provisioned services without the need to interact or be involved with the cloud provider and its staff?

   A. Resource pooling

   B. Measured service

   C. Multitenancy

   D. On-demand self-service

6. Which of the following properties of an application will lead to the biggest cost-savings potential with a move into a cloud environment?

   A. Heavy utilization

   B. Light utilization

   C. Cyclical utilization

   D. Internal utilization

7. Which of the following standards pertains to the accreditation of cryptographic modules?

   A. FIPS 140-2

   B. PCI DSS

   C. NIST 800-53

   D. ISO/IEC 27001

8. Which model lays out a vision for IT Service Management, encompassing best-practice recommendations covering a wide variety of IT services and operations?

   A. SABSA

   B. ITIL

   C. TOGAF

   D. NIST SP 500-293

9. Which phase of the cloud secure data lifecycle is where data is viewable to customers or users?

   A. Use

   B. Share

   C. Store

   D. View

10. Which cloud storage type is typically accessed via an API or web service call?

   A. Volume

   B. Structured

   C. Unstructured

   D. Object

11. Which data security and privacy practice uses an opaque value for sensitive data fields that can be mapped back to the original value if needed?

   A. Anonymization

   B. Tokenization

   C. Obfuscation

   D. Masking

12. Which phase of the cloud data lifecycle represents the first opportunity to apply security controls to protect data?

   A. Create

   B. Use

   C. Share

   D. Store

13. Which of the following is *NOT* one of the main methods of data discovery processes?

   A. Checksums

   B. Metadata

   C. Labels

   D. Content analysis

14. Which jurisdiction has implemented policy regulations that are known as the "right to be forgotten" protections?

   A. United States

   B. Russia

   C. European Union

   D. APEC

15. Which of the following functions can be controlled by IRM technologies, where typical operating system controls would not be sufficient?

   A. Read

   B. Copy

   C. Delete

   D. Write

16. Which of the following will always dictate the minimum requirements for data retention and archiving periods?

   A. Company policies

   B. Application needs

   C. Regulations

   D. Administrator requests

17. Which of the following event data types is a cloud customer most likely to be supplied with a SaaS implementation?

   A. Firewall

   B. Authentication

C. Patching

D. Billing

18. Which security concept is the most important consideration with the use of an external key management system?

A. Confidentiality

B. Availability

C. Integrity

D. Privacy

19. Which of the following is not one of the defined security controls domains within the Cloud Controls Matrix, published by the Cloud Security Alliance?

A. Financial

B. Human resources

C. Mobile security

D. Identity and access management

20. Which concept is utilized by a cloud provider to determine how to allocate resources requested by cloud customers when the cloud infrastructure does not have enough resources to meet all requests?

A. Limits

B. Reservations

C. Holds

D. Shares

21. Which type of hypervisor runs within a host operating system, rather than directly tied to the underlying hypervisor hardware?

A. Type 1

B. Type 3

C. Type 2

D. Hosted

22. What will govern the level of access and insight a cloud customer has with the cloud provider they are hosting applications and data with?

A. SLAs

B. Regulation

C. Jurisdiction

D. Classification

23. When is a system vulnerable within a cloud environment but would not be within a traditional data center?

    A. When powered off

    B. During development

    C. During patching

    D. During booting

24. Which of the following components is not a key participant within a federated identity system?

    A. User

    B. Application

    C. Relying party

    D. Identity provider

25. Which of the following will typically be used by a cloud provider to offer assurance of security to cloud customers and mitigate the need for customers to audit the underlying infrastructure?

    A. Contracts

    B. SLA

    C. Certification

    D. Baselines

26. What metric is intended to measure the duration of operational recovery to meet a predetermined point after a disaster has occurred?

    A. RPO

    B. RSL

    C. SRE

    D. RTO

27. There are many different causes that can lead to a declared disaster for a system. Which of the following would not be considered a reason for a declared disaster and the triggering of a BCDR plan?

    A. Earthquake

    B. Flood

    C. Key personnel loss

    D. Utility outage

28. Which of the following metrics are tested during a BCDR exercise to ensure management objectives are being achieved?

   A. RPO and RTO

   B. RPO and costs

   C. Costs and RTO

   D. Costs and downtime

29. What type of common vulnerability is exploited by sending commands through input fields in an application in an attempt to bypass application security?

   A. Cross-site scripting

   B. Cross-site request forgery

   C. Insecure direct object references

   D. Injection

30. What type of security testing uses testers who have knowledge of the systems, and in most cases access to the source code as well, and is performed against offline systems?

   A. DAST

   B. SAST

   C. Pen

   D. RASP

31. What type of software is often considered secured and validated via community knowledge?

   A. Proprietary

   B. Object-oriented

   C. Open source

   D. Scripting

32. During which stage of the SDLC process should security be consulted and begin its initial involvement?

   A. Testing

   B. Design

   C. Development

   D. Requirement gathering

33. What security concept does the letter *R* represent in the DREAD threat risk model?

   A. Reversibility

   B. Reproducibility

   C. Redundancy

   D. Resiliency

34. For security purposes, a university keeps its student and faculty data separated from each other within a system. What security concept does this strategy illustrate?

    A. Sandboxing

    B. Isolation

    C. Segregation

    D. Compartmentalization

35. Which of the following would be appropriate to use in conjunction with an RSA token for a multifactor authentication system?

    A. Thumb drive

    B. Access card

    C. Password

    D. Mobile device code generator

36. What is the recommended relative humidity level for a data center, per recommendations from ASHRAE?

    A. 40–60 percent

    B. 20–30 percent

    C. 50–70 percent

    D. 24–36 percent

37. Which protocol allows for the use of storage commands over a TCP network rather than a physical connection?

    A. IPSec

    B. SCSI

    C. VPN

    D. iSCSI

38. DRS is used for managing all aspects of clustered systems. Which of the following represents what DRS stands for?

    A. Dynamic resource state

    B. Distributed resource scheduling

    C. Distributed resource selection

    D. Dynamic resource scheduling

39. Which strategy involves using a fake production system to lure attackers in order to learn about their tactics?

    A. IDS

    B. Honeypot

C. IPS

D. Firewall

40. Which network protocol allows for the centralized administration and configuration of network settings for systems hosted within the network?

   A. DNS

   B. IPSec

   C. DHCP

   D. VLAN

41. What type of management involves minimizing the impact of disruptions to services or operations?

   A. Incident management

   B. Problem management

   C. Continuity management

   D. Availability management

42. One approach to dealing with risk is often compared to taking insurance against risk becoming realized. What type of risk mitigation strategy does this refer to?

   A. Accept

   B. Avoid

   C. Mitigate

   D. Transfer

43. An eDiscovery order typically encompasses data that fits within all of the following categories of an organization's processes except which one?

   A. Possession

   B. Custody

   C. Control

   D. Creation

44. Which United States program was designed to attempt to bridge the differences between US and European privacy requirements for the purposes of commerce?

   A. GLBA

   B. Safe harbor

   C. HIPAA

   D. SOX

45. What type of reports are considered restricted and commonly used to detail the financial reporting controls of an organization?

    A. SAS-70

    B. SOC 2

    C. SOC 1

    D. SOC 3

46. Which of the following represents the most commonly used metrics for risk categorization?

    A. Minimal, low, moderate, high, critical

    B. Low, medium, high

    C. Low, moderate, high

    D. Low, medium, high, critical

47. When forming a contract with a cloud provider, which of the following would not be a direct component of the actual contract?

    A. Definitions

    B. Incident response

    C. Metrics

    D. Uptime requirements

48. Modern systems and applications bridge many different services and systems. What is the overall management of an entire system commonly referred to as?

    A. Holistic management

    B. Supply-chain management

    C. Comprehensive management

    D. Configuration management

1. B	17. D	33. B
2. C	18. B	34. A
3. A	19. A	35. C
4. B	20. D	36. A
5. D	21. C	37. D
6. C	22. A	38. B
7. A	23. A	39. B
8. B	24. B	40. C
9. B	25. C	41. A
10. D	26. D	42. D
11. B	27. C	43. D
12. D	28. A	44. B
13. A	29. D	45. C
14. C	30. B	46. A
15. B	31. C	47. D
16. C	32. D	48. B

Total Score: _____

Comprehensive Answers and Explanations

1. Which cloud service category is most associated with auto-scaling offerings for a cloud customer?

   A. IaaS

   B. PaaS

   C. SaaS

   D. DaaS

   ☑ **B.** Platform as a Service (PaaS) is most associated with auto-scaling, as PaaS offers a fully configured and deployable hosting environment, where the cloud customer's application code and data are the additional components needed to make everything fully functional. It allows for programmatic and automatic expansion of an environment to meet current need with minimal additional configuration required from the cloud customer, as opposed to IaaS.

   ☒ **A, C,** and **D** are incorrect. Although Infrastructure as a Service (IaaS) allows for auto-scaling as well, PaaS entails the least overhead for the cloud customer and enjoys the greatest ease of automatic expansion. Software as a Service (SaaS) and Desktop as a Service (DaaS) are environments maintained by the cloud provider, and although they do offer auto-scaling in many instances, they are not applications deployed specific to the cloud customer.

2. Which of the following is *NOT* considered one of the core building-block technologies of cloud computing and services offered by cloud providers?

   A. CPU

   B. Memory

   C. Operating systems

   D. Storage

   ☑ **C.** Operating systems are not one of the key components of the cloud computing resources and services offered by a cloud provider. Depending on the cloud service category, operating systems may not even be a factor at all, such as with IaaS, where they are the sole responsibility of the cloud customer, and they are certainly not a universal factor across all cloud service categories.

   ☒ **A, B,** and **D** are incorrect. CPU, memory, and storage are they key building blocks of cloud computing that are universal across all cloud service categories. They form the basis for measured services and resource pooling.

3. If an organization desires to utilize multiple cloud providers for the purposes of redundancy and disaster recovery strategies, which cloud deployment model would be the most appropriate?

A. Hybrid

B. Private

C. Public

D. Community

☑ **A.** A hybrid cloud solution utilizes multiple different cloud deployment models to meet an organization's needs. It allows an organization to use different providers and types of services, but in a way where the systems are compatible and interchangeable.

☒ **B, C,** and **D** are incorrect. Public, private, and community cloud deployment models are single systems that do not enjoy the diversity of a hybrid cloud across multiple providers or deployment models.

4. Which of the following strategies to ensure data deletion and unrecoverability is the most likely to be available within a cloud environment?

A. Degaussing

B. Cryptographic erasure

C. Overwriting

D. Shredding

☑ **B.** Cryptographic erasure involves the purposeful destruction of encryption keys that were used to protect data. Destroying the keys ensures that the encryption cannot be undone or recovered, or at least not within any time frame that would be useful or practical. Because this process is entirely software based, it would be available in any cloud environment.

☒ **A, C,** and **D** are incorrect. Degaussing and shredding are physically destructive methods used against storage media, which due to resource pooling and multitenancy, would almost certainly never be available in a cloud environment. Even in the case of a private cloud, they would be highly unlikely because multiple different systems and applications share the same physical storage. Overwriting, although software based, would be very difficult to ensure in a cloud environment because data is constantly moving between different systems, and ensuring that all locations are known, or even able to be overwritten, is virtually impossible.

5. Which key aspect of cloud computing allows the cloud customer to administer their configurations or provisioned services without the need to interact or be involved with the cloud provider and its staff?

A. Resource pooling

B. Measured service

C. Multitenancy

D. On-demand self-service

☑ **D.** On-demand self-service allows a cloud customer to provision resources or change configurations on their own, without the need to interact with the staff of the cloud provider. This is typically accomplished through a web portal and tools provided by the cloud provider.

☒ **A, B,** and **C** are incorrect. Resource pooling and multitenancy both pertain to having a large pool of resources and services that are shared between different applications and customers with a cloud environment, but neither concept specifically pertains to administration. Measured service pertains to only incurring billing and charges for services the cloud customer actually uses, and for the duration of their use, but does not pertain to their administration.

6. Which of the following properties of an application will lead to the biggest cost-savings potential with a move into a cloud environment?

A. Heavy utilization

B. Light utilization

C. Cyclical utilization

D. Internal utilization

☑ **C.** An application that experiences cyclical utilization, where some periods have high utilization and others have low, has the potential to realize substantial cost savings within a cloud environment due to measured service. With a traditional data center, an application needs to be built to handle the highest possible utilization, with substantial resources sitting idle at other times. Within a cloud environment, systems can be expanded for high-utilization periods and then scaled down during lower periods, thus saving money.

☒ **A, B,** and **D** are incorrect. High utilization and low utilization steady-states would not realize costs savings in a cloud environment versus a traditional data center, where they can be planned and designed for. Internal utilization versus public utilization would not result in a cost difference.

7. Which of the following standards pertains to the accreditation of cryptographic modules?

A. FIPS 140-2

B. PCI DSS

C. NIST 800-53

D. ISO/IEC 27001

☑ **A.** The FIPS 140-2 criterion is published by the federal government of the United States and pertains to the accreditation of cryptographic modules. Although it was published in 2002, long before cloud computing came into existence, the heavy usage of and reliance on encryption within cloud computing makes it relevant to the cloud security professional.

☒ **B, C,** and **D** are incorrect. The Payment Card Industry Data Security Standard (PCI DSS) is an industry regulation, published by the major credit card brands, and required of vendors that utilize processing and networks for the major card brands. The NIST 800-53 regulates systems and data utilized by the US federal government for all non-national security systems. ISO/IEC 27001 is a widely recognized international security certification and guidelines program.

8. Which model lays out a vision for IT Service Management, encompassing best-practice recommendations covering a wide variety of IT services and operations?

   A. SABSA

   B. ITIL

   C. TOGAF

   D. NIST SP 500-293

   ☑ **B.** The IT Infrastructure Library (ITIL) is a collection of papers and concepts to lay out a vision for IT Service Management (ITSM). It is essentially a collection of best practices to give companies of all sizes (but more targeted to large companies) a framework for providing both IT services and user support.

   ☒ **A, C,** and **D** are incorrect. The Sherwood Applied Business Security Architecture (SABSA) provides a group of components that can be used in part or whole as an approach to security architecture of any system. The Open Group Architecture Framework (TOGAF) is meant to be an open enterprise architecture model that is intended to be a high-level design approach. The NIST Cloud Technology Roadmap, put out by the NIST of the US federal government in special publication "SP 500-293," is a comprehensive guide for US government agencies and their use of and migration to cloud computing platforms.

9. Which phase of the cloud secure data lifecycle is where data is viewable to customers or users?

   A. Use

   B. Share

   C. Store

   D. View

   ☑ **B.** The "share" phase of the cloud secure data lifecycle is where data is made available to the users or customers of an application or system.

   ☒ **A, C,** and **D** are incorrect. The "use" phase is where data is accessible to the application for processing or modification. The "store" phase is where data is committed to storage of any type. The "view" phase is not part of the cloud secure data lifecycle.

10. Which cloud storage type is typically accessed via an API or web service call?

    A. Volume

    B. Structured

C. Unstructured

D. Object

☑ **D.** Object storage is data storage that operates as an API or a web service call. Rather than being in a file tree structure and accessible as a traditional hard drive, data is stored as objects in an independent system and given a key value for reference and retrieval.

☒ **A, B,** and **C** are incorrect. Volume storage is allocated to a server with IaaS and functions the same as a traditional file system that's managed by the operating system. Structured storage, used with PaaS, resembles database storage with predefined structures, and unstructured storage is also used with PaaS to host support files such as images and style sheets.

11. Which data security and privacy practice uses an opaque value for sensitive data fields that can be mapped back to the original value if needed?

A. Anonymization

B. Tokenization

C. Obfuscation

D. Masking

☑ **B.** Tokenization is the practice of utilizing a random and opaque "token" value in data to replace what otherwise would be a sensitive or protected data object. The token value is usually generated by the application with a means to map it back to the actual real value.

☒ **A, C,** and **D** are incorrect. Masking and obfuscation involve replacing sensitive values in data sets with random or garbage values. They are typically used when making data sets for testing in non-production environments, where the format of the data is important but the exact values are not. Anonymization involves removing indirect identifiers from data so that it cannot be traced back to a specific individual.

12. Which phase of the cloud data lifecycle represents the first opportunity to apply security controls to protect data?

A. Create

B. Use

C. Share

D. Store

☑ **D.** Immediately after the "create" phase has been completed, the data must be committed to some sort of storage system, such as a database or file system. This represents the first time where security controls can be applied to the data, based on the type of storage system used and the classification of the data.

☒ **A, B,** and **C** are incorrect. The "create" phase is simply where data is created or generated, but not until the data is stored or written can security controls be applied. The "use" and "share" phases occur after the "store" phase, so neither would be the first instance where security controls can be applied.

13. Which of the following is *NOT* one of the main methods of data discovery processes?

    A. Checksums

    B. Metadata

    C. Labels

    D. Content analysis

    ☑ **A.** Checksums, where a value is derived based on the overall data object, are often used for ensuring the integrity of data. If any alterations to the file have been made from the original, the checksum of the file will compute to a different value. Checksums would not be used for data discovery.

    ☒ **B, C,** and **D** are incorrect. Metadata, labels, and content analysis are the three main types of data discovery. Metadata involves the use of information about the data (filenames, creator, dates, and so on) to determine classification. Labels use data categories and their headings, such as database fields, to determine classification, and content analysis runs searches against the actual data for pattern matching and keywords.

14. Which jurisdiction has implemented policy regulations that are known as the "right to be forgotten" protections?

    A. United States

    B. Russia

    C. European Union

    D. APEC

    ☑ **C.** The European Union is widely recognized as implementing the most comprehensive and strong data privacy and security regulations. The "right to be forgotten" provisions protect a user's right and ability to have their presence and information removed from search engine indexes and results.

    ☒ **A, B,** and **D** are incorrect. The United States lacks a national privacy regulation that is universal, and Russia and the Asian-Pacific Economic Cooperation (APEC) have only implemented varying degrees of privacy regulations. None has implemented requirements as stringent or comprehensive as the EU's "right to be forgotten" provisions.

15. Which of the following functions can be controlled by IRM technologies, where typical operating system controls would not be sufficient?

    A. Read

    B. Copy

    C. Delete

    D. Write

☑ **B.** Information rights management (IRM) technologies extend the security controls available to protect data beyond those offered by the operating systems. The ability to control the copying of a file is one of those controls. With standard operating system controls, if a user can read a file, they can also copy the file, which is something that IRM can control.

☒ **A, C,** and **D** are incorrect. Read, delete, and write are all operations that can be controlled by operating system permissions and security controls.

16. Which of the following will always dictate the minimum requirements for data retention and archiving periods?

    A. Company policies

    B. Application needs

    C. Regulations

    D. Administrator requests

    ☑ **C.** Regulatory requirements, either from law or industry, will always dictate the minimum retention period for any log data in order to maintain compliance or certification.

    ☒ **A, B,** and **D** are incorrect. Company policies, administrator requests, and any application requirements may expand upon the minimum requirements specified by regulation, but they cannot be strict without violating compliance requirements.

17. Which of the following event data types is a cloud customer most likely to be supplied with a SaaS implementation?

    A. Firewall

    B. Authentication

    C. Patching

    D. Billing

    ☑ **D.** With the entire responsibility for both the system and application being with the cloud provider for a SaaS implementation, the customer is mostly like going to receive only very limited event data. Among the event data types that are universal for cloud customers to receive with SaaS is billing data for their usage of services.

    ☒ **A, B,** and **C** are incorrect. Firewall, authentication, and patching data will almost certainly not be available to cloud customers in a SaaS implementation, nor would they be of much value because the responsibility for them lies with the cloud provider.

18. Which security concept is the most important consideration with the use of an external key management system?

    A. Confidentiality

    B. Availability

C. Integrity

D. Privacy

  ☑ **B.** With the use of an external key management system, where the keys are hosted and managed on a system that is kept segregated from the systems using and depending on them, availability becomes the most pressing security concern for production operations. If availability is not maintained, especially with storage and data-at-rest encryption used widely with cloud implementations, an entire system or application may be rendered useless and inaccessible.

  ☒ **A, C,** and **D** are incorrect. The confidentiality of private keys as well as their integrity are important considerations for an external key management system, but availability is the best choice based on the example provided. Privacy relates to user data and would not be pertinent to the example used within the question.

19. Which of the following is not one of the defined security controls domains within the Cloud Controls Matrix, published by the Cloud Security Alliance?

  A. Financial

  B. Human resources

  C. Mobile security

  D. Identity and access management

  ☑ **A.** Financial is not one of the security controls domains of the Cloud Control Matrix (CCM).

  ☒ **B, C,** and **D** are incorrect. Human resources, mobile security, and identity and access management are all specific domains of the CCM.

20. Which concept is utilized by a cloud provider to determine how to allocate resources requested by cloud customers when the cloud infrastructure does not have enough resources to meet all requests?

  A. Limits

  B. Reservations

  C. Holds

  D. Shares

  ☑ **D.** The concept of shares within a cloud environment is used to mitigate and control customer requests for resources, which the environment may not have the current capability to allow. Shares work by prioritizing hosts within a cloud environment through a weighting system that is defined by the cloud provider.

  ☒ **A, B,** and **C** are incorrect. Limits are put in place to enforce maximum utilization of memory or processing by a cloud customer. A reservation is a minimum resource that is guaranteed to a customer within a cloud environment. A hold is not a concept within cloud computing that relates to the particulars of the question.

21. Which type of hypervisor runs within a host operating system, rather than directly tied to the underlying hypervisor hardware?

A. Type 1

B. Type 3

C. Type 2

D. Hosted

☑ **C.** A Type 2 hypervisor runs within a host operating system rather than being tied directly to the underlying hardware in the way a Type 1 hypervisor is.

☒ **A, B,** and **D** are incorrect. A Type 1 hypervisor is tied directly to the hardware of the hypervisor and does not run within any other software. Both Type 3 and "hosted" hypervisors are not real types.

22. What will govern the level of access and insight a cloud customer has with the cloud provider they are hosting applications and data with?

A. SLAs

B. Regulation

C. Jurisdiction

D. Classification

☑ **A.** The service level agreement (SLA) between the cloud customer and cloud provider will dictate and govern the type, level, and immediacy of access and insight available with the underlying infrastructure and operations.

☒ **B, C,** and **D** are incorrect. Both regulation and jurisdiction may provide some requirements for access and information from the cloud provider to the cloud customer, but neither is the best answer in this case. Classification refers to the sensitivity of the data, but does not pertain to access or insight that a cloud customer is given with the cloud provider.

23. When is a system vulnerable within a cloud environment but would not be within a traditional data center?

A. When powered off

B. During development

C. During patching

D. During booting

☑ **A.** Within a cloud environment, or any virtualized environment, virtual images are files that exist on a file system (typically within object storage in a cloud environment). Due to this factor, even when a virtual machine is powered off, the images are still potential vulnerabilities that an attacker can attempt to exploit.

☒ **B, C,** and **D** are incorrect. Despite the unique nature of a cloud environment and virtualization, there isn't a significant difference when systems are being booted, patched, or are in development as compared to a traditional data center.

24. Which of the following components is not a key participant within a federated identity system?

    A. User

    B. Application

    C. Relying party

    D. Identity provider

    ☑ **B.** Although access to an application is typically the end result of going through a federated identity system, it is not one of the core components of the actual federated system.

    ☒ **A, C,** and **D** are incorrect. The user who initiates the federated identity process, the identity provider that validates the user's authentication and releases their attributes, and the relying party that consumes the authentication and attribute assertions are all key components of a federated identity system.

25. Which of the following will typically be used by a cloud provider to offer assurance of security to cloud customers and mitigate the need for customers to audit the underlying infrastructure?

    A. Contracts

    B. SLA

    C. Certification

    D. Baselines

    ☑ **C.** A standard strategy for providing security assurances to cloud customers is for the cloud provider to obtain certification for its security controls and policies from a prominent and reputable certification source. This will allow cloud customers to assume security controls up to the scope of the certification, and then perform their own audits from that point on.

    ☒ **A, B,** and **D** are incorrect. Contracts and SLAs will be used to require and verify that certifications and other compliance strategies are implemented and verified by the cloud provider, but they are not themselves the source of the assurance. Baselines, which are used to ensure a level-set of system configurations, will often form an integral component of certification, but this is not the best answer in this case.

26. What metric is intended to measure the duration of operational recovery to meet a predetermined point after a disaster has occurred?

    A. RPO

    B. RSL

    C. SRE

    D. RTO

☑ **D.** The recovery time objective (RTO) is the time that it would take to recover operations in the event of a disaster to the point where management's objectives for BCDR are met.

☒ **A, B,** and **C** are incorrect. The recovery point objective (RPO) is defined as the amount of data a company would need to maintain and recover in order to function at a level acceptable to management. The recovery service level (RSL) is a percentage measure of the typical total production service level that needs to be restored to meet BCDR objectives in the case of a failure. SRE is provided as an answer but is not pertinent to the question.

27. There are many different causes that can lead to a declared disaster for a system. Which of the following would not be considered a reason for a declared disaster and the triggering of a BCDR plan?

    A. Earthquake

    B. Flood

    C. Key personnel loss

    D. Utility outage

    ☑ **C.** The loss of key personnel, although detrimental to a system or operations, would not trigger a declared disaster or the invocation of a BCDR plan because it would not directly affect a system or its users, nor would it be a reason to move services or data to an alternative hosting location.

    ☒ **A, B,** and **D** are incorrect. An earthquake, flood, and utility outage are all widespread events that have the potential to affect an entire data center, and as such could be reasons for the triggering of a declared disaster and invocation of a BCDR plan.

28. Which of the following metrics are tested during a BCDR exercise to ensure management objectives are being achieved?

    A. RPO and RTO

    B. RPO and costs

    C. Costs and RTO

    D. Costs and downtime

    ☑ **A.** With any BCDR test, the main objective is to ensure the BCDR plan is designed to meet both the recovery point objective (RPO) and the recovery time objective (RTO) established by management.

    ☒ **B, C,** and **D** are incorrect. During a BCDR test, the overall costs are not considered part of the testing or plan. Downtime is provided as a similar concept to the RTO, but is not the best or correct response.

29. What type of common vulnerability is exploited by sending commands through input fields in an application in an attempt to bypass application security?

    A. Cross-site scripting

    B. Cross-site request forgery

    C. Insecure direct object references

    D. Injection

    ☑ **D.** An injection attack is where a malicious actor sends commands or other arbitrary data through input and data fields with the intent of having the application or system execute the code as part of its normal processing and queries.

    ☒ **A, B,** and **C** are incorrect. Cross-site scripting is an attack where a malicious actor is able to send untrusted data to a user's browser without going through any validation or sanitization process, or where the code is not properly escaped from processing by the browser. Insecure direct object references occur when a developer has in their code a reference to something on the application side, such as a database key, the directory structure of the application, configuration information about the hosting system, or any other information that pertains to the workings of the application that should not be exposed to users or the network. A cross-site request forgery attack forces a client that a user has used to authenticate to an application to send forged requests under the user's own credentials to execute commands and requests that the application thinks are coming from a trusted client and user.

30. What type of security testing uses testers who have knowledge of the systems, and in most cases access to the source code as well, and is performed against offline systems?

    A. DAST

    B. SAST

    C. Pen

    D. RASP

    ☑ **B.** Static application security testing (SAST) is a method used to test and analyze the code and components of an application. It is considered "white-box" testing in that the people running the tests have knowledge of and access to the source code and systems involved.

    ☒ **A, C,** and **D** are incorrect. Dynamic application security testing (DAST) is considered "black box" testing of an application and is run against live systems. The people running the test do not have any special knowledge of the system. Pen testing is typically a "black-box" test and is run in the same manner and with the same toolsets that an attacker would attempt to use against an application. Runtime application self-protection (RASP) is typically run against systems that have the ability to tune and focus their security measures based on actual environment variables and the particular attack methods being used against them.

31. What type of software is often considered secured and validated via community knowledge?

   A. Proprietary

   B. Object-oriented

   C. Open source

   D. Scripting

   ☑ **C.** The most popular and widely used open source software packages have undergone extensive code review, testing, collaborative development, and scrutiny, which is not possible with proprietary software packages that are closed source and protected. With this level of scrutiny and the ability for any organization to evaluate and analyze the code from these packages, many consider them to be among the most secure and stable packages available in the industry.

   ☒ **A, B,** and **D** are incorrect. Proprietary software is closed source and not available for review or validation outside of the company that has created it, and as such would not be considered secure via community knowledge. Both object-oriented and scripting are types of coding and software development and do not depend on community knowledge for security.

32. During which stage of the SDLC process should security be consulted and begin its initial involvement?

   A. Testing

   B. Design

   C. Development

   D. Requirement gathering

   ☑ **D.** Requirements gathering and feasibility is the first stage, and it is appropriate for security to be included as part of this stage. Security should be included at the project's inception or at least from the very earliest stages to ensure proper controls and technologies are being used, as well as to ensure that security is always considered with each decision made.

   ☒ **A, B,** and **C** are incorrect. The testing, design, and development phases of the SDLC all come after the initial requirements gathering phase, and as such they would be too late to begin to involve security to ensure project success and objectives are being met.

33. What security concept does the letter *R* represent in the DREAD threat risk model?

   A. Reversibility

   B. Reproducibility

   C. Redundancy

   D. Resiliency

   ☑ **B.** The *R* of the DREAD threat risk model refers to reproducibility, which in this case means a quantitative measure as to the ease and sophistication required to reproduce an exploit.

☒ **A, C,** and **D** are incorrect. Reversibility refers to the ability for a cloud customer to completely remove all data and services from a cloud environment, with assurance that the data has been securely and completely removed. Resiliency and redundancy both pertain to an application or service adjusting to problems or load issues to maintain an acceptable level of performance, but they are not related to the DREAD threat risk model.

34. For security purposes, a university keeps its student and faculty data separated from each other within a system. What security concept does this strategy illustrate?

   A. Sandboxing

   B. Isolation

   C. Segregation

   D. Compartmentalization

   ☑ **A.** Sandboxing involves the segregation and isolation of information or processes from other information and processes within the same system or application, typically for security concerns. This is generally used for data isolation, such as keeping different communities and populations of users isolated from others with similar data.

   ☒ **B, C,** and **D** are incorrect. Segregation, isolation, and compartmentalization are all similar concepts, but none is the correct term in this case.

35. Which of the following would be appropriate to use in conjunction with an RSA token for a multifactor authentication system?

   A. Thumb drive

   B. Access card

   C. Password

   D. Mobile device code generator

   ☑ **C.** A password would be appropriate to use in conjunction with an RSA token for a multifactor authentication system because a password is something a user knows, whereas the RSA token represents something the user has. As such, they are factors from two different categories.

   ☒ **A, B,** and **D** are incorrect. An access card, thumb drive, or mobile device with a code generator would not be appropriate to use in conjunction with an RSA token for a multifactor authentication system because each one is something a user possesses. Therefore, they are all the same type of factor.

36. What is the recommended relative humidity level for a data center, per recommendations from ASHRAE?

   A. 40–60 percent

   B. 20–30 percent

   C. 50–70 percent

   D. 24–36 percent

☑ **A.** The recommended relative humidity rate for a data center, per the American Society of Heating, Refrigeration, and Air Conditioning Engineers (ASHRAE), is 40–60 percent.

☒ **B, C,** and **D** are incorrect. None of the other options available is the recommended relative humidity rate per ASHRAE.

37. Which protocol allows for the use of storage commands over a TCP network rather than a physical connection?

   A. IPSec

   B. SCSI

   C. VPN

   D. iSCSI

   ☑ **D.** The most prevalent communications protocol for network-based storage is iSCSI, which is a protocol that allows for the transmission and use of SCSI commands and features over a TCP-based network.

   ☒ **A, B,** and **C** are incorrect. SCSI is used for storage commands and functions over a physical connection, not a network. IPSec is used for secure communications and encryption between two devices, and a virtual private network (VPN) is used to allow for secure connections and tunneling from public networks into a trusted zone.

38. DRS is used for managing all aspects of clustered systems. Which of the following represents what DRS stands for?

   A. Dynamic resource state

   B. Distributed resource scheduling

   C. Distributed resource selection

   D. Dynamic resource scheduling

   ☑ **B.** Distributed resource scheduling (DRS) is used within all clustering systems as the method for clusters to provide high availability, scaling, management, and workload distribution and balancing of jobs and processes.

   ☒ **A, C,** and **D** are incorrect. None of the other options presented is what the acronym DRS stand for.

39. Which strategy involves using a fake production system to lure attackers in order to learn about their tactics?

   A. IDS

   B. Honeypot

   C. IPS

   D. Firewall

☑ **B.** A honeypot is a system isolated from the production system but designed to appear to an attacker as part of the production system and containing valuable data. However, the data on a honeypot is bogus data, and it is set up on an isolated network so that any compromise of it cannot impact any other systems within the environment.

☒ **A, C,** and **D** are incorrect. An intrusion detection system (IDS) monitors for specific types of network signatures and events and then alerts staff to any such instances, whereas an intrusion prevention system (IPS) can actively block such events, rather than just alerting about them. A firewall is used to block network traffic based on origin and destination IP addresses, combined with port and protocol.

40. Which network protocol allows for the centralized administration and configuration of network settings for systems hosted within the network?

A. DNS

B. IPSec

C. DHCP

D. VLAN

☑ **C.** The Dynamic Host Configuration Protocol (DHCP) is used to assign an IP address and the associated network configuration settings to a system within a network from a centralized administrative system, rather than having the settings on the host themselves.

☒ **A, B,** and **D** are incorrect. Domain Name Service (DNS) resolves common names for servers, systems, or services to their associated IP address for network connectivity. IPSec is used for secure communications and network transmissions between two hosts. VLANs are used for segregating a physical network into logical networks.

41. What type of management involves minimizing the impact of disruptions to services or operations?

A. Incident management

B. Problem management

C. Continuity management

D. Availability management

☑ **A.** Incident management is focused on limiting the impact of disruptive events on an organization and their services, and returning their state to full operational status as quickly as possible.

☒ **B, C,** and **D** are incorrect. Continuity management, or business continuity management, is focused on planning for the successful restoration of systems and services following an unexpected outage, incident, or disaster. The focus of problem management is to analyze and identify potential issues and to put processes and mitigations in place to prevent predictable problems from ever occurring in the first place. Availability management is focused on making sure system resources, processes, personnel, and toolsets are properly allocated and secured to meet SLA requirements for performance.

42. One approach to dealing with risk is often compared to taking insurance against risk becoming realized. What type of risk mitigation strategy does this refer to?

A. Accept

B. Avoid

C. Mitigate

D. Transfer

☑ **D.** Risk transfer is the process of having another entity assume the risk from the organization. One thing to note, though, is that risk cannot always be transferred to another entity. A prime example of transfer is through the use of insurance policies to cover the financial costs of successful risk exploits; however, this will not cover all issues related to risk transference because an organization can face nonfinancial penalties, such as the loss of reputation, business, or trust.

☒ **A, B,** and **C** are incorrect. Through risk mitigation, an organization takes steps, such as buying new systems or technologies, to try to prevent any exploits from happening. In an instance where the cost to mitigate outweighs the cost of accepting the risk and dealing with any possible consequences, an organization may opt to simply deal with an exploit if and when it occurs. Risk avoidance is when an organization opts to limit or remove vulnerable services or systems rather than taking on another risk strategy for them.

43. An eDiscovery order typically encompasses data that fits within all of the following categories of an organization's processes except which one?

A. Possession

B. Custody

C. Control

D. Creation

☑ **D.** Whether or not an organization is the creator of specific data is not one of the core components of what typically encompasses an eDiscovery order.

☒ **A, B,** and **C** are incorrect. An eDiscovery order typically encompasses data that is under the control, custody, or possession of an organization.

44. Which United States program was designed to attempt to bridge the differences between US and European privacy requirements for the purposes of commerce?

A. GLBA

B. Safe harbor

C. HIPAA

D. SOX

    ☑ **B.** The Safe Harbor regulations were developed by the Department of Commerce and meant to bridge the gap between the privacy regulations of the European Union and the United States. With the lack of an adequate privacy law or protection from the federal level in the US, European privacy regulations generally prohibit the exporting (or sharing) of personally identifiable information (PII) from Europe to the United States.

    ☒ **A, C,** and **D** are incorrect. The Gramm-Leach-Bliley Act (GLBA) is focused on PII as it relates to financial institutions. The Health Insurance Portability and Accountability Act (HIPAA) is focused on the security controls for and confidentiality of medical records. The Sarbanes-Oxley (SOX) Act regulates accounting and financial practices used by organizations.

45. What type of reports are considered restricted and commonly used to detail the financial reporting controls of an organization?

    A. SAS-70

    B. SOC 2

    C. SOC 1

    D. SOC 3

    ☑ **C.** The SOC 1 reports are the effective direct replacement for the SAS-70 reports. They are focused specifically on controls for financial reporting. The SOC 1 reports are considered restricted-use reports in that they are intended for a small and limited scope of controls auditing, and are not intended to be expanded into greater use. They are focused specifically on internal controls as they relate to financial reporting.

    ☒ **A, B,** and **D** are incorrect. Although SAS-70 reports are very similar to SOC 1 reports, they have been deprecated and replaced by the SOC 1 reports, and as such this is not the best answer. SOC 2 reports expand greatly on SOC 1 reports and apply to a broad range of service organizations and types, whereas SOC 1 is only for financial organizations. SOC 3 reports are similar to SOC 2 reports in scope, design, and structure, with the main difference between SOC 2 and SOC 3 being the audience they are intended for: SOC 3 reports are designed for public consumption.

46. Which of the following represents the most commonly used metrics for risk categorization?

    A. Minimal, low, moderate, high, critical

    B. Low, medium, high

    C. Low, moderate, high

    D. Low, medium, high, critical

    ☑ **A.** The most commonly used metrics for risk categorization are minimal, low, moderate, high, and critical.

    ☒ **B, C,** and **D** are incorrect. The other options represent some but not all of the metrics commonly used for risk categorization.

47. When forming a contract with a cloud provider, which of the following would not be a direct component of the actual contract?

A. Definitions

B. Incident response

C. Metrics

D. Uptime requirements

☑ **D.** Uptime (or availability) requirements are not typically a direct component of a contract with a cloud provider. The uptime and availability requirements would be a key component of the service level agreement (SLA).

☒ **A, B,** and **C** are incorrect. The contract should include agreed-upon definitions of any terms and technologies. How the cloud provider will handle incident response for any security or operational incidents, as well as how communication will be provided to the cloud customer, are key components of a contract. The contract will clearly define what criteria should be measured as far as system performance and availability are concerned, as well as the agreement between the cloud customer and cloud provider as to how these criteria will be collected, measured, quantified, and processed.

48. Modern systems and applications bridge many different services and systems. What is the overall management of an entire system commonly referred to as?

A. Holistic management

B. Supply-chain management

C. Comprehensive management

D. Configuration management

☑ **B.** With the nature of modern applications being built on a myriad of different components and services, the supply chain of any system or application can rapidly expand to a scale far outside a single organization.

☒ **A, C,** and **D** are incorrect. The other options provided are similar-sounding terms but none is the appropriate answer for this question.

Analyzing Your Results

Congratulations on completing the CCSP pre-assessment. You should now take the time to analyze your results with these two objectives in mind:

- Identifying the resources you should use to prepare for the exam
- Identifying the specific topics you should focus on in your preparation

Use this table to help you gauge your overall readiness for the CCSP examination:

Number of Answers Correct	Recommended Course of Study
1–25	I recommend you spend a significant amount of time reviewing the material in the *CCSP Certified Cloud Security Professional All-in-One Exam Guide* before using this practice exams book.
26–37	I recommend you review the following objective map to identify the particular areas that require your focused attention and use the *CCSP Certified Cloud Security Professional All-in-One Exam Guide* to review that material. Once you have done so, you should proceed to work through the questions in this book.
38–48	I recommend you use this book to refresh your knowledge and prepare yourself mentally for the exam.

Once you have identified your readiness for the exam, use the following table to identify the specific objectives that require your focus as you continue your preparation:

Chapter	Exam Weight	Objective	Question Number in Pretest
1: Architectural Concepts and Design Requirements Domain 19 percent			
		Cloud computing concepts	2, 5
		Cloud reference architecture	1, 3
		Security concepts relevant to cloud computing	4
		Design principles of secure cloud computing	6, 9
		Identify trusted cloud services	7
		Cloud architecture models	8
2: Cloud Data Security Domain 20 percent			
		Understanding the cloud data lifecycle	12
		Design and implement cloud data storage architectures	10, 18
		Design and apply data security strategies	11
		Data discovery and classification techniques	13
		Relevant jurisdictional data protections for PII	14, 19
		Data rights management	15
		Data detention, deletion, and archiving strategies	16
		Auditability, traceability, and accountability of data events	17

Chapter	Exam Weight	Objective	Question Number in Pretest
3: Cloud Platform and Infrastructure Security Domain 19 percent			
		Cloud infrastructure components	20, 21
		Risks associated with cloud infrastructure	22, 23
		Design and plan security controls	24, 25
		Disaster recovery and business continuity management planning	26, 27, 28
4: Cloud Application Security Domain 15 percent			
		Training and awareness in application security	29
		Cloud software assurance and validation	30
		Verified secure software	31
		Understand the software development lifecycle (SDLC) process	32
		Applying the secure software development lifecycle	33
		Cloud application architecture	34
		Identity and access management	35
5: Operations Domain 15 percent			
		Support the planning process for data center design	36
		Implement and build the physical infrastructure for the cloud environment	37
		Run physical infrastructure for the cloud environment	38
		Manage physical infrastructure for the cloud environment	39
		Run logical infrastructure for the cloud environment	40
		Ensure compliance with regulations and controls	41
		Conduct risk assessment to logical and physical infrastructure	42
6: Legal and Compliance Domain 12 percent			
		Legal requirements and unique risks within the cloud environment	43
		Privacy issues and jurisdictional variation	44
		Audit processes, methodologies, and required adaptations for a cloud environment	45
		Implications of cloud to enterprise risk management	46
		Outsourcing and cloud contract design	47
		Executive vendor management	48

About the CD-ROM

The CD-ROM included with this book comes complete with Total Tester customizable practice exam software with 250 practice exam questions, and a secured PDF copy of the book.

NOTE If you do not have a CD-ROM drive, you may download the Total Tester by simply going to this URL:

www.totalsem.com/1260031365d/

Also, to access the secured book PDF, visit McGraw-Hill Professional's Media Center by going to this URL:

https://www.mhprofessionalresources.com/mediacenter/

Enter your e-mail address and this 13-digit ISBN: 978-1-260-03136-2. You will then receive an e-mail message with a download link for the book PDF.

System Requirements

The software requires Windows Vista or later and 30MB of hard disk space for full installation, in addition to a current or prior major release of Chrome, Firefox, Internet Explorer, or Safari. To run, the screen resolution must be set to 1024×768 or higher. The secured book PDF requires Adobe Acrobat, Adobe Reader, or Adobe Digital Editions to view.

Total Tester Premium Practice Exam Software

Total Tester provides you with a simulation of the CCSP exam. Exams can be taken in Practice Mode, Exam Mode, or Custom Mode. Practice Mode provides an assistance window with references to the book, explanations of the correct and incorrect answers, and the option to check your answer as you take the test. Exam Mode provides a simulation of the actual exam. The number of questions, the types of questions, and the time allowed are intended to be an accurate representation of the exam environment. Custom Mode allows you to create custom exams from selected domains or chapters, and you can further customize the number of questions and time allowed.

To take a test, launch the program and select CCSP from the Installed Question Packs list. You can then select Practice Mode, Exam Mode, or Custom Mode. All exams provide an overall grade and a grade broken down by domain.

Installing and Running Total Tester Premium Practice Exam Software

From the main screen you may install the Total Tester by clicking the Total Tester Practice Exams button. This will begin the installation process and place an icon on your desktop and in your Start menu. To run Total Tester, navigate to Start | (All) Programs | Total Seminars, or double-click the icon on your desktop.

To uninstall the Total Tester software, go to Start | Control Panel | Programs And Features, and then select the Total Tester program. Select Remove, and Windows will completely uninstall the software.

Secured Book PDF

The entire contents of the book are provided in secured PDF format on the CD-ROM. This file is viewable on your computer and many portable devices.

- **To view the PDF on a computer**, Adobe Acrobat, Adobe Reader, or Adobe Digital Editions is required. A link to Adobe's website, where you can download and install Adobe Reader, has been included on the CD-ROM.

 NOTE For more information on Adobe Reader and to check for the most recent version of the software, visit Adobe's website at www.adobe.com and search for the free Adobe Reader or look for Adobe Reader on the product page. Adobe Digital Editions can also be downloaded from the Adobe website.

- **To view the book PDF on a portable device**, copy the PDF file to your computer from the CD-ROM and then copy the file to your portable device using a USB or other connection. Adobe offers a mobile version of Adobe Reader, the Adobe Reader mobile app, which currently supports iOS and Android. For customers using Adobe Digital Editions and an iPad, you may have to download and install a separate reader program on your device. The Adobe website has a list of recommended applications, and McGraw-Hill Education recommends the Bluefire Reader.

Technical Support

For questions regarding the Total Tester software or operation of the CD-ROM, visit **www.totalsem .com** or e-mail **support@totalsem.com**.

For questions regarding the secured book PDF, visit **http://mhp.softwareassist.com** or e-mail **techsolutions@mhedu.com**.

For questions regarding book content, e-mail **hep_customer-service@mheducation.com**. For customers outside the United States, e-mail **international_cs@mheducation.com**.